Russian Politics

PETER LANG
New York • Washington, D.C./Baltimore • Bern
Frankfurt am Main • Berlin • Brussels • Vienna • Oxford

Donald D. Barry

Russian Politics

The Post-Soviet Phase

PETER LANG
New York • Washington, D.C./Baltimore • Bern
Frankfurt am Main • Berlin • Brussels • Vienna • Oxford

Library of Congress Cataloging-in-Publication Data

Barry, Donald D.
Russian politics: the post-soviet phase / Donald D. Barry.
p. cm.
Includes bibliographical references (p.) and index.
1. Russia (Federation)—Politics and government—1991–. 2. Soviet Union—Politics and government—1985–1991. 3. Post-communism—Russia (Federation). 4. Democracy—Russia (Federation). 5. Constitutional law—Russia (Federation). 6. Political culture—Russia (Federation).
7. Russia (Federation)—Forecasting. I. Title.
JN6695.B37   320.947—dc21   98-47868
ISBN 0-8204-4414-6

Die Deutsche Bibliothek-CIP-Einheitsaufnahme

Barry, Donald DeLyle.:
Russian politics: the post-soviet phase / Donald D. Barry.
–New York; Washington, D.C./Baltimore; Bern;
Frankfurt am Main; Berlin; Brussels; Vienna; Oxford: Lang.
ISBN 0-8204-4414-6

Cover design by Dutton & Sherman Design

The paper in this book meets the guidelines for permanence and durability
of the Committee on Production Guidelines for Book Longevity
of the Council of Library Resources.

© 2002 Peter Lang Publishing, Inc., New York

All rights reserved.
Reprint or reproduction, even partially, in all forms such as microfilm,
xerography, microfiche, microcard, and offset strictly prohibited.

Printed in the United States of America

A Dianne,

moglie amata e amica

Table of Contents

Preface		ix
Acknowledgments		xi
1	The USSR—From Quasi-Totalitarian State to More Open Politics	1
2	From Open Politics to Collapse	25
3	Russia and the Near Abroad	51
4	Evolution of Russian Political Institutions: 1991–1993	65
5	The Constitution: Foundation for the Rule of Law?	81
6	Political Parties and Elections: Underdeveloped Politics	103
7	Operation of the Major Political Institutions	133
8	Social Problems and the New Russian Economy	157
9	Russia's Hard Road Toward Democracy	169
Appendix A: The Constitution of the Russian Federation		187
Appendix B: Chronology, 1985–2000		233
Index		243

Preface

One of the author's objectives in this book is to review the major political developments of Russia's first post-Soviet decade, using as a backdrop the remarkable activities of the late Soviet period. Interwoven with this discussion of events is an analysis of institutional structures and practices, with particular emphasis on the present political arrangements in Russia, created after the crisis of the autumn of 1993.

Any analysis of politics cannot fail to take note of important economic and social considerations, and so these factors find their way into this book as well. But the major focus is on political, and particularly institutional, developments. As a number of other writers on Russia have noted, keeping up with and making sound statements about the fast-paced developments that have characterized post-Soviet Russia are difficult tasks. Russia has not yet reached a point of political equilibrium, where institutional arrangements are well established and operate with reasonable predictability. This is another way of saying that after ten years of independent existence, Russia is still in transition.

If this situation has led the author to any firm conclusion regarding contemporary Russian politics, it is this: one should be wary of the analyst, Russian or foreign, who pronounces with inflated certainty as to where Russia is going politically and what the solutions to its manifold problems are. And if analyses if this kind are founded on supposed national character traits of Russians and Russia, then the reader should be particularly on guard.

I write these words just several days after an article entitled "Russia Is Finished" appeared in a leading American magazine. This is representative (though somewhat extreme in its judgment) of a number of recent writings of this genre. Such assessments seem to me to be highly premature. Since we don't yet have an adequate perspective with which to write with much confidence about Russia's post-Soviet phase, the more proper course, and one that gives due respect to readers trying to understand Russian politics, is to observe events closely and analyze the meaning of political and institutional developments as carefully as possible, keeping predictions and prescriptions to a minimum. I have tried to observe this guideline in the writing that follows.

In an introductory book of this kind, some hard choices had to be made regarding the subjects to be covered and the level of detail to be included. In choosing to emphasize politics at the national level, important aspects of regional and local politics were given scant attention.

In transliterating Russian words I have generally followed the Library of Congress system, except with regard to a few commonly used names (e.g., Yeltsin instead of El'tsin; Yavlinsky, rather than Yavlinskii). When used in the text, Russian words are generally italicized. Two exceptions are "glasnost" and "perestroika," which gained widespread and common usage in English during the Gorbachev era. They are italicized only when introduced for the first time.

Donald D. Barry
May 1, 2001

Acknowledgments

The author would like to acknowledge his considerable debt to colleagues in the field, from whom he has learned much over the years about Russian politics. The citations in the chapter references testify not only to this personal debt, but also to the large amount of quality work being done in the supposedly declining field of Russian Studies. On a more personal note, I want to thank the following colleagues, who have given generously of their knowledge and counsel, both on this volume and over a period of years: Gianmaria Ajani, Ger van den Berg, F.J.M. Feldbrugge, George Ginsburgs, Eugene Huskey, Andrei Loeber, Yuri Luryi, Peter Maggs, Richard Newell, Nicolai Petro, Stanislaw Pomorski, Albert Schmidt, Robert Sharlet, William Simons, Oles Smolansky and Wim Timmermans.

A number of good friends from Russia contributed considerably to my understanding of that country. Among the most important of these are Elena Dolgopolova, Yuri Feofanov, Mikhail Iofa, Ekaterina Mishina, Zoya Mishina and Viktor Mozolin. A quartet of close friends, now deceased, whose impact on my understanding of Russia and the Soviet Union was enormous, are George Barabashev, Avgust Mishin, Valery Savitsky and Raymundas Rayatskas. The last mentioned was a Lithuanian whom I was privileged to know for over thirty years.

At Lehigh University, among many who facilitated my work on this project were Dorothy Windish, departmental coordinator for political science; Roseann Bowerman, from Information Resources, who knows how to open doors and find resources; Sandy Edmiston, a formatting genius who saved the day on numerous occasions; and Dessi Sherban, a former graduate student in political science, who provided valuable research assistance. Many people at Peter Lang Publishing contributed greatly to this book. I want to thank in particular Phyllis Korper, editor, and Jacqueline Pavlovic, production supervisor.

Chapter 1
The USSR—From Quasi-Totalitarian State to More Open Politics

Top Leaders and the Evolution of Soviet Politics

It would be hard to get general agreement among analysts as to *precisely* when the USSR abandoned its traditional political system. But the time span of the outward signs of this transition occupied a rather narrow range of years. In the 1984 election for the USSR parliament, the results were about the same as they had been for the past 45 years: one candidate ran for each legislative seat, and in every district the candidate was reportedly elected by about 99 percent of the vote.

In the next parliamentary election, five years later, a considerably different picture presented itself. Many of the seats were contested, and among those elected were a large number of people with views strongly opposed to those of the traditional political leaders. By this time, the spring of 1989, the country known since the 1920s as the USSR (Union of Soviet Socialist Republics, or Soviet Union) had barely 18 months to live.

Obviously, during that five-year period, a great deal happened that worked to undermine the old system. But this is not to say that times prior to this period were unimportant in the system's demise. There was, as Peter Juviler has aptly put it, a "creeping openness" in some earlier periods that set the stage for the momentous events of the late 1980s and early 1990s (Juviler 1998, 3).

Seven top leaders are associated with the communist period of rule in Russia from the time of the Bolshevik Revolution in November 1917 to the collapse of the Soviet Union in December 1991 (see Table 1.1). Two of these, Andropov and Chernenko, served for such short periods that they are given scant attention in present-day analyses of the Soviet period. The other five served long enough to have put their own personal stamps on the times when they held the top political post. The successive eras of Soviet history are associated with their names.

But if these eras differed in some important respects, they were united in one grand feature: political power was exercised by those belonging to

Table 1.1
Top Soviet Leaders and their Posts

Leader	Years in Power	Principal Post	Other Post
V.I. Lenin	1917 to 1924	Prime Minister	
J.V. Stalin	1926–7 to 1953	General Secretary, Communist Party, 1922 to 1952; First Secretary, 1952 to 1953	Prime Minister, 1941 to 1953
N.S. Khrushchev	1954 to 1964	First Secretary, 1953 to 1964	Prime Minister, 1958 to 1964
L.I. Brezhnev	1964 to 1982	First Secretary, 1964 to 1966; General Secretary, 1966 to 1982	Chairman, Supreme Soviet, 1977 to 1982
Iu.V. Andropov	1982 to 1984	General Secretary, 1982 to 1984	Chairman, Supreme Soviet, 1983 to 1984
K.U. Chernenko	1984 to 1985	General Secretary, 1984 to 1985	Chairman, Supreme Soviet, 1984 to 1985
M.S. Gorbachev	1985 to 1991	General Secretary, 1985 to August 1991	Chairman, Supreme Soviet, 1988 to 1990; President, 1990 to December 1991

just one group, an organization that came to be known as the Communist Party of the Soviet Union (CPSU). Other parties were not tolerated, and the communist party sought to exercise pervasive influence over all sanctioned political activity. That one feature characterized the country for about 70 years, and when the one-party system was seriously challenged in the late 1980s, so was the existence of the USSR.

Vladimir Ilich Lenin was responsible for establishing the Bolshevik faction of the Russian Social Democratic Labor Party in 1903 and for fashioning the party as a small elite group of professional revolutionaries. The Bolsheviks succeeded in seizing power in Russia in November 1917 but were immediately faced by serious challenges from the debilitating effects of the First World War and an ensuing civil war, in which the opponents of the Bolsheviks tried to drive the Lenin government from power.

Although an ardent Marxist socialist, Lenin sought to combat the economic dislocations threatening to paralyze Russia by the adoption in 1921 of the NEP (New Economic Policy), a program designed to revive the economy by allowing small-scale private economic activity in the areas of agriculture, light industry and trade. The policy saved the young Soviet state.

Lenin was the unquestioned leader of the Bolsheviks and a member of its ruling bodies from the earliest days. But he was also head of the government, chairman of the council of people's commissars (a body later to be named council of ministers). In May 1922 Lenin suffered the first of a series of strokes that increasingly removed him from the center of political activity. He died in 1924.

Joseph Vissarionovich Stalin was able to use his key position as general secretary of the party to defeat all rivals in the struggle for power after Lenin's death. Toward the end of his life Lenin came to realize the potential for abuse in the way Stalin was shaping the general secretaryship and sought, without success, to have Stalin removed from the post. From Stalin onward, until late in the Gorbachev period, the primary post was that of general secretary (the name of the post was "first secretary" from 1952 to 1966).

Stalin was not content merely to drive his political rivals from office.

He arranged for the physical elimination of large numbers of them, through execution after meaningless trials or through outright murder. But his machine of terror reached far beyond political opponents. Millions of others, mostly innocent victims, met death or served long terms in prison under wretched conditions during those horrible years. Under Stalin a highly active secret police made irrational fear an instrument of political and social control. The Communist Party was for a period of time eclipsed in significance by Stalin's highly personal rule.

But in addition to systematic terror, Stalin's reign—the longest of any Soviet leader—was also characterized by a radical change in other features of the system. His "revolution from above" at the end of the 1920s created an economic and political upheaval that rivaled the Bolshevik Revolution itself in its consequences. The NEP was abandoned, accompanied by the forced collectivization of agriculture, with brutal repression of all those who resisted. A highly structured planned economy, with rapid industrialization as its centerpiece, became Stalin's obsessional goal. To achieve this, pervasive control over all aspects of human activity was undertaken by the authorities. A cult of Stalin took on fantastic proportions. If ever the controversial term "totalitarianism" could be said to have applied to a political system, it was during the long decades of Stalin's rule.

After Stalin's death in 1953, Nikita Sergeevich Khrushchev emerged as party first secretary and later assumed the post of prime minister as well. His period in power is most associated in the public mind with the de-Stalinization campaign, to which Khrushchev himself contributed significantly with his "secret speech," delivered at the Twentieth Party Congress in 1956.

Two short-lived periods of political "thaw" took place under Khrushchev, but they did not lead to long-term political reform. Khrushchev attacked Stalin in the name of "a return to Leninist norms." Stalin, in Khrushchev's view, was a terrible aberration in a system that was basically right. His aim, therefore, was to take the Soviet Union further down the road toward its communist goals.

But after a number of initial successes (in space flights, agriculture, and in making some strides toward opening the Soviet Union to the outside world), things turned sour. The debacle of the Cuban Missile Crisis (1962) hurt his reputation both at home and abroad. His pledge to "overtake and surpass" the United States in economic achievements quickly came to be seen as wildly unrealistic. Relations with China, the USSR's number one ally, became severely strained. A series of abortive administrative reforms angered important forces in the Communist Party, the bureaucracy and the military.

In retrospect, it is clear that Khrushchev's grasp on power was not as secure as it may have seemed. A 1957 plot to oust him from power had nearly succeeded. In 1964 he was cast aside by a cabal of many of his close associates—the only top leader until Gorbachev to leave his position before death.

Taking over for Khrushchev in the top party post was Leonid Ilich Brezhnev. He and his colleagues sought to impose order and stability in place of what they called Khrushchev's "harebrained schemes." They restored many of the traditional practices that had been put in place under Stalin, minus the widespread use of terror and the subordination of the party hierarchy to the supreme autocrat. Gone were the exposés of the crimes of Stalin and the rehabilitation of his victims. The reputation of Stalin himself was partially restored to respectability.

With a return to greater restraints on expression after Khrushchev's periods of partial liberalization, the dissident movement became a notable feature of the Brezhnev era. The dissenters were intellectuals, for the most part, who made their views known largely through underground publications, some of which found their way to the West. They won sympathy abroad as well as among some of their more passive fellow citizens for their courage in the face of harsh treatment by the regime—prison, incarceration in mental hospitals, dismissal from work, and a range of other sanctions. Leading the state's campaign against the dissenters was the Committee for State Security (KGB), headed for many years under Brezhnev by his successor as general secretary, Yuri Andropov.

The Brezhnev regime could show its hard side, but the USSR was not nearly as isolated from the world as it was in Stalin's time. Some of its policies showed the effects of this exposure. Although emigration was not permitted in general, an *ad hoc* policy was adopted that allowed many thousands of Soviet Jews to leave the country for Israel and elsewhere. And by the signing of international agreements, the regime paid lip service to the protection of human rights—for which they were often challenged when it was shown that they were not living up to the agreements.

On the other hand, the Brezhnev years demonstrated that the leadership could be firm about what it considered to be squarely in the USSR's self-interest. The emphasis on a steady military buildup resulted in formidable achievements during these years. And the military suppression of the "Prague Spring" in Czechoslovakia in 1968, in order to assure that Soviet-style one-party rule would be maintained, was a warning to the USSR's neighbors to the east and to the world as a whole that this regime would go to considerable lengths to preserve its empire.

One of the results of the stability of the Brezhnev era was the gradual aging of the leadership group. The average age of full members of the ruling Politburo surpassed 70 at the end of the Brezhnev era, about ten years higher than when he had come to power. Brezhnev served 18 years as general secretary, second only to Stalin. During his last years he was in poor health, and the country appeared to drift. But the Soviet system had developed no mechanism for replacing superannuated leaders. Either they were ganged up on and removed, as in the case of Khrushchev, or they held their positions until death. During the liberalization under Gorbachev, the final years of Brezhnev's tenure came to be referred to in the USSR as "the period of stagnation."

Yuri Vladimirovich Andropov, upon his accession to power, seemed to understand the difficult situation in the country. He set about quickly to improve labor discipline and combat corruption, among other reform measures. But illness overtook him rather quickly, and after lingering, out of the public eye, for a period of time, he died in February 1984 after less than 16 months on the job.

The selection of 72-year-old Konstantin Ustinovich Chernenko to succeed Andropov showed that the conservatives in the Kremlin still exercised considerable power. Chernenko was a long-time party apparatchik and close colleague of Brezhnev, but there appeared to have been little else to recommend him beyond his ties to the old-line segment of the leadership. In any case, there was scarcely a chance to determine what Chernenko might have stood for, as he died in office barely a year after taking over.

Chernenko was succeeded by Mikhail Sergeevich Gorbachev. Gorbachev had nearly been chosen leader after Andropov's death, and the Politburo moved swiftly to select him this time. With his appointment, a new and critical era in Soviet history was about to begin.

For the first 65 years of the Soviet regime, only four leaders—Lenin, Stalin, Khrushchev, and Brezhnev—held the top political post. Now, in a period of 28 months, three more had assumed that position. Lenin and Stalin were in their forties when they took the reins of power, while Khrushchev and Brezhnev were in their late fifties. Andropov was 68 and Chernenko was 72. None of these leaders left voluntarily; all died in office except Khrushchev, who was removed at age 70. Gorbachev, in assuming the general secretaryship just a few days after his 54th birthday in March 1985, became the youngest Soviet leader since Stalin.

How It Was: The Distribution of Power Under the Old System

As suggested above, the key characteristic of politics in the Soviet period was the one-party system. Through the Communist Party, the country's political leaders sought to monopolize all significant political activity and to exercise influence in areas of life tangential to politics as well. The way in which power was organized within the party, therefore, was of foremost importance. And when party control began to falter under Gorbachev, it had a profound impact on politics and social life as it had existed in the country for generations. A few words about the traditional methods of exercising power in the Soviet Union, therefore, are in order.

Although the Bolsheviks dealt brutally with their opponents outside the party, some semblance of democracy within the party was tolerated for a time after the Revolution. Even during Lenin's time, however, intra-party democracy suffered serious restrictions, and under Stalin all traces of it had been eliminated. When the period of Stalin's highly personal rule had ended, an oligarchic party structure was solidly institutionalized. A look at the operation of the main organs in the party structure will make this clear.

The *Party Congress* was described in the party statute as the supreme organ of power. It was a meeting of representatives of party bodies from around the country. In that way, it provided a link between the permanent party elite and the grassroots, the so-called primary party organizations (PPOs), to which all individual members belonged. In the early postrevolutionary years congresses met frequently, typically once a year. As Stalin's control was consolidated, the intervals between meetings lengthened. During the last three decades of the Soviet Union, congresses were usually convened at five-year intervals. Another feature of the Party Congress that contributed to its inability to perform significant functions was its size. Congresses held in the early years after the Revolution were attended by several hundred delegates at most. During the period of Brezhnev and his successors, congresses of 5,000 attendees were typical. It was not surprising, therefore, that the Party Congress wielded no significant power. By its unanimous assent it approved a slate of candidates, composed in advance, for the next higher body in the hierarchy, the *Central Committee*.

The Central Committee's main function was to run the party in the intervals between congresses. In Lenin's day the Central Committee was a select body, small enough to oversee day-to-day operations. In later years, however, it reached bloated proportions (counting full and candidate members, nearly 500 persons) and no longer performed this role. As the main link between the Congress and the even more elite party bodies, the Central Committee had a crucial potential function, but one that it was seldom called upon to play. Rather, its meetings—typically two one-day sessions per year—served as a backdrop for the airing of party policy statements and concerns by the top leaders. The Central Committee was also responsible for choosing the top party bodies, the *Politburo* and the *Secretariat*. But here too the function was essentially an empty one, amounting to the approval of nominees decided upon in advance by the top elite.

The Politburo began as a temporary body, created in October 1917 to secure the success of the Bolshevik Revolution. It was brought back as a permanent standing committee of the Central Committee in 1919. As authority came to be more and more exclusively exercised, it grew in power. Throughout Soviet history the Politburo remained a small body, composed during most of its last three decades of about a dozen full members and a half-dozen candidate (nonvoting) members (Löwenhardt,

Ozinga and van Ree 1992, 86).

The Politburo was the top policy-making body of the CPSU. It decided broad policy, defined priorities, and determined how resources were to be allocated, in addition to addressing issues of particular concern. Its membership always included a number of leaders of key organizations in the Soviet system: the top man in the Communist Party (general secretary); the head of the government (chairman of the council of ministers); the leaders of the party organizations of some of the key constituent republics of the USSR (the first secretary of the Ukrainian party organization was usually a member of the Politburo in Moscow, for instance). In addition, in the latter decades of its existence, the Politburo also usually included the ministers in charge of several of the most important government ministries, such as the secret police (KGB), defense and foreign affairs. This "interlocking directorate" feature of the Politburo created an elite representing a number of the most strategic hierarchies in the power structure.

Besides the general secretary, membership in the Politburo was usually accorded to several of the other members (secretaries) of the Secretariat, the second body at the apex of the party. Because of the partial overlap of Politburo and Secretariat membership, what could be called the "top elite" in the country usually totaled about 25 persons during the last decades of Soviet rule. Obviously, Politburo members who were also on the Secretariat were particularly well positioned. In recent times, those who succeeded to the general secretaryship did so while occupying posts on both bodies.

If the Politburo was in charge of policy making, then it can be said that the basic task of the Secretariat was policy execution. It was involved in administering the party on a day-to-day basis, including the handling of personnel matters, functions central to the operation of the modern bureaucratic state. But given the pervasiveness of party dominance across a range of activities in the USSR, it is clear that the power exercised by the Secretariat extended to much more than merely administering internal party business.

The Secretariat was in charge of the party apparatus, an organization that comprised several hundred thousand officials during its last several decades. Although overall supervision was the responsibility of the general secretary, the apparatus was divided into a number of broad functional areas, each subdivided into specific departments. The functional areas were headed by a secretary or other responsible party official. A partial list of the departments gives some sense of the reach (or attempted reach) of party influence: agriculture, construction, culture, defense industry, economics, heavy industry, international, liaison with foreign communist parties, light industry and consumer goods, machine building, propaganda, science and educational institutions, trade and domestic services, transportation and communications (Joint Economic Committee 1983, 18).

The apparatus was, in a way, a second government bureaucracy, in fact a bureaucracy superior to that of the government. The departments in the Secretariat had general responsibility for supervising the work of specific ministries. One long-term internal complaint about policy administration in the USSR was that the party apparatus too often supplanted the government bureaucracy rather than merely guiding its operation. Given the broad extent of state ownership and control in the USSR—over virtually the whole economy, all educational institutions, all of the sanctioned media of communication, every cultural organization (museums, orchestras, theaters, ballet companies, etc.)—it becomes clear how pervasive (and stifling) party influence could be. In a general sense, this control was administered by the Secretariat.

This high level of party-state dominance made possible another feature of the political system: the ability of the party to oversee the appointment of persons to key posts, not just in the party, but in the government, the economy, the educational system, and other areas. This system was known by the Russian word *nomenklatura*. As the meaning of the term evolved, the holders of such posts came to be referred to as "the *nomenklatura*," part of the elite of Soviet society. Many of the well-placed members of the Soviet *nomenklatura* successfully survived the upheavals of the late Soviet period and have risen to elite status in post-Soviet Russia and elsewhere in the former Soviet Union.

Finally, the phenomenon of party dominance in the Soviet Union was imposed in yet another way: through analogous Communist Party structures, with analogous mechanisms for exercising political control, at the republic, regional and local levels in various parts of the country.

Although these subunits enjoyed some autonomy, Moscow went to considerable lengths to maximize its centralized authority and power.

The Gorbachev Era: Decline of the Old System

At the beginning of this chapter the abandonment of the old political system in the USSR was given as the period between 1984 and 1989. Now it is time to look at those years more closely. During most of that period Gorbachev was at the helm (as noted previously, he took over the general secretaryship in March 1985).

In that connection, a few words should be said about Gorbachev's role in the process of change. Certainly Gorbachev was the most important Soviet politician of his era. That said, it is also true that he *alone* wasn't responsible for the changes of the period. He came along when the mood of many people, concerned by the drift of the country and the apparent ineffectiveness of its aging leadership, favored change. There was plenty of support for the idea of moving the USSR in a more modern, more liberal direction. Furthermore, many of the ideas for change advocated by Gorbachev were not new. Some had been endorsed by members of the dissident community in the Soviet Union (Brown 1996, 8). Some had been put forward cautiously by establishment economists, lawyers, and other professionals. And when Gorbachev did move to institute change, he relied on the counsel of countless colleagues and advisors, from fellow Politburo members and other party and government officials to specialists in a wide range of technical and scholarly fields.

It should also be pointed out that Gorbachev's period in power coincided with a time when other significant factors were affecting the country. These included the nationalities problem; the increasing openness of the USSR to outside influences; population dynamics, which were challenging Russian and Slavic dominance in the country; and the comparative stagnation in Soviet economic growth and technological progress. These matters would come to influence the USSR in profound ways, over which Gorbachev was to have little control.

In short, change in the USSR involved numerous considerations, and was far more complex than merely the succession to the top post of a new man. Nevertheless, it is without question that the changes in question *did* take place under Gorbachev, and there is little doubt that, particularly in the early years of reform, he was at the forefront of the process. The late 1980s and early 1990s were unquestionably the Gorbachev era.

Mikhail Gorbachev was born in March 1931 in the village of Privolnoe in the Stavropol region of southern Russia. He came from a family of peasants and collective farmers. While still in his teens Gorbachev established a commendable record, both as a student and a farm laborer. Largely on the basis of these achievements he gained entry to the law school of Moscow University, from which he graduated in 1955.

The years in Moscow had a great impact on Gorbachev's development. In addition to receiving his higher education, he lived through the last years of the Stalinist reign and the first faint hints of the post-Stalin thaw in the Soviet capital. Shortly after his return to his native region the destalinization campaign burst into the open, highlighted by Khrushchev's "secret speech" at the Twentieth Party Congress in February 1956. The phrase "children of the Twentieth Congress" came into wide currency in the 1980s to describe the generation of young men and women who reached their political maturity in the mid-1950s and then participated in the reform movement 30 years later. Gorbachev was clearly one of these "children."

After the university, Gorbachev chose not the legal field but professional politics. While at Moscow University he had joined the Communist Party and become an organizer in the *komsomol* (communist youth organization). After his return to the Stavropol region, he continued in *komsomol* work, rising to leadership positions before switching to the local Communist Party apparatus. He had been the leader (first secretary) of the Stavropol region party organization for eight years when he was chosen, in 1978, to return to Moscow as secretary of the Central Committee for agriculture. At age 47 he had reached the elite ranks of the top 25 persons in the political hierarchy.

Gorbachev's rise up the career ladder was swift but otherwise not particularly remarkable. He followed a path typical of countless other Soviet politicians of his era and earlier. And once in Moscow his ascent continued in predictable fashion, except that only a few, of course, reach the pinnacle of power. He became a candidate member of the Politburo in

1979 and a full member in 1980. All the while he continued to fulfill a variety of functions as one of the Central Committee secretaries. When he was chosen general secretary in 1985, his selection was almost a foregone conclusion.

Gorbachev's first year and a half in power gave little hint of the radical transformation that would eventually overtake the country. It was, as one commentator put it, a "wordy era" (Keep 1995, 337), in which much was said about the ills of the system, and numerous resolutions and other documents were adopted. In terms of actual accomplishment, however, the record was rather modest and not radically out of line with the direction Gorbachev's predecessors had taken.

But to the careful observer, there was a hint of the changes to come. In a number of speeches, including one in December 1984, several months before he had become general secretary, Gorbachev talked about the need to create "a qualitatively new state of society" and to achieve a "profound transformation" of society and the economy. Perhaps more important, he employed several concepts that later expanded in meaning and came to be closely associated with his period of rule. Among them, the most important were *glasnost* and *perestroika*.

Glasnost can be translated as "openness," "publicity" or "candor." Gorbachev was not the first to use the term in a political context; it can be found in Russian political tracts of the nineteenth century. It was used by Soviet dissidents during the 1960s and 1970s in calling for greater freedom of expression. It even found its way into statements by Brezhnev. And Andropov, who was in a sense a mentor of Gorbachev, invoked the term in calling for the party to be more responsive to the people in fighting corruption and mismanagement.

And it seems to have been in this sense—the idea that the authorities should be more open with the people in discussing problems in the system—that Gorbachev first called for glasnost. But as the use of the term continued, its meaning expanded, and for many it was seen not just as a tool for the political authorities but as a "facilitating concept" (Brown 1996, 125) that writers, journalists and the growing ranks of the democratically minded employed to push for something akin to freedom of speech. It took some time for this transmutation to take place, however.

Perestroika had similarly modest beginnings. The term, which means "restructuring," can be found in speeches by Gorbachev as early as the 1970s. Both then and later, when used by Gorbachev early in his time as general secretary, his field of vision regarding the concept was limited to reforming the economy. From late 1986 onward Gorbachev began to speak differently, both as to what perestroika should embrace and about the kind of reform the country needed.

At a Central Committee meeting in January 1987 he expanded perestroika to include political reform, stating that democratization was "at the core of restructuring" (White 1992, 29). Later that year Gorbachev's book, *Perestroika: New Thinking for Our Country and the World*, was published in English and became an immediate bestseller. It confirmed his expansive view of perestroika. In the book, Gorbachev spelled out his views on a range of topics. He made it clear that perestroika was not just about economics but embraced important components of domestic politics and even international politics as well. And his frequent use of the terms "revolution" and "revolutionary" suggested that he envisaged a significant break with past practices. "Politics," wrote Gorbachev, "is undoubtedly the most important thing in any revolutionary process. This is equally true of perestroika. Therefore, we must attach priority to political measures, broad and genuine democratization, the resolute struggle against red tape and violations of law, and the active involvement of the masses in managing the country's affairs. All this is directly linked with the main question of any revolution, the question of power" (Gorbachev 1987, 54).

Certainly there were some ambiguities in these words. As became clear later, his conception of democratization was considerably different from the standard understanding of the process in the West, for he held strongly to the view that democratization was to take place within the context of a one-party system. And even elsewhere in the book one finds statements that seem to contradict his more radical prescriptions for change. In the sentence that follows the passage quoted above, Gorbachev assures the reader that "we are not going to change Soviet power, of course, or abandon fundamental principles."

But when compared with statements of Soviet leaders of the past, what Gorbachev had to say in the book appeared spontaneous and fresh. Its temperate, confident tone avoided saber-rattling and threats. Even though the book was prepared primarily for a foreign audience, one could see that here was a man whose purpose was to change the way in which the Soviet system operated.

But this was all still in the future. During 1985 and much of 1986 he moved cautiously, talking far more about reform than actually implementing it. He revived Andropov's campaign to tighten labor discipline and called for more vigilant criminal investigation of official corruption. He and his lieutenants spoke endlessly of economic acceleration (*uskorenie*), but only within the context of the system as it existed. On the agricultural front he succeeded, in late 1985, in having five ministries and one state committee abolished, replacing them with a single State Committee for the Agro-Industrial Complex (*Gosagroprom*). For a variety of reasons, however, *Gosagroprom* never lived up to its advance billing. It was abolished in 1989, and its tasks were transferred to republic-level agencies.

But the policy development most associated with the early Gorbachev era was the anti-alcohol campaign. This is somewhat ironic, since others on the Politburo were mainly behind the effort, although Gorbachev embraced the idea once it was initiated (White 1996, esp 66–68; Brown 1996, 141). Started in the spring of 1985, its purpose was primarily to improve worker performance and combat alcohol-induced violations of public order. A number of concrete measures were taken to curtail the sale of vodka and other alcoholic beverages. Some vodka distilleries were closed. Vineyards were plowed under. The serving of alcoholic beverages at state functions was banned. But the campaign did not achieve the intended results. Large numbers of citizens turned to making alcoholic beverages at home, and the treasury suffered significantly from the loss of revenue on sales of alcohol, a government monopoly. Moreover, the crusade against alcohol was enormously unpopular with large numbers of citizens. By mid-1987, in the midst of the launching of the more serious stage of perestroika, the campaign began to be dismantled. A year later, its outward signs had virtually disappeared.

Why was it that Gorbachev proceeded so slowly during the early period? Some analysts assert that he came to the job with no particular reform agenda in mind, and that only when he had occupied the top job for a period of time and had seen the depth of the problems facing the Soviet Union did he come to the conclusion that more radical change in the system was necessary. Then, because he was a product of the traditional Soviet system, he needed time to outgrow the habits of the typical apparatchik before he could embark on the path toward comprehensive change (Hosking 1990, 127–29).

Others believe that Gorbachev came to office with the intention of effecting bold reform but that he was constrained in several ways from moving immediately. Archie Brown, who holds this view, argues that what was required to allow Gorbachev's turn toward radical reform was a combination of "learning, power and pressure" (Brown 1996,12–14). Gorbachev needed his first years to size up the situation and to gain experience in the job. He consulted widely with members of the leadership sympathetic with his views, as well as reform economists and other intellectuals. It was also necessary to strengthen his grip on the levers of power. In considerable part this was accomplished by replacing those who were likely to oppose reform with younger, more progressive politicians. As the reform process advanced, however, and glasnost permitted ever more demands from diverse political, ethnic and economic interests, Gorbachev felt increasing pressure to push reform further. The process itself, in other words, created a momentum of its own.

The question of whether Gorbachev took office as a serious reformer or was pushed in that direction by events cannot be answered with certainty. What can be discussed with reasonable assurance is the course that the reform took between late 1986 and 1989.

Several Key Appointments

Over the course of his years in power Gorbachev succeeded in replacing a number of holdovers from the past with politicians more to his liking. Even so, he was never able to gain complete control over the Politburo or Central Committee. Opposition to many of Gorbachev's policy initiatives was sustained and bitter, particularly when it became clear that his actions were leading to a weakening of the political role of the Communist Party. In addition, Gorbachev made some errors in judgment, choosing men for key posts who would later turn against him. Space limitations prevent a thorough analysis of Gorbachev's personnel policies, but a brief review of several of his early appointments will be instructive.

Barely a month after Gorbachev came to power, Nikolai Ryzhkov and Yegor Ligachev were named full members of the Politburo without serving the usual period of candidate membership first. Within a few months Ryzhkov was appointed prime minister, replacing 80-year-old Nikolai Tikhonov, and Ligachev assumed the position of second-in-command to Gorbachev on the Secretariat. In time, both would demonstrate serious differences with Gorbachev over the nature of reform. Ryzhkov proved more conservative on economic matters. Ligachev, while seeming to endorse glasnost and perestroika, found a whole range of Gorbachev's actions too extreme. But both remained in their posts through much of the Gorbachev period, Ligachev until mid-1990 and Ryzhkov until early 1991.

Two other 1985 appointees who would prove more supportive of Gorbachev's reform efforts were Alexander Yakovlev and Eduard Shevardnadze. Yakovlev had impressed Gorbachev during the latter's visit to Canada in 1983, where Yakovlev was serving as ambassador. It was at this time that their political friendship was forged. Yakovlev was named head of the propaganda department of the Central Committee in August 1985, and thereafter his advancement was exceedingly swift: to secretary of the Central Committee in March 1986, to candidate Politburo member in January 1987 and to full member in June (while maintaining his position on the Secretariat). More important than the posts that he achieved was his closeness to Gorbachev in ideas and reform impulses. Journalist Robert Kaiser's description captures the nature of the relationship well:

> [Yakovlev] is the second great personality of the Gorbachev revolution, fully its co-author in many respects. Without his influence, events at many key junctures would have developed differently. From the outset he was Gorbachev's ambassador to the intellectuals, the new leader's first critical constituency. He was the architect of *glasnost* and the most important protector of the liberal editors who, beginning in the summer of 1986, began to give the Soviet Union its first critical and independent press. Yakovlev also helped create and cultivate the new Gorbachev image at home and abroad, and he was the co-author of Gorbachev's "new thinking" in foreign policy. Perhaps most important, he was a soul mate of Gorbachev, a lonely man on a lonely mission. (Kaiser 1992, 106)

Shevardnadze was, in some respects, a highly unusual appointment. He was promoted to full Politburo membership in July and made foreign minister, replacing 76-year-old Andrei Gromyko, who had run the Soviet Union's foreign affairs establishment for 28 years. As the long-time head of the Georgian party organization (he had held the post for 13 years when appointed foreign minister), Shevardnadze's foreign experience was limited.

But he and Gorbachev had known each other since the 1960s, when both held responsible *komsomol* positions, Gorbachev in the Stavropol region and Shevardnadze in nearby Georgia. And prior to Gorbachev's appointment as general secretary, they had consulted with each other on the state of affairs in the USSR, agreeing that the system was in need of significant reform (Brown 1996, 81). In Shevardnadze, Gorbachev found a colleague whom he could trust, and one who shared his vision of perestroika for the Soviet Union's foreign policy.

Finally, among many other appointments by Gorbachev early in his tenure, undoubtedly the most notable was that of Boris Yeltsin. Yeltsin was born in 1931, a month before Gorbachev, near the Ural Mountains city of Sverdlovsk in central Russia. He received a technical education and worked in the construction industry before moving to professional party work in his late thirties. After serving in the top party post in Sverdlovsk (the city was renamed Ekaterinburg during the later stages of perestroika) for nearly ten years, he was called to Moscow in 1985. Ironically, Yegor Ligachev was one of those who recommended bringing Yeltsin to Moscow. As events unfolded over the next several years, Ligachev and Yeltsin became bitter adversaries.

Yeltsin first served in the central party apparat as chief of the department of construction and Central Committee secretary responsible for construction, but before the year was out he was named to the important post of first secretary of the Moscow party organization, replacing 71-year-old Victor Grishin. Early in 1986 he was named a candidate Politburo member.

Yeltsin quickly established himself as one of the more radical members of the leadership, as well as one of the more outspoken. At times he acted like a populist politician of the West by trying to establish a common bond with the people. This took various forms, including occasionally riding the subway to work, dropping in at local food stores, and visiting the homes of regular Muscovites. Early on he made a reputation by attacking the excessive privileges of the country's elite. But his colorful personality was not generally appreciated by his colleagues in the leadership. When, at an October 1987 Central Committee meeting, he harshly attacked the lack of progress of perestroika, singling out Ligachev (and, by implication, Gorbachev) for criticism (Kaiser 1992, 180), he exceeded the then acceptable limits of permissible behavior. Shortly thereafter he was vilified at a party meeting called specially for the purpose and removed from his positions. Gorbachev offered Yeltsin a relatively insignificant ministerial post, which Yeltsin accepted. If the country's political ground rules had remained as they were, that would have been the last anyone heard of Boris Yeltsin the politician. But by challenging the leadership Yeltsin had become a hero in the eyes of many, and when important Gorbachev-initiated political change came soon thereafter, Yeltsin was able to thrust himself back into the new political life of the country. This time, however, he was an antagonist of Gorbachev rather than an ally.

Toward Radical Reform: The Political Agenda

A number of events signaled the move toward more open politics. Undoubtedly one of the most promising of these was the December 1986 release of Andrei Sakharov from internal exile in the city of Gorky, hundreds of miles from Moscow. Sakharov, a brilliant physicist who had once done important secret work for the state (he was known as the father of the Soviet hydrogen bomb), had gained the enmity of the authorities for his outspoken advocacy of human rights and defense of those persecuted by the regime. He had been arrested in Moscow and banished to Gorky in 1980, during the Brezhnev era. His exile, a lawless act, had become one more black mark against the Soviet human rights record. Sakharov's release (in which Gorbachev played a direct role) was one of the early signs that something really different was under way in Soviet politics. In the three years left to Sakharov after his return to Moscow, he became something of a thorn in Gorbachev's side. He continued his defense of human rights and, as a deputy in the Soviet Union's new parliament, he clashed with Gorbachev over a number of issues.

But 1986 was not a year of unmixed liberalization. During the year the works of several previously banned writers began to be published (the poets Gumilev and Pasternak and the emigré novelist Nabokov, for instance). And new editors of several publications, who would soon push the limits of glasnost, were appointed. On the other hand, the Chernobyl accident took place in April 1986. The world first heard about it from foreign sources, as the Soviet authorities, including Gorbachev, attempted at first to minimize its importance. And in 1986 an American correspondent, Nicholas Daniloff, was arrested on trumped-up spy charges and held by the KGB, to be released a month later in a trade of prisoners after strong U.S. objections.

In spite of this mixed picture, it was clear that Gorbachev was continuing to pursue his reform agenda. The period of radical political reform took off in earnest in 1987. Under the banner of glasnost, discussions of once-taboo subjects became regular occurrences. And the first head-on effort to change the operation of political institutions was launched.

A Central Committee plenary meeting that had been postponed three times, surely because of the sensitive matters to be addressed, was held in January 1987. At the meeting Gorbachev expanded upon the concept of democratization, which had been little more than a slogan up to this time. Parts of the speech were quite traditional in form, containing a thorough cataloging of Soviet achievements and numerous references to Lenin for ideological support. But the overall message was explosive. Gorbachev proposed that in elections for party offices, more than one candidate should run. This principle would apply to all levels up to the union republic, and the elections would be conducted by secret ballot. He also recommended that "further democratization should also apply to the central leading bodies of the party," but in saying this he drew back from specifically proposing contested elections.

He also raised the question of convening, in the summer of the following year, an all-union party conference, to deal, as Gorbachev put it, with "further democratizing the life of the Party and society as a whole" (Gorbachov 1987, 122–23 and 148). This was an unusual move on Gorbachev's part. Under the party rules, another party *congress* could not be called until 1990. The rules did permit the convoking of a party *conference* during the period between congresses, but the practice had fallen into disuse, the last one having been called in 1941. So in making the proposal, which was later accepted by his colleagues, Gorbachev was seeking to speed up the process of political reform.

Gorbachev returned to the theme of democratization several more times during 1987, but resistance within the party was sufficient that actual accomplishments were meager. And conservative forces in society and in high party posts continued to show their strength. Somewhere along the line Gorbachev decided that since intra-party reform was proving difficult, he would need to take the process outside the party.

The Nineteenth All-Union Party Conference, a gathering of 5,000 delegates that met in Moscow in the summer of 1988, attracted intense interest both at home and abroad. By the time of the conference glasnost had opened the bounds of permissible political discussion considerably. But the Communist Party still monopolized political action and remained essentially unreformed. The ethnic awakening that would soon be such a prominent part of the scene was only beginning to surface. And the economy had so far experienced only tepid reform. The conference marked a turning point in several ways.

It was the first large party gathering in which the scenario was not fully scripted in advance. Some lively discussion occurred, including a sharp exchange between Yeltsin and Ligachev. And in the end, in spite of some outspoken criticism of the direction of perestroika, Gorbachev got much of what he wanted.

There was to be a curtailment of party power and the restructuring of the party's main operating principles accompanied by the creation of new parliamentary structures, chosen in a way that promised to be at least partly democratic. The size of the party apparatus was to be reduced and its functions restricted, making the state less dependent on party dictation. Another effort was to be made to democratize the party, including limiting high party officials to no more than two consecutive five-year terms.

The one-party system was to remain in place, however, with party leaders very much involved in governmental administration. First party secretaries at every level (local, republic, national) were expected to serve as the heads of corresponding parliamentary bodies. The new supreme parliament, the USSR Congress of People's Deputies, would be comprised of deputies elected from the traditional election districts (territorial and national-territorial) as well as from so-called social organizations, such as the Communist Party, the trade unions and other mass bodies. It was with regard to election from these social organizations that the potential for nondemocratic practices seemed greatest. Nevertheless, the conference resolution that embodied many of these proposed changes stated that in elections to parliamentary bodies, "the unrestricted nomination of candidates, broad and free discussion of candidates, the inclusion on the ballot of a larger number of candidates than there are seats to fill, [and] strict observance of democratic election procedures" were to be among the guiding principles ("On Perestroika" and "On Democratization and Political Reform" 1988).

If some of these provisions seem mutually contradictory, it is because they were. Gorbachev did not have a completely free hand in fashioning political reform as he saw fit. Moreover, his own vision of reform was far from clear. He sought to reduce the party's power yet maintain a one-party system. He intended to democratize the electoral system, but only up to a point. These sets of goals proved to be mutually exclusive.

As he proceeded further into this uncharted territory, he encountered a number of problems he had not foreseen. If such problems had been limited only to the nature of the political institutions he was creating, his task might have been manageable. But a series of major economic, social, and ethnic challenges, controllable when the system was less open, gradually took on huge proportions. Like the sorcerer's apprentice, he had unleashed forces that he could no longer control. The way in which this process played itself out under Gorbachev is discussed in the next chapter.

References

Brown, Archie. 1996. *The Gorbachev Factor.* Oxford: Oxford University Press.

Gorbachev, Mikhail. 1987. *Perestroika: New Thinking for Our Country and the World.* New York: Harper and Row.

Gorbachov, M. S. 1987. "On Restructuring the Party's Personnel Policy: Report to the Plenary Meeting of the CPSU Central Committee, 27 January 1987." *Speeches and Writings of M. S. Gorbachev, Volume 2.* Oxford: Pergamon Press.

Hosking, Geoffrey. 1990. *The Awakening of the Soviet Union.* Cambridge: Harvard University Press.

Joint Economic Committee, Congress of the United States. 1983. *Soviet Economy in the 1980s: Problems and Prospects.*

Juviler, Peter. 1998. *Freedom's Ordeal: The Struggle for Human Rights and Democracy in the Post-Soviet States.* Philadelphia: University of Pennsylvania Press.

Kaiser, Robert G. 1992. *Why Gorbachev Happened.* New York: Simon and Schuster.

Keep, John L. H. 1995. *Last of the Empires: A History of the Soviet Union, 1945–1991.* Oxford: Oxford University Press.

Löwenhardt, John, James R. Ozinga and Erik van Ree. 1992. *The Rise and Fall of the Soviet Politburo.* London: UCL Press.

"On Perestroika" and "On Democratization and Political Reform." 1988. Resolutions adopted at the 19th Conference of the Communist Party of the Soviet Union. *Izvestiia,* July 2. Condensed translations in *Current Digest of the Soviet Press* 40: 36, 12–15.

White, Stephen. 1992. *Gorbachev and After.* Cambridge: Cambridge University Press.

White, Stephen. 1996. *Russia Goes Dry: Alcohol, State and Society.* Cambridge: Cambridge University Press.

Chapter 2
From Open Politics to Collapse

Political Reform

The Nineteenth Conference of the party had set the course for political reform. Now the changes it had accepted had to be brought into being. This required that the still-compliant parliament, the USSR Supreme Soviet, adopt a series of amendments to the 1977 Constitution. This it quickly did in December 1988. Among the most important of the changes were the following:

1. A new "highest organ of state power," the Congress of People's Deputies, was created. In being so designated, the Congress took the place of the old Supreme Soviet. A new Supreme Soviet, with an altered role, was also created. The Congress was to be made up of 2,250 deputies, chosen on three bases: 750 from territorial units based on population size; 750 from nationality-territorial units; and 750 from social organizations, such as the Communist Party, trade unions and others.

2. The Congress was to meet once a year, in a session lasting just a few days. Among its duties was to name from its members a Supreme Soviet, a smaller standing parliament that was to act as "the continuously functioning legislative, management and control organ of USSR state power." Although both the Congress and the Supreme Soviet had the power to adopt laws, it was expected that the smaller body would exercise more authority. And if it could be populated largely by those in sympathy with the present leadership, a large measure of control over the system would be achieved. This is clearly what Gorbachev hoped for.

3. Structures parallel to these were to be established on the union republic and lower levels. Quite soon, however, sources of resistance to this arrangement developed, and the Constitution had to be changed further. This matter will be discussed below, in connection with the challenges from the republics.

4. Changes were made in the Constitution to accommodate the idea of contested elections. At the same time, a new electoral law was adopted that set forth detailed provisions on choosing the new parliament.

With the new electoral arrangements in place, the stage was set for the campaign and election, which occupied the first several months of 1989. As indicated, the USSR Congress of People's Deputies was to be composed of three sets of 750 deputies: two sets elected by the general population, from population-territorial districts and national-territorial districts; and the third 750 from a variety of all-union social organizations. Many of the latter had long been controlled by the Communist Party. If this control could be maintained, the party would be able to count on a considerable level of "automatic" support at Congress meetings. And to a great extent this is what happened. The Communist Party itself, through its Politburo, put up a slate of 100 candidates for the 100 deputy seats it was allowed to fill. The party body that was designated to do the actual selection of deputies, the Central Committee, duly approved the list. The same process took place in a number of other social organizations, although some of them actually nominated a few more candidates than there were seats available, thus requiring some genuine voting at the organizations' mass meetings (Kiernan 1993, 65–66; White 1992, 46–47).

A particularly interesting situation developed in the USSR Academy of Sciences, which was entitled to 20 seats. The academy's election screening committee eliminated the name of Andrei Sakharov (who had been proposed by numerous academy organizations), as well as those of other liberal scientists, from the list of proposed candidates. But supporters in the academy's general meeting of delegates were able to defeat the leadership's efforts to bypass Sakharov. In the end he and several other reformers gained seats in the Congress as representatives of the Academy of Sciences.

The election of the 1,500 other deputies was potentially more democratic (Barry and Barner-Barry 1991, 90–93). They would be chosen in single-member districts, by secret ballot, with no limit on the number of candidates. But the liberal provisions of the electoral law were often thwarted in practice. Party authorities were still in charge in localities around the country, and they could, if so inclined, resort to a number of means to control the process, including limiting electoral contests to a single candidate (as happened in 384 of 1,500 contests).

But by 1989 an awakening of sorts had begun in the country, and the authorities were no longer omnipotent. The press had become more outspoken, and some publications in particular were willing to report violations of the letter and spirit of the electoral law. Moreover, new political forces, such as popular fronts, political clubs and nationality movements, had come into being, and were prepared to push their interests in the elections. So if the elections were not completely democratic, neither were they the charades of the past. Nearly 3,000 candidates contested the 1,500 seats.

One unusual feature of the electoral law was the requirement that the winning candidate receive an absolute majority of the total vote. In single-member-district contests in a number of countries, for instance Great Britain and the United States, the candidate need only win a plurality of the vote, that is, more votes than any other candidate, in order to gain a seat. In most parliamentary elections in France in recent years, a candidate has been required to gain an absolute majority of the vote in the first ballot in order to win a seat. But if this is not achieved, a plurality suffices on the second ballot. The 1989 arrangement in the USSR was a throwback to the old electoral system, which also required an absolute majority. But under the old single-candidate arrangements, the requirement made little practical difference. Now it complicated the picture, sometimes necessitating more than one round of voting in order for a victor to be named.

A further peculiarity of the electoral system was the way of marking ballots. One voted in favor of a candidate by crossing out the names of all other candidates. One could cross out all of the names, thus voting for "none of the above," even when only one name was on the ballot. In the runup to the election, a grassroots campaign of sorts developed, the point of which was to urge a protest vote against candidates in one-person races, thus depriving them of the ability to obtain an absolute majority of the vote. This strategy worked in a number of cases.

The election results brought some surprises. Communist Party members constituted a large percentage of those elected, larger, in fact, than in the past. This was not particularly unexpected, since the Communist Party was still the only party in existence. But the data show that the composition of the party contingent was different in this parliament: high-level professional politicians were less well represented than previously, while the percentage of lower-echelon party members increased.

Moreover, there were some spectacular victories and defeats. Boris Yeltsin won a resounding victory in one of the Moscow constituencies against a party-supported establishment candidate, gaining over 89 percent of the vote. His populist campaign, built around attacking party privileges, proved enormously popular with the public. Interestingly, Yeltsin did not resign from the party until more than a year later. But this electoral victory was the beginning of the revival of his political career.

A number of other liberals were chosen over more conservative candidates. And recently awakened nationality interests scored well in their areas. The Lithuanian movement Sajudis won about 90 percent of the republic's seats, for instance. In Latvia the republic's conservative prime minister was defeated as were the mayors of Moscow and Kiev. Perhaps the most spectacular defeats were in the city of Leningrad, however. A whole series of high party officials failed to gain seats, most importantly Yuri Solovyov, the first secretary of the Leningrad party organization, who was also candidate member of the Politburo. He failed in his effort although running unopposed, a humiliation that quickly ended his political career.

In spite of these spectacular results, the new Congress was by no means a radical body. Many areas of the country elected rather conservative candidates, and the large majority of deputies chosen from social organizations held traditional political values. Still, Gorbachev was now about to be faced with increased challenges. When he headed a party organization that controlled an essentially closed political system, the range of forces to be reckoned with was relatively narrow. But as the country opened up, new voices, many with messages that departed from the conventional political wisdom, were increasingly heard. And now, with a new political institution that promised to exercise some real power, political authority was further dispersed.

Gorbachev was able to maintain reasonable control of the political process, particularly at the beginning of the Congress's operation. But it soon became clear that he was no longer at the forefront of reform. A number of politicians were advocating more radical solutions to the country's political, social and economic problems, and several nationality groups would soon push for changes more extreme than Gorbachev had ever imagined. Gorbachev soon became a centrist, not just in terms of his policy positions but also as a man in the middle, between increasingly vocal forces advocating more radical change on the one hand and those clinging to the status quo or wishing for a return to pre-perestroika days on the other. Gorbachev's success, and indeed his continued ability to remain at the helm, would depend upon his ability to mediate between these forces while addressing the problems that soon began to confront him on all sides.

As the Congress opened for its first session in May 1989, however, no one could anticipate the astonishing speed with which events would move. Gorbachev had little trouble being chosen to the top post of the new parliament, Chairman of the Supreme Soviet. The selection of deputies to serve in the smaller standing parliament, the Supreme Soviet, appeared in large part to favor the conservative forces (Brown 1996, 190–91). One of the glaring omissions from the ranks of the Supreme Soviet was Boris Yeltsin, in spite of his immense popularity with the population at large. This was corrected when a liberal deputy from Siberia, who had been chosen to the Supreme Soviet, stood down in Yeltsin's favor.

The first Congress session showed the Soviet Union and the world that the new parliament was like none other in the country's history of over 70 years. Great public attention was focused on the proceedings, which were televised live (a reported 20 percent falloff in industrial production took place during the first few days of the session). Deputies clamored to speak, as the meetings took on a spontaneous, feisty air. Formerly taboo subjects were discussed openly. In one of the early speeches, for instance, a deputy attacked the KGB as a "threat to democracy." Politburo members were criticized by name and labeled as incompetent. Gorbachev struggled to keep order, on occasion showing his authoritarian side (he once simply turned off Andrei Sakharov's microphone in order to end his remarks).

Compared with the rather chaotic Congress, the smaller Supreme Soviet operated in a more businesslike way. Although Gorbachev was able to achieve much of what he wanted from parliament, the going wasn't always smooth. For instance, several of the nominees for posts in the Council of Ministers were rejected by the Supreme Soviet, and further rejections would have taken place if a change in the Supreme Soviet's voting rules had not been pushed through. Moreover, groups of deputies were showing signs of organizing in order to promote common objectives. The most important of these aggregations came to be known as the Inter-Regional Group, a radical caucus led by several prominent deputies, including Boris Yeltsin. As would soon become clear, the agenda of the Inter-Regional Group was considerably different from that of Gorbachev and his allies.

In short, then, the new experiment with parliamentary government had gotten off to a somewhat chaotic but promising start. Problems were being discussed openly, political forces were beginning to organize, and it had been demonstrated that the old rules of the game, in which all important decisions were dictated in a top-down fashion, had been seriously challenged. If matters could have proceeded in this mode, the foundations of genuine parliamentary government might have been laid. But too many problems were looming outside the parliamentary arena that threatened the relative calm that had recently prevailed. The most important of these had to do with economic choices, nationality challenges and foreign policy initiatives.

Economic Choices

Gorbachev had inherited a deeply troubled economy. The impressive growth rates of the 1960s and 1970s had disappeared by the mid-1980s. The gap between the Soviet Union and its Western adversaries, which Khrushchev had promised to eliminate a generation earlier, was widening. Soviet industrial equipment was extremely outmoded, and the country was being left behind in the scientific-technological revolution. In spite of continued tinkering with the socialized system of agriculture and the infusion of significant investments, the Soviet Union was having difficulty feeding its population.

In attempting to match the West militarily and with regard to global influence, domestic investment—particularly in areas that directly affected the population—had long been underfunded. Thus, medical care was free but was of poor quality and difficult to obtain for most citizens. Housing was inexpensive but in pathetically short supply. In fact, the whole consumer sector was plagued by endemic shortages.

These were, of course, matters of which all Soviet citizens were well aware. But with the advent of glasnost and permission to discuss them openly, the new leadership had assumed a certain responsibility. Improvement, based on economic reform, was the order of the day. Reform unquestionably implied some loosening of the central control of all aspects of economic life that had characterized the system for so long. Could this be accomplished without some decentralization of *political* control? Gorbachev would need to convince his more conservative colleagues in the Communist Party that economic reform would not threaten the party's preeminent position. This was a challenge that came to be of increasing significance as reform proceeded on several fronts.

It is without question that in the years that followed, a number of changes in the economic system were brought about by Gorbachev and his colleagues. But did Gorbachev have an economic *plan*, or even a general sense of where he was going in embarking on these changes? Views differ on this subject, but some analysts have concluded that Gorbachev had little idea of how economic reform could be achieved (Hough 1997, 104–106).

As mentioned in Chapter 1, reform started slowly. Under the banner of *uskorenie* (acceleration), attempts were made to tighten labor discipline, including the ill-fated anti-alcohol campaign. And a giant State Committee for the Agro-Industrial Complex (*Gosagroprom*) was created to replace five ministries whose functions included aspects of agriculture. But this innovation was abandoned several years later. Late in 1986 a Law on Individual Labor Activity was adopted, which allowed limited forays into private economic activity by individuals and family members in such fields as tutoring, tailoring and automobile or appliance repair.

The Law on the State Enterprise, adopted in 1987, was intended to give these units much greater autonomy in carrying out their functions. Since these enterprises were the basic economic organizations of the USSR's socialized economy, freeing them from the extensive political control under which they had traditionally operated implied a considerable change in the system. Unfortunately, in its implementation the law did not achieve its objectives (Moskoff 1993, 2–13).

The next year, 1988, saw the adoption of one of the most well-known pieces of economic legislation of the Gorbachev period, the Law on

Cooperatives. Cooperatives were designed to be small to medium-sized units engaged in production and providing services. In practice cooperatives took many forms, including catering, consumer goods production, providing domestic services, restaurants and the like (White 1992, 119).

Although the number of cooperatives expanded quickly and came eventually to employ millions of workers, resentment against them was considerable. It came from a variety of sources: those who objected to the high prices some cooperatives charged, those envious of cooperative successes, and those who saw cooperatives merely as disguised private enterprise, covered by a fig leaf of socialist mythology. In spite of the law, cooperatives often received little support from the local authorities, and thus became easy victims of the growing organized crime movement, forced to pay protection money or simply taken over by mafia organizations.

The reform measures so far discussed had little positive effect on Soviet economic performance, which continued to show disappointing results in the last years of the 1980s (White 1992, 121–32). This led a number of liberal economists to look for even more radical reform. What Archie Brown called "the most dramatic episode in the history of attempted economic reform of the Gorbachev era," the so-called 500 Days program, developed in the latter months of 1990 (Brown 1996, 150). This proposal, crafted by a group of economists led by Stanislav Shatalin and Grigory Yavlinsky, envisaged large-scale privatization of the economy and the creation of market institutions within a period of just over 16 months. Much of the authority for implementing the plan was ceded to the Soviet Union's constituent republics. It would be difficult to overstate the significance of this proposal, which would have eventually wiped out the state socialist economic system under which the country had lived for seven decades.

At first Gorbachev endorsed the plan, as Yeltsin had earlier. But under pressure from a number of more conservative forces, including his own prime minister, Gorbachev sought a compromise that scaled back the more radical features of the Shatalin-Yavlinsky program. Whether or not the "500 Days" was a workable plan will never be known. But Gorbachev's vacillation at the crucial time led its adherents to lose faith in him as a genuine reformer. For the Soviet period, economic innovation was essentially over.

Nationality Challenges

Although numerous problems beset Gorbachev during his nearly seven years in power, it is fair to say that the one he least anticipated, and was least prepared for, was the issue of nationality conflict. When he awoke to the seriousness of the problem, he seemed to believe (or hope) that economic recovery would dampen nationalist yearnings (Olcott 1999, 138). Since significant economic improvement did not come during the Gorbachev era, this idea remained untested. But ethnic consciousness, and its accompanying problems, quickly manifested itself.

Since traditional Soviet ideology stressed internationalism as a positive feature of the political system, it was easy to justify the repression of nationalist sentiments as contrary to the interests of the state. This strategy had worked well for the Moscow leadership during much of Soviet history. By placing compliant (if sometimes corrupt) leaders in charge of the ethnic territories (the so-called union republics and subsidiary nationality-based regions), the central authorities, aided by an efficient security apparatus, were able to maintain firm control over the nationality-based areas of the USSR.

But this policy, like much else in Soviet practice, became a victim of the very tactics that Gorbachev selected in order to revive the system. By encouraging glasnost, Gorbachev was asking people to talk about what was on their minds, what was bothering them. It is quite clear that Gorbachev and his lieutenants did not intend that the Soviet system would immediately be thrown wide open. But as taboos fell and more subjects became allowable for discussion, the authorities' control over the process diminished. Thus did ethnic grievances gradually become a permitted topic.

Even before this process got seriously under way, however, the ethnic factor showed its potential for disrupting the old ways. During the period 1985–1987 Gorbachev secured the replacement of a number of top leaders in the republics. In the first of these moves, in December 1985, the long-term party chief of Kazakhstan, an ethnic Kazakh, was replaced by a Russian. This went against the long-standing practice in which a republic's first secretary was from the indigenous nationality, and the second secretary was often a Russian. When demonstrations and rioting in the capital city of Kazakhstan ensued and were suppressed with force, a new stage in inter-ethnic relations had been reached. The days of easy central control of nationality affairs were over.

The riots in Kazakhstan grew out of the attempt to assert greater *central* control (which most Kazakhs naturally saw as *Russian* control) over the periphery. But not all ethnic resentment was directed against the Russians. The problem in the region known as Nagorno-Karabakh, which remains unresolved to this day, was essentially a territorial issue between two relatively small Soviet nationalities. Nagorno-Karabakh is a region largely inhabited by Christian Armenians, but located within the republic of Azerbaijan, whose dominant ethnic group, the Azeris, have a Moslem tradition. Although Nagorno-Karabakh had the status of an autonomous republic within Azerbaijan, its inhabitants objected to having their affairs largely administered from Baku, the Azerbaijan capital. They alleged all manner of discrimination, which was resented not only in Nagorno-Karabakh, but also in the neighboring Soviet republic of Armenia. During the decades of authoritarian Soviet rule, this dispute was kept largely under wraps. Glasnost brought long-simmering grievances into the open and led in 1988 to a movement to return Nagorno-Karabakh to the "motherland" (Keep 1995, 365). Fighting ensued, and at times took on the character of an all-out war. Although Moscow attempted to control the situation, both sides became embittered toward the central authorities for failing to resolve the problem to their satisfaction.

Nor were these the only ethnic conflicts along the Soviet Union's southern fringe. In the Caucasus republic of Georgia, two extremely small nationalities, the 164,000 South Ossetians and the 95,000 Abkhazians, sought greater autonomy from Georgia proper. The Black Sea city of Sukhumi and other sites in Abkhazia witnessed numerous bloody battles between Georgians and Abkhazians. Nationalism in the republic of Moldavia (now Moldova) created a reaction from several of the non-Romanian ethnic groups there. When a 1989 law made Romanian the official language of the republic, other minorities, particularly the Russians and the Ukrainians, protested. A more serious threat to Moldovan territorial integrity has been the effort of residents in the Dniestr River region and to its east (mostly Russians and Ukrainians) to create a separate Transdniestr Republic (Fowkes 1997, 141).

But undoubtedly the major challenge to Soviet unity came from the north, in the three Baltic republics of Estonia, Latvia and Lithuania. Forcibly incorporated into the USSR in 1940, these three states had experienced a shorter period of Soviet rule than did the other union republics. Perhaps for this reason, they were quicker to seek increased autonomy within the USSR, and from there it became a short step to overt talk of independence.

Among the issues that bothered the Balts, particularly the largely Protestant Estonians and Latvians, was the population composition of their lands. Estonia had gone from being about 90 percent Estonian at the time of annexation to just over 60 percent at the end of the 1980s. During that same period, the proportion of Latvians in Latvia dropped from over three-quarters to just over half. By contrast, in Lithuania, a country with a strong Catholic tradition, the Lithuanian portion of the population had remained steady at about 80 percent for the previous several decades.

Another matter that engendered activism in the Baltic states was concern about environmental degradation that each of the countries had experienced. The most overtly political issue, however, was the secret agreements with Germany that led to the USSR's annexation of Latvia, Lithuania and Estonia. At first the demand was merely for acknowledgment of the existence of these "secret protocols." But by the time of a massive demonstration in all three republics on the 50th anniversary of the Nazi-Soviet Pact (August 23, 1989), sentiment in the Baltic states seemed to be leaning in the direction of demanding outright independence from the USSR (Strayer 1998, 152–56).

Another way in which the Baltic states were out front in separatist leanings was in their electoral behavior. In the 1989 elections to the new USSR-level Congress of People's Deputies, described earlier in this chapter, a large majority of the deputies elected in each of the Baltic states belonged to movements not associated with the republic communist parties (Sajudis in Lithuania, and Popular Front parties in Latvia and Estonia). Shortly after the Congress began to meet in Moscow in mid-1989, the deputies from Lithuania left the session, never to return. When the elections took place for the republic congresses of people's deputies in early 1990, Sajudis won a majority of seats in the Lithuanian parliament. At its first session the parliament declared Lithuanian independence. Gorbachev termed the act invalid, and considerable strife followed in the next seventeen months, before independence became a reality. But with this act Lithuania pointed the direction toward which the Soviet Union was going.

This section has discussed several of the numerous ethnic problems that Gorbachev faced during his years in power. But no examination of this issue would be complete without addressing Russian nationalism. Nationalist sentiments had long existed in Russia, even during the time when the prevailing communist ideology might have been expected to curb them. Two major factors were at work in the increasing manifestations of Russian nationalism under Gorbachev. First, with the advent of glasnost, old grievances could be given freer expression. And second, the changes associated with the Gorbachev era created new resentments.

The most obvious concerns were undoubtedly economic. Those from Russia who had traveled around the USSR noted the higher standard of living in several other republics. In shopping in their own collective farm markets, Russians saw stalls dominated by sellers from the Caucasus region, charging what many considered inflated prices. Some Russian regional leaders, whose territories included many millions of people and involved huge economic operations, resented the lobbying access in Moscow of certain ethnic regions (e.g., Estonia, with 1.5 million people) because of their status as union republics (Hough 1997, 241).

Less tangible matters also caused complaints. Russia's lack of a Russian branch of the Academy of Sciences and of a separate Communist Party organization (both of which all of the other republics had) were often cited. The fact that Russians dominated both the USSR Academy of Sciences and the Communist Party of the Soviet Union was not the issue; it was simply that Russia did not have its own organizations.

A more serious issue had to do with language. Russian was not only the first language of the Russian Soviet Federated Socialist Republic (the RSFSR—the Soviet Union's largest constituent unit). It was also the first or second language in all of the other republics, understood and spoken by much of the population across the whole USSR. Moreover, most Russians living in the other republics of the Soviet Union (they numbered 25 million during the Gorbachev era) did not learn the local language. They assumed that the other nationality groups should know Russian (which, as indicated, was typically the case). But when nationalist sentiments began to assert themselves in the republics, the situation changed. A number of the republics adopted language laws that stressed the importance of the local language. This appeared to threaten the comfortable situation that most Russians had traditionally enjoyed as residents of the other republics.

Other factors also fueled the growth of Russian nationalist sentiments. Some Russian patriots condemned the whole Soviet experience, including the "Western" influence of Marx and communism, as profoundly anti-Russian. These sentiments were translated into political action in a wide variety of initiatives and organizational forms, from the extreme right wing chauvinistic and anti-Semitic *Pamyat* (Memory) society to moderate organizations, such as the Fund for Soviet Culture, headed by the respected scholar Dmitri Likhachev (Keep 1995, 385; Strayer 1998, 167). Undoubtedly the strongest challenge to Gorbachev, however, came from Boris Yeltsin, who used nationalist themes—reform in the context of "Russian sovereignty"—to carry out his political and personal struggle against the USSR's leader.

Unlike some other republics, however, where a variety of forces united temporarily to pursue a single goal—their common interest in autonomy and even independence from central control—the Russian nationalists were extremely diverse in their objectives. They lacked what Robert Strayer has called "a clear or single target" (Strayer 1998, 170). Thus, nationalism in Russia did not coalesce into a powerful enough force to dominate the political scene. But the diverse strands of nationalist sentiment have continued to play important roles in Russian politics, often clashing with each other over a range of issues.

Foreign Policy Initiatives

As with Gorbachev's initiatives on the domestic side, his efforts to reorient relations with the outside world took some time to unfold. A number of key personnel changes were made over a period of several years, the most important of which was the replacement of Andrei Gromyko as Minister of Foreign Affairs by Eduard Shevardnadze. Gromyko had been Soviet foreign minister for 28 years. He and Gorbachev seemed to be on cordial terms, but Gromyko was too closely associated with the policies of the past. He was elevated to the largely ceremonial post of chairman of the Presidium of the Supreme Soviet (often referred to loosely as the presidency). In Shevardnadze Gorbachev was choosing a longtime and trusted colleague. As a person with no ties to the foreign affairs establishment, the flexible and resourceful Shevardnadze had the capacity to lead the ministry in new directions.

Among a number of others upon whom Gorbachev came to rely in foreign policy, of chief importance was Aleksandr Yakovlev. During Gorbachev's years in power Yakovlev held several positions, rising eventually to full Politburo member in charge of ideology and foreign policy. Yakovlev's influence derived not so much from his official titles as from his closeness to Gorbachev as an advisor and confidant.

As important as Gorbachev's foreign policy initiatives were in their own right, it is certainly true that they were closely tied to the country's domestic situation. Military expenditures were consuming about a quarter of the USSR's national budget, which seriously hampered the country's potential for domestic reform. Gorbachev hoped that a negotiated reduction in arms expenditures would permit him to embark on comprehensive internal changes. Much of what he initiated in the foreign policy realm should be seen in this light.

"New political thinking," or simply "new thinking" (*novoe myshlenie*) was the byword for Gorbachev's foreign policy ideas, much as perestroika was used to characterize his plans for the domestic scene. Commentators have observed that the proposals comprising the new thinking were not particularly new (e.g., Sakwa 1991, 316; White 1992, 219). Several of the ideas had been put forward earlier by Soviet scholars and other specialists, and some of the terminology dated back to the time of previous USSR leaders. But the sheer number of initiatives and the relative openness of their discussion were qualitatively new departures from the past. And the eventual political fallout from the actions taken brought about unprecedented change.

Foreign policy developments of the Gorbachev era embraced a wide range of issues. The assessment of their success or failure depends upon one's perspective. The general diminution of international tensions, the reduction of the number of "hot spots" of superpower contention, and agreement between the USSR and the West on a large number of issues were seen as positive accomplishments by large numbers of people in the Soviet Union and abroad. But these same policies contributed to the collapse of alliances and cooperative economic arrangements that had long been centerpieces of Soviet foreign policy (the Warsaw Pact and the Council for Mutual Economic Assistance, for instance, ceased to exist before Gorbachev left office). They undoubtedly encouraged nationality groups within the Soviet Union to hope for greater autonomy or even independence. And Gorbachev's more open style exposed to the outside world the manifold weaknesses of the Soviet system, which were much harder to document when the country operated in its traditional closed manner. These results could not help but bother many in the Soviet Union, particularly those in the country of a rightist persuasion.

Among the most noteworthy foreign policy developments under Gorbachev were the following. The withdrawal of Soviet troops from Afghanistan was achieved in 1989. This removed one of the principal barriers to improved relations with the West and extricated the USSR from a draining ten-year military action. Large cuts in Soviet conventional forces, and in missiles and other weapons systems, were also achieved. Through the efforts of Gorbachev and Shevardnadze, Soviet influence was cut back in Latin America, Southeast Asia and Africa. But undoubtedly the most important and far-reaching development was in Eastern Europe.

In a remarkable speech at the United Nations in New York in December 1988, Gorbachev disavowed force as an instrument of foreign policy and endorsed freedom of choice for all nations as a universal principle. The so-called Brezhnev Doctrine had been the justification for the invasion of Czechoslovakia in 1968 by Warsaw Pact forces, led by the Soviet Union. Its purpose, which was to prevent any Eastern European country from straying from the socialist bloc, emphasized anything but freedom of choice. Was Gorbachev now repudiating the Brezhnev Doctrine? Although it took some time to test the proposition, clearly he was. When the former Soviet satellites of Eastern Europe moved the next year to withdraw from the Soviet bloc, Gorbachev did nothing to prevent them from doing so. His words had certainly encouraged this action, and with the successes of the Eastern European countries in breaking free from the Soviet orbit, there was greater hope for those in the Soviet Union who aspired to a loosening of Moscow's control over their territories.

1990 and Beyond

Nineteen ninety was a transition year in Gorbachev's fortunes as Soviet leader. As the year began, he still enjoyed a high level of public support, both in Russia and in the Soviet Union as a whole (Brown 1996, 238). By the time he received the Nobel Peace Prize in October, he had been hit by a series of setbacks theretofore unprecedented during his period of rule. And when he gave his New Year address to the country on December 31, he called 1990 "one of the most difficult years in our history" (Kaiser 1992, 482). The sources of his difficulties are not hard to discern. They relate in large part to the problem areas just discussed, and to the backlash that developed when the political authorities proved incapable of solving, or at least controlling, the situation.

The year brought no relief to the consumer on the economic front. In fact, in May, when the government called for higher prices, including substantial increases in the cost of bread, panic buying cleared the shelves of many goods. Later there were "cigarette riots" in several cities, and food rationing was instituted in Leningrad. As already discussed, 1990 was also the year of the "500 Days" proposal, which Gorbachev vacillated over before rejecting.

Lithuania led the republics in seeking autonomy from central control. Massive demonstrations for independence took place in Vilnius, the capital city, in January. In February the nationalist Sajudis movement won a majority of seats in the Lithuanian parliament. And in March the parliament declared Lithuania independent. Intense pressure from Moscow over the succeeding months kept independence from being realized for the time being. But the Lithuanian leaders made it clear that the republic would not go back to the old days of being a compliant province. Sentiment for autonomy from Moscow was not unique to Lithuania. Before the year was out every one of the 15 USSR republics had declared either independence or "sovereignty." The vagueness of the latter term made it difficult to determine the intentions of those republics that chose it. Sovereignty implied something less than a full breaking of ties with Moscow, but it was probably seen in some republics as an intermediate step before independence was declared. Certainly it indicated a strong desire to loosen the degree of central control. As the year proceeded, several republics declared that their laws took precedence over those of the central government. What ensued came to be known as the "war of laws." Gorbachev fought back, using the special powers recently granted by parliament to try to assert the predominance of national law. But he also pursued another strategy, aimed at the voluntary cooperation of the republics in creating a new kind of state arrangement. This manifested itself in the form of a new union treaty, the first draft of which was circulated in the fall of 1990. Gorbachev's efforts on this matter continued over the next year, and ended only with the collapse of the USSR.

Two developments in the winter and spring of 1990 show that the ferment was also affecting the central political institutions. Radicals, led by Andrei Sakharov, had been clamoring for the elimination of Article 6 of the Soviet Constitution, which granted the Communist Party a monopoly on political power. It is said that Gorbachev privately also wanted Article 6 changed, but only later, in the context of the adoption of a completely new constitution (Brown 1996, 193-94). But as political developments, particularly in some of the republics, seemed to be headed in the direction of a multiparty system in any case, Gorbachev and his allies decided to accept what seemed to be inevitable.

The party Central Committee approved the elimination of the party's monopoly in February 1990, reportedly over the bitter objections of a number of party conservatives (Hough 1997, 268; Kaiser 1992, 320–21). And the next month parliament made the necessary changes to the constitution. The words in the preamble referring to "the leading role of the Communist Party—the vanguard of the people," were eliminated. Article 6 was not dropped altogether, but its provisions that described the party as "the leading and guiding force of Soviet society and the nucleus of its political system" and assigned it the function of determining the general lines of domestic and foreign policy were replaced by a statement to the effect that the Communist Party, "other political parties," and other organizations may participate in the operation of the political system.

The other important change directly affected Gorbachev's position of power in the political hierarchy. This was the creation of a completely new institution, the presidency of the USSR. Perhaps because the status and power of the Communist Party were diminishing, but certainly also because Gorbachev could see the need for more authority than he could muster as chairman of the Supreme Soviet, he agreed to the creation of the presidency. As recently as six months earlier he had insisted that the presidency was not needed. But along with the demise of the party came a variety of internal problems, most notably violent ethnic unrest in various parts of the country, the increasingly separatist sentiment of leaders and movements in several union republics, and a series of debilitating strikes, particularly by coal miners, in mid-1989. By early 1990 Gorbachev came to see the need for a stronger executive to cope with these problems. So at the same session of parliament that altered Article 6 of the constitution, the necessary constitutional changes were made to establish a presidency with broad executive powers.

The constitution provided that the president was to be popularly elected. Regarding the first incumbent for the office, however, Gorbachev proposed an exception allowing the president to be chosen by the Congress of People's Deputies. Over strong objection by many deputies and some segments of the public, Gorbachev carried the day. Before the parliamentary session was over, Gorbachev was chosen as the USSR's first (and last) president (Barry and Barner-Barry 1991, 78–81). Would his popular election, rather than parliamentary selection, have made any difference, 17 months later, when the USSR collapsed and he resigned the presidency? Probably not. But the fact that he did not begin his term as chief executive by seeking a popular mandate was considered by many to be an inauspicious start.

A sign that Gorbachev's image was no longer inviolate came on May 1, when he and other leaders viewing the May Day parade from atop the Lenin Mausoleum were jeered by participants in the parade. The leaders left the mausoleum rather than submit to the censure. More serious challenges to Gorbachev's authority came from other politicians, however. The winter and spring of 1990 brought elections to the parliaments of the union republics. As on the USSR level the previous year, the thorough orchestration that had created legislatures completely submissive to the Communist Party was abandoned. Thus, as already discussed, the Lithuanian parliament elected in February declared the republic's independence the following month. Although the RSFSR (Russian) parliament elected in 1990 did not go this far, it presented serious problems for Gorbachev nonetheless. First and foremost, it provided a forum from which Boris Yeltsin could challenge the Soviet leader. At the first session of the Congress of People's Deputies in May, Yeltsin was chosen chairman of the Supreme Soviet, the smaller standing parliament.

The fact that it took three ballots before Yeltsin was selected for this post indicates that his level of support was not particularly high. And in years to come, relations between Yeltsin and the Russian parliament would become extremely antagonistic. But in 1990 parliament went along with Yeltsin's efforts to promote Russia's interests, even declaring Russian laws superior to USSR laws, and thus exacerbating further the "war of laws" (Hough 1997, 335–38).

Several important developments also took place regarding the Communist Party. Communists in Russia finally organized a separate party organization in June, and chose a conservative leadership at the founding congress. The next month, the 28th (and last) Congress of the Communist Party of the Soviet Union took place. Once Gorbachev had assumed the presidency of the USSR, in March, he paid less attention to party affairs. This neglect of the party, as well as Gorbachev's support for changing Article 6 of the constitution, had led to resentment against him from some segments of the party leadership. And in the early days of the Congress delegates showed considerable hostility toward Gorbachev. Nevertheless, he was reelected to the top party post (though over 1,000 delegates to the Congress voted against him), and Yegor Ligachev, the conservative leader who had become increasingly critical of Gorbachev, was defeated in his bid for the position of deputy leader. One of the most dramatic moments of the Congress came near its end, when Boris Yeltsin took the rostrum to resign from the party, and then strode from the hall.

Gorbachev's "Turn to the Right"

Buffeted by the problems just described and subjected to increasingly bold criticism from both the left and the right, Gorbachev made a series of policy and personnel changes in the fall of 1990 that were apparently intended to placate conservative forces. This was widely referred to as Gorbachev's "turn to the right" (Brown 1996, 269; Strayer 1998, 185).

Because of his temporizing and vacillation, Gorbachev had lost the support of many of his more liberal colleagues, not to mention radicals like Yeltsin. But he was also faced with increasingly vocal and organized criticism from the right. At a meeting in November with a large number of military officers, Gorbachev heard alarming news about the decaying state of the armed forces and resentment within the military. The restiveness of the extreme right had been observable for some time. But by late 1990 it appeared to be gathering force. Of particular concern was a conservative group in parliament known as Unity, whose members included a number of professional military men upset by what they saw as growing Soviet weakness under Gorbachev.

Gorbachev's turn to the right took several forms. He criticized and then sought to limit the freedom of Soviet television; he allowed the KGB a new role in investigating economic crime; and, in a move to restore law and order, he allowed the army to supplement the regular police in patrolling the streets in some cities.

Also important were a number of institutional and personnel changes. He abolished the Presidential Council, which had among its members a number of liberal intellectuals, and parceled its tasks among other government agencies. He established a Security Council, which included a number of the conservative voices within the government. And he arranged for the creation of the post of vice president. Gennady Yanaev, a former *komsomol* and trade union official whom Gorbachev seemed not to have known well, was named to the post. The liberal Minister of Interior, Vadim Bakatin, was dismissed in favor of Boris Pugo, a Latvian hardliner. In early 1991 Gorbachev replaced his moderate premier, Nikolai Ryzhkov, with Valentin Pavlov, who was soon to try to increase his powers at the expense of Gorbachev.

Most outspoken among Gorbachev's conservative colleagues was

KGB chairman Vladimir Kryuchkov. Gorbachev had named Kryuchkov, a long-time KGB operative, to head that agency in 1988. In 1990 and early 1991, as Kryuchkov saw the threat to the USSR's stability increasing, he became more vocal in his public statements. At a meeting of the Congress of People's Deputies in December he asserted that "destructive elements" were seeking to subvert Soviet rule and blamed Western intelligence agencies for causing disruption in the country. He hinted that force might be needed to needed to establish order (White 1992, 237; Kaiser 1992, 481). Also at this meeting of the parliament, Eduard Shevardnadze, the Minister of Foreign Affairs, co-architect of the country's foreign policy, and one of the important liberal voices in the government, resigned from his post, warning of the "onset of dictatorship" (Brown 1996, 278).

Undoubtedly the most important sign of the resurgence of conservative power in the government came in January 1991, when the Soviet authorities moved against the Baltic states. As mentioned earlier, the Baltic republics, and especially Lithuania, had led the way in declaring their desire for independence from Soviet rule. Gorbachev had tried all manner of persuasion and enticement to quash such separatist inclinations, but had not resorted to overt force. But by the end of the year he seemed to have lost control over the situation. Matters came to a head in January, when Soviet security forces carried out armed attacks in Lithuania and Latvia, killing 19 people and wounding hundreds of others. Gorbachev's prior knowledge and approval of these actions remains a matter of dispute. After the first attacks he does seem to have acted to prevent further military action. But his denial of responsibility for the assaults satisfied neither right nor left, and caused irremediable damage to his claim to be a democratic politician.

The Last Months of the USSR

Four events or developments dominated the last months of the Soviet Union's existence in 1991: the efforts to negotiate and adopt a new union treaty; the referendum of March 17; the August coup attempt; and the slide into chaos at the end of the year. From 1989 on, Gorbachev had been preoccupied with adopting a new union treaty to replace the one that had been in operation in the USSR since 1922. To head off the clamoring for greater autonomy from many parts of the country, he proposed a new arrangement with loosened central control within a preserved federal structure. To this end, four successive versions of a union treaty, each granting greater powers to the republics, were drafted and discussed between November 1990 and August 1991. The first draft was not well received by the republics, even the usually compliant Central Asian territories. Significant changes were demanded.

Gorbachev then decided upon a tactic that he hoped would strengthen his hand. In December 1990 he received approval from parliament to call an all-union referendum on the future of the Soviet state. The question that all voters in the USSR were to be asked was: "Do you consider necessary the preservation of the Union of Soviet Socialist Republics as a renewed federation of equal sovereign republics, in which the rights and freedoms of an individual of any nationality will be fully guaranteed?" He believed that if the people supported him, his leverage in dealing with the republics would be increased. This move was, in the words of a report by the Commission on Security and Cooperation in Europe, "a desperate attempt to maintain the Soviet Union's territorial integrity and, most important, central control" (Commission on Security and Cooperation in Europe 1991, 1).

But the republics did not fully cooperate. Six of them—Lithuania, Latvia, Estonia, Georgia, Armenia and Moldova—refused to participate (although in the event some voting took place in some of the regions of these republics). To make matters worse, the first four held their own referendums on independence instead. Moreover, a number of republics altered the procedure, either by changing the wording of the question or by adding other questions, to be voted on in individual republics. Thus, for instance, in Ukraine, voters were asked if they favored a declaration of a state of sovereignty for Ukraine (over 80 percent did). And in the RSFSR, citizens voted on creating the position of popularly elected president of Russia (70 percent backed the proposal).

Nevertheless, there was some basis for Gorbachev and his followers to express satisfaction with the results. About 80 percent of eligible voters were reported to have turned out, and of these over 76 percent voted yes. In the two largest republics, the RSFSR and Ukraine, the level of support was reported as 73 percent and 70 percent, respectively. However, virtually no voting took place in six republics, and support for Gorbachev's position was much lower in many of the USSR's biggest cities. Gorbachev and his lieutenants put the best possible spin on the results and moved forward to seek agreement on the union treaty.

As the negotiations proceeded, several other notable events took place. Boris Yeltsin was elected president of the RSFSR in June. He won by a comfortable margin, receiving 57 percent of the vote. One of his opponents, little known theretofore, was the populist Vladimir Zhirinovsky, who managed to get over six million votes, good for third place in the race. A few days after this election, with Gorbachev absent from the USSR parliament, Soviet prime minister Pavlov sought to increase his powers by taking some of the authority of the president. Conservatives in parliament quickly lined up behind Pavlov, and it was only several days later that Gorbachev got the decision reversed (Kaiser 1992, 414–16). In retrospect, this episode was a precursor to what was to take place that August.

A number of events in the summer of 1991 sharpened the controversy between the forces of left and right. Among these was a decree promulgated by newly-elected Russian President Yeltsin in July. It banned political parties from operating at work sites in the RSFSR. This was clearly directed at the Communist Party and unquestionably added to the anxiety of conservatives.

In early August the union treaty finally appeared ready. Gorbachev and the heads of Russia, Kazakhstan and Uzbekistan were prepared to sign it, with other republics joining later. The treaty provided for a "Union of Sovereign States." All direct references to communism and socialism were absent, not only from the country's name but also from the document itself (White 1992, 179–80). With the signing of the treaty set for August 20, Gorbachev left for a short vacation at his home on the Crimean coast. It was at this point that the coup attempt took place. On August 18 Gorbachev and his family were placed under house arrest, with all meaningful outside communication cut off. Gorbachev's power was usurped by a "State Committee for the State of Emergency," a group that included the USSR's vice president, prime minister, minister of defense, minister of interior, and head of the KGB, all officials who had been directly selected by Gorbachev himself. Also involved was Anatoly Lukyanov, chairman of the Supreme Soviet and close advisor of Gorbachev, and a his friend since their days together at Moscow University Law School. The most important objective of the coup plotters was to prevent the signing of the union treaty.

All accounts agree that the putschists were ill prepared to carry out their plot. When resistance developed, most notably from Russian president Boris Yeltsin and others, the coup collapsed. Although a number of accounts state or imply that Gorbachev was a party to the putsch, these allegations find little support in a close examination of events. Gorbachev's major failings in this episode were his poor choice of aides for key posts and his continued trust in them after they had ceased to deserve that trust.

As has often been said, Gorbachev returned from his house arrest to "another country." Although he resumed his duties as president of the USSR, his political authority had been seriously diminished. Boris Yeltsin, the hero of the resistance, had become the dominant political figure in the country. The credibility of the Communist Party had been gravely damaged because of the association of numerous high party leaders with the conspiracy. And when Gorbachev, in an early post-coup press conference, sought to defend the party and urge its renewal, public scorn spilled over on to him.

But perhaps the largest victim of the "three days in August" was hope—that the USSR, under whatever name it might be known, could look forward to any kind of viable future. Yeltsin quickly issued decrees suspending the operation of the Communist Party on RSFSR territory and seizing its property. Gorbachev, under pressure from colleagues still loyal to him, resigned as general secretary of the party and recommended that the party Central Committee disband itself. Yeltsin's decrees against the Communist Party were later to be challenged in the Russian Constitutional Court. But for the present they had the intended effect of making the party virtually powerless.

A direct effect of the trauma of the coup was the accelerated process of independence in the republics. On September 6 Lithuania, Latvia and Estonia were recognized by the Soviet Union as independent. Several other republics had declared their independence or were about to do so. Still Gorbachev doggedly tried to revive the process of adopting a union treaty, but now with support coming mainly from the Central Asian republics and Kazakhstan. Russia paid lip service to joining in, but as Archie Brown characterized the situation: "While Yeltsin went through the motions of participation, behind the scenes he and his closest advisors were preparing to take full power in Russia rather than to share it with even much weakened union authorities" (Brown 1996, 303).

In his anxiety to placate the remaining republics, Gorbachev brought about the demise of the USSR Congress of People's Deputies, in the process yielding further federal power to the territories. But by this time the situation was beyond his control. Unbeknownst to Gorbachev, the leaders of the three Slavic republics (Russia, Ukraine and Belarus) held a meeting in a hunting lodge in Belarus on December 8. They in effect declared their independence from the Soviet Union by asserting that "the USSR is ceasing to exist." In its place they called for the creation of a voluntary Commonwealth of Independent States.

Gorbachev offered legal objections to this action, asserting that "the fate of a multinational state cannot be determined by the will of the leaders of three republics" and noting that the declaration "was discussed by neither the population nor the supreme soviets in whose name it was signed." The leaders of some of the non-Slavic republics raised more practical concerns: that they had been left out of the process. But several days later the presidents of Kazakhstan and the Central Asian republics met and confirmed their willingness to join Russia, Ukraine and Belarus in this new venture. Gorbachev's legal protests were swept aside by what had become a political *fait accompli* (Barry 1992, 531).

Thus, Gorbachev was a president without a country. He resigned on December 25, 1991. When the Soviet flag was replaced in the Kremlin by the Russian tricolor two days later, the once-mighty Soviet Union truly had ceased to exist.

References

Barry, Donald. 1992. "The USSR: A Legitimate Dissolution?" *Review of Central and East European Law* 18:527–33.

Barry, Donald, and Carol Barner-Barry. 1991. *Contemporary Soviet Politics*. 4th ed. Englewood Cliffs, NJ: Prentice-Hall.

Brown, Archie. 1996. *The Gorbachev Factor*. Oxford: Oxford University Press.

Commission on Security and Cooperation in Europe. 1991. *Referendum in the Soviet Union: A Compendium of Reports on the March 17, 1991 Referendum on the Future of the U.S.S.R.*. Washington, DC: U.S. Government Printing Office.

Fowkes, Ben. 1997. *The Disintegration of the Soviet Union: A Study in the Rise and Triumph of Nationalism*. New York: St. Martin's Press.

Hough, Jerry F. 1997. *Democratization and Revolution in the USSR, 1985–1991*. Washington, DC: Brookings Institution Press.

Kaiser, Robert G. 1992. *Why Gorbachev Happened*. New York: Simon and Schuster.

Keep, John L. H. 1995. *Last of the Empires: A History of the Soviet Union, 1945–1991*. Oxford: Oxford University Press.

Kiernan, Brendan. 1993. *The End of Soviet Politics: Elections, Legislatures, and the Demise of the Communist Party*. Boulder, CO: Westview Press.

Moskoff, William. 1993. *Hard Times: Impoverishment and Protest in the Perestroika Years*. Armonk, NY: M. E. Sharpe.

Olcott, Martha Brill. 1999. "Growing Autonomy for the Republics." In *The Collapse of the Soviet Union,* ed. Paul A. Winters. San Diego, CA: Greenhaven Press.

Sakwa, Richard. 1991. *Gorbachev and His Reforms, 1985–1990*. Englewood Cliffs, NJ: Prentice-Hall.

Strayer, Robert. 1998. *Why Did the Soviet Union Collapse? Understanding Historical Change*. Armonk, NY: M.E. Sharpe.

White, Stephen. 1992. *Gorbachev and After*. Cambridge: Cambridge University Press.

Chapter 3
Russia and the Near Abroad

When the USSR ceased to exist, 15 new countries, the former constituent republics of the Soviet Union, came into being. For convenience, they are often referred to as the Newly Independent States (NIS) or the former Soviet Union (FSU). In Russia the other 14 republics, where considerable numbers of ethnic Russians continue to live, are often called collectively the Near Abroad (the three Baltic states, Latvia, Lithuania, and Estonia, are sometimes excluded from this designation). This chapter sketches the main contours of Russia's relations with the Near Abroad after the Soviet Union's collapse.

The Commonwealth of Independent States

As indicated in the last chapter, the demise of the USSR was accompanied by the creation of the Commonwealth of Independent States (CIS). But in terms of the evolution of governmental structures and operations, the CIS is in no sense a successor to the USSR. It is not a state, and in its decade of existence it has shown little development toward becoming a state. If anything it has gone in the opposite direction. Nonetheless, there are good reasons for examining this organization. It was created on the basis of the demise of the USSR. The original intention appeared to be to cloth it with some of the attributes of a unified state, albeit a loosely organized one. And the contours of its continued existence speak to the efforts of the individual member countries to find what they consider appropriate relationships and forms of cooperation with fellow members.

The founding document for the CIS was the Accord of the presidents of the three Slavic Republics of the USSR (Russia, Ukraine, Belarus) of December 8, 1991, the same statement containing the key words, "the USSR is ceasing to exist"("Accord on the Commonwealth of Independent States"1991). About two weeks later the leaders of eight other former Soviet republics signed a "protocol" to the Accord, making them co-founders of the Commonwealth. Lithuania, Latvia and Estonia did not join, and Georgia delayed becoming a member until 1993. The substantive provisions of the declaration included the following:

1. A pledge to guarantee the territorial integrity of the member states, and the protection of residents and citizens of any state, regardless of the republic in the Commonwealth where they lived.

2. Several provisions on military matters, including the preservation of a common military and strategic space under a common command and common control over nuclear armaments.

3. A pledge to undertake a number of mutual activities through common coordinating institutions, including foreign policy, economic policy, transportation and communication systems, environmental protection, migration policy and fighting organized crime.

4. An agreement to assume the international obligations of the former USSR. This was accompanied by a declaration that the laws of the USSR were no longer valid in the member republics.

5. A statement that disputes regarding the interpretation of the agreement were to be solved through negotiation. Any party could suspend the agreement or individual articles of it with a one-year notice (Barry and Barner-Barry 1992, 26–27).

Among a large number of other documents adopted by the member states, a charter of the CIS, containing the substance of most of these provisions, was signed in February 1993. Article 1 of the charter declares: "The Commonwealth is not a state and does not possess supranational powers" ("Charter of the Commonwealth of Independent States" 1997, 506). Nevertheless, some believe that Russia sees the organization as a vehicle for the restoration of the Russian empire or at least as a means to enhance its influence over other former Soviet republics. Whatever Russia's intentions may be, the development of the CIS as a viable institution has so far been quite limited.

The highest organ of the CIS is the Council of Heads of State, made up of the presidents of each of the member republics. The CIS Charter prescribes that this body will meet twice a year for regular sessions. The Council of Heads of Government (prime ministers) is in charge of coordinating the cooperation of member states in the economic and social spheres, although it may consider other matters of common interest as well. It holds regular sessions four times a year. The Interparliamentary

Assembly is comprised of delegations from the parliaments of each of the member states. Its basic function is to seek cooperation in the adoption of joint proposals for consideration by the national parliaments.

In addition to these leading bodies, a large number of other organizations have been created for cooperation in narrower policy areas. Examples are the Foreign Ministers Council, the Defense Ministers Council, the Joint Armed Forces High Command, the Council of Commanders of Border Troops, the Economic Court, and the Commission on Human Rights ("Charter of the Commonwealth of Independent States" 1997, 508–10).

This impressive organizational framework has been used to adopt a large number of documents, which on the surface suggests a high level of cooperation among member countries. But the fact is that members may choose to join or not join a given agreement. When one looks more closely, therefore, the consensus among CIS members across a wide range of issues is considerably lower than it might at first appear. For example, a 1998 report estimates that of 886 high-level CIS documents adopted, only 130 were signed by all 12 member states (Sakwa and Webber 1999, 396).

This lack of consensus derives from what one analysis described as the two contradictory objectives that prevailed when the CIS was created. The organization was seen, on the one hand, as "a vehicle which would facilitate the journey of the former Soviet republics toward independence" (Sakwa and Webber 1999, 379). Indeed, then Ukrainian President Kravchuk once referred to the CIS as a means of "civilized divorce" (Kremenyuk 1994, 80). On the other hand, the CIS was perceived as an organization through which a variety of modes of cooperation could also be achieved.

No doubt all CIS members have welcomed cooperation in some areas and on some levels. But the interest of many members in preserving their freedom of action and autonomy has proved stronger. The position of Russia in this equation is without question of crucial importance. Russia is the dominant member of the CIS, in terms of size, resources, military power, economic potential, and by virtually any other measure one could imagine. Naturally, therefore, Russia has taken a significant role in CIS operations, and has dominated the leadership positions of the organization (Sakwa and Webber 1999, 404). This alone would be enough to cause anxiety for other CIS members, even without the memory of Russia's decades-long dominance of the USSR. Moreover, some CIS member states have particular reasons to want extra breathing room from Russia. Azerbaijan, for instance, resents what it considers Russia's support for the Armenian side in the Nagorno-Karabakh dispute. Georgia has expressed similar misgivings about Russia's relations with the Georgian province of Abkhazia. Ukraine has indicated a desire to establish closer ties with the West, and wants to limit its commitments within the CIS for this reason. These are just a few of the grounds for the reluctance among some CIS members to make a fuller commitment to the organization (Olcott, Åslund and Garnett 1999, 1–30).

As a result, there has developed within the CIS a kind of schism between several countries that tend to support greater organizational integration (Armenia, Belarus, Kyrgyzstan, Tajikistan and, in part, Kazakhstan) and the "sceptics" (Azerbaijan, Georgia, Moldova, Turkmenistan, Uzbekistan and Ukraine), which want to maintain looser ties. For the latter, according to a leading analysis, the benefits of CIS cooperation "are overshadowed by suspicions of Russia's motives within the Commonwealth, and the shared view that the CIS is an impediment to the development of independent and multifaceted foreign policy orientations" (Sakwa and Webber 1999, 400–401).

Thus, the CIS has not developed as some of its founders had envisaged. It has provided a means for limited cooperation among 12 former Soviet republics, which have largely pursued their own domestic and foreign policy agendas.

Manifestations of Russian Independence

By the time the Soviet flag was replaced atop the Kremlin on the day Gorbachev resigned, Yeltsin was moving fast to put the symbols of the Russian state in place. The nuclear codes were quickly transferred from President Gorbachev to President Yeltsin. And just as swiftly, the attributes of Gorbachev's official position disappeared. His dacha and presidential limousine were taken, and Yeltsin moved into Gorbachev's Kremlin office without giving the latter a chance to move out (Grachev 1995, 185–194).

Earlier, even before the CIS accord of December 8, 1991, Yeltsin and his lieutenants had set about stripping the USSR of many of its Russia-based assets. The list of such actions is long, so a few representative examples will suffice. Oil, gas and other energy resources were nationalized by the RSFSR in September 1991. In November, all activities associated with the mining, producing and marketing of precious metals and stones were brought under Russian republic control. In that same month Russia asserted authority over much of the banking system that had been under USSR jurisdiction. These developments, part of Yeltsin's "autumn putsch," foreshadowed the swift events of December that finally ended the Soviet Union's existence (Dunlop 1993, 267–69).

On issues that extended beyond the RSFSR's physical borders, however, solutions did not come so easily. CIS mechanisms, as well as bilateral and multilateral agreements between Russia and its neighbors, then came into play. The number of problems to be addressed and resolved was large, none more serious than military and security matters.

Yevgeny Shaposhnikov was made USSR Minister of Defense in August 1991, after his predecessor had been arrested as a member of the coup plot. When the CIS was created, he was appointed commander-in-chief of the CIS Unified Armed Forces. Shaposhnikov urged strongly that the whole CIS remain a single defense space, and at first Russian President Yeltsin appeared to agree. But a number of the other CIS countries, led by Ukraine, insisted on having their own armies. Ukraine shocked Russia by claiming that all Soviet troops stationed on Ukrainian soil would come under the jurisdiction of Ukraine. It further asserted that the Black Sea Fleet, stationed at Sevastopol on the Crimean peninsula (land that had been given by Khrushchev from Russia to Ukraine in 1954), belonged to Ukraine. It would take Russia and Ukraine several years to sort out these and other contentious issues.

What quickly became clear, based on the actions of a number of republics, was that a single unified CIS military force was not to be. By May 1992 most CIS member states, including Russia, had created their own ministries of defense and had begun establishing their own armies. When, that same month, a CIS collective security treaty was proposed, only six member states chose to sign it. Shaposhnikov remained at his post into the next year, but essentially occupied an empty position ("The Military

Evolution" 1997, 441–42).

A different pattern unfolded with regard to nuclear arms. Such weapons (both tactical and strategic) were in place in only four of the CIS republics: Russia, Ukraine, Belarus and Kazakhstan. A number of agreements, reached at the inception of the CIS, provided that all of these weapons would be gradually transferred to Russia. On this issue, outside influence, as well as financial and technical aid, particularly from the United States, played a significant role in bringing the agreements to fruition. With the removal of the weapons to Russia, CIS activity in this area came to an end (Sakwa and Webber 1999, 383).

When the CIS was created it was agreed that Russia would become the USSR's successor state, taking over the Soviet Union's membership in the United Nations and other international organizations. Soon thereafter Russia also negotiated bilateral agreements with all CIS members, except Ukraine whereby it would assume all Soviet foreign debt in exchange for claiming all of the USSR's assets abroad.

Russian-Ukrainian Issues

The Crimea was part of Russia (then the RSFSR) until 1954, when it was given to Ukraine by the Soviet leadership in Moscow to mark the 300th anniversary of Russian-Ukrainian union. At the time, the transfer had little political significance because it amounted to an administrative shifting of land in what was a pseudo-federal, but essentially unitary, state. But with the loosening of controls by Moscow in the late 1980s, the rise of nationalist sentiments leading to widespread claims of sovereignty and independence and, finally, the breakup of the USSR, the Crimean peninsula, along with numerous other disputed territories across the former Soviet Union, became a major problem. The Crimea is a region of considerable economic and strategic importance, and one to which many people have strong emotional ties. Blessed with one of the best climates in the area, it is the site of many health resorts, vacation spots and homes of political leaders (Gorbachev was at his opulent dacha in the Crimean seaside town of Foros when the coup was initiated in August 1991). Moreover, it possesses excellent port facilities and is the home of the Black Sea Fleet, another source of contention between Russia and Ukraine.

Approximately 70 percent of the territory's 2.5 million people are Russian and only 20 percent are Ukrainian, figures that Russian nationalists cite in arguing for Moscow's claim to the region. The Crimea was once the home to 250,000 Crimean Tatars, who were subjected to mass deportation by Stalin in 1941 after being falsely accused of collaborating with the Nazis. In connection with this act, the administrative unit known as the Crimean Autonomous Soviet Socialist Republic was abolished. Although they were absolved of the collaboration charge and rehabilitated in the 1960s, Crimean Tatars only began returning to the peninsula during the Gorbachev period. Their return has met resistance from the Russian-Ukrainian population.

With the rise of Ukrainian nationalism and the breakup of the Soviet Union, Russian anxiety about the Crimea has grown. In May 1992 the Russian parliament voted overwhelmingly to declare the 1954 transfer of the Crimea to Ukraine unconstitutional and void. This declaration came less than six months after all CIS member states pledged, in their founding agreement, to "recognize and respect each other's territorial integrity and the territorial integrity of each other's borders."

Early in 1992 Ukraine announced its intention to create its own army, decreed that military property on Ukrainian soil belonged to Ukraine, and demanded that all military personnel in Ukraine take an oath of allegiance to the republic. Of the significant amount of military property located in Ukraine, the most important component was the Black Sea Fleet, whose home port is Sevastopol in the Crimea.

It soon became clear that Ukraine did not intend to use the entire Black Sea Fleet for its own needs, any more than it expected its army to be as large as the 700,000 military men and women stationed on its soil. The key issue was the rivalry and growing distrust between Ukraine and Russia. Also of importance was the commercial value of unneeded military equipment, which could be sold off by the state that asserted control over it. A temporary solution was reached in mid-1992 when the Russian and Ukrainian presidents agreed to establish a temporary joint command for the fleet.

For the leaders of both Ukraine and Russia, the task has been to placate nationalists at home by not seeming to give up too much while being sufficiently conciliatory to provide the chance for solutions to outstanding problems to be reached. The difficulty of maintaining this balance, across a number of issues, explains in part why the process has been so protracted.

The year 1997 represented a breakthrough of sorts in Russian-Ukrainian relations. In May the two countries signed a set of agreements on the Black Sea Fleet. The next month the Russian and Ukrainian presidents approved a long-term political treaty. The treaty covers a number of issues, including Russia's assumption of the foreign debt of Soviet-era Ukraine in return for Kiev's foreign assets of that period. The treaty also recognized Ukraine's territorial integrity, including sovereignty over the Crimea. Although the treaty has not yet been approved by the Russian parliament, its chances of adoption appear to be considerably enhanced by the recent improvement in relations with Ukraine.

Under the Black Sea Fleet agreements, which were approved by the Russian parliament in 1999, Russia assumed ownership of 83 percent of the fleet. It is permitted to lease port facilities and maintain its ships at Ukrainian sites (Braun 2000, 102).

In its negotiations with Ukraine, Russia holds a number of advantages. Its economy, in spite of numerous problems, is in considerably better shape than Ukraine's. Moreover, Ukraine is dependent on Russia for a number of resources, most notably natural gas. And a large percentage of Ukrainian foreign trade is with Russia, a pattern that Ukraine has found difficult to change. As the CIS country with the largest debt to Russia, Ukraine's leverage in dealing with the problems just discussed has been considerably diminished ("Russia Slowly Moving to Recover 7 Billion Dollars of CIS debt" 2000; Smolansky 1995).

Bilateral and Regional Agreements

The agreements between Russia and Ukraine discussed above were bilateral in form, outside the framework of the CIS. Russia has concluded bilateral compacts with all member states of the CIS, but its chief partner in this form of agreement is Belarus, its neighbor to the west. Through a series of treaties and accords since 1994, the two countries have worked toward a tighter form of integration. Whether an actual merging of Belarus and Russia will eventually materialize is questionable, but the term "union" is routinely used in describing the relationship. Since the breakup of the USSR, no two CIS countries have developed closer ties than Belarus and Russia. But a host of anticipated problems associated with their further integration (including, most notably, the loss of sovereignty for Belarus and a considerable economic burden for Russia) have led to significant opposition on both sides of the Russia-Belarus border ("A Ghost Lurks" 2000, 60; Braun 2000, 107–110). Other CIS members, but particularly Ukraine, have pointedly distanced themselves from the embrace of this political union.

Several regional arrangements have been created among CIS countries. Particularly significant from the Russian standpoint are those that include countries other than Russia. One such organization is the Central Asian Economic Community, comprising Kazakhstan, Uzbekistan, Kyrgyzstan and Tajikistan. Its accomplishments to date have been modest, and in any case the member countries maintain close economic and military ties to Russia. A potentially more significant body is GUUAM (Georgia, Ukraine, Uzbekistan, Azerbaijan and Moldova). This group envisages a number of bases for cooperation, including common trade and tariff agreements. It also has a shared interest in the development of a trans-Georgia pipeline, linking Azerbaijan with Turkey and helping to supply the energy needs of Ukraine and Moldova. Since this pipeline would be heavily financed by Western, particularly U.S., interests, it is of considerable concern to Russia. It should be noted that the members of GUUAM are among the "CIS sceptics" discussed above, who, for a variety of reasons, seek distance from Russia and looser ties within the CIS (Vavilov 1999, 1; Sakwa and Webber 1999, 401).

Russia and the Baltic States

In the previous chapter some of the factors that set the Baltic states apart from the other Soviet republics were discussed. Of major importance were: their forced incorporation into the USSR in 1940, and the resentment caused by the immigration—particularly to Latvia and Estonia—of large numbers of ethnic Russians. It was the Baltic states, led by Lithuania, that spearheaded the campaign for sovereignty, and then outright independence, and suffered most from Moscow's backlash during Gorbachev's "turn to the right" at the end of 1990. And it was Lithuania, Latvia and Estonia that achieved their independence in the wake of the coup attempt against Gorbachev, three months before the USSR's final collapse.

Boris Yeltsin had been sympathetic with the plight of the Baltic states as they sought to achieve independence in late 1990 and early 1991. He was among the strongest Russian critics of the use of force by Soviet troops in Vilnius and Riga in January 1991. He went so far as to sign agreements of mutual assistance with the three Baltic states soon after these attacks (Kaiser 1992, 396; Simes 1999, 46). It is true, of course, that in taking this stance, Yeltsin's motives were by no means purely altruistic. He was attempting to strengthen his own hand in his struggle against the Soviet leadership, particularly against Gorbachev (Dunlop 1993, 59–60). But as president of an independent post-Soviet Russia, Yeltsin found his country's relationship with the Baltic states considerably more complicated.

Early in the post-Soviet period, restrictive procedures were introduced for granting citizenship in Estonia and Latvia. These were seen by Russia (and by many in the West as well) as discriminating against the large Russian minorities in these countries. Apparently this policy has not had the intended effect. Migration to Russia from the Baltic states appears to have stabilized in recent years, presumably in large part because of the considerably lower standard of living in most parts of Russia (Pikayev 1998, 143). Estonia and Latvia have for a number of years maintained territorial claims against Russia, further exacerbating relations. Lithuania has no official land disputes with Russia, but some Lithuanians consider the Russian Baltic Sea enclave of Kaliningrad to be part of traditional Lithuanian territory.

But most upsetting to Russia is the move by the Baltic states to draw closer to the West, most importantly by seeking membership in NATO. This, in the nearly unanimous view of Russian politicians, would compromise the country's vital interests. Russians see the Baltic area not only as part of Russia's traditional sphere of influence, but also as a historic weak point in Russia's defense capability.

The Baltic states, then, remain an area of particular concern for Russia, because its influence is on the wane there. Yet good relations are clearly important for both sides. Trade between the two regions, while down in comparison with the early 1990s, is still significant. And in spite of efforts to acquire alternative energy sources from other parts of the world, the Baltic states remain heavily dependent on oil and gas from Russia. Moreover, cooperation in other areas has become increasingly important. For instance, combating traffic from Russia in drugs and stolen property, and in the transport of illegal aliens from Asia and Africa, is of concern not only to the Baltic states, which serve as one of the transit corridors for this activity, but to the whole of Western Europe as well.

Conclusion

Russia emerged from the fall of the Soviet Union in the same position relative to its nearest neighbors as it had been in prior to the country's demise. It was unquestionably the largest and most powerful of the states that had comprised the USSR. But as a separate country Russia was considerably weakened in comparison with its status as the dominant Soviet republic. Three sets of factors explain this change:

1. Within the Soviet Union, Russia dominated a country of nearly 300 million people. As an independent country Russia's population is about half that of the Soviet Union. Its land area, while still enormous, is about three quarters of the size of the USSR. More important than the mere loss of population and territory, however, is the feeling that Moscow, in its relations with the other former USSR republics, is now dealing not with parts of its own *empire*, where it could dictate to member states on matters large and small, but with *independent countries*. Even though several of these countries maintain, out of necessity, close economic, military and even cultural ties with Russia, the change in status has had profound psychological effects on relations among these former units of the USSR.

2. In the relatively closed conditions of the traditional USSR, virtually all economic power was concentrated in the hands of the state. Through the priorities chosen by the leaders, the USSR was transformed into a powerful industrial nation, albeit one with a number of weaknesses. Although the consumer economy suffered under these priorities, incremental improvements for a time gave the populace hope. Moreover, a social safety net

delivered at least minimal support for the population as a whole. Long before the final demise of the USSR, however, the flaws in the system had become evident. The process of its decline only accelerated during the Gorbachev era. As an independent state Russia emerged as an economically impoverished country (as did most of its Near Abroad neighbors). Its experience with privatization and the adoption of a market economy have so far only exacerbated its difficult economic circumstances.

3. The USSR was unquestionably a military superpower, with the largest army in the world and an impressive array of nuclear and conventional weapons. Moreover, it was a military machine dominated by Russians and Russia. Even before the Soviet Union's demise the country had experienced the debacle of the war in Afghanistan. After the USSR's collapse, further weaknesses of the Russian military have been exposed. The poor showing in the campaign in Chechnya in the mid-1990s demonstrated Russia's inability to put down a determined separatist movement within its own borders. Russia's renewal of the fighting in Chechnya at the end of the decade may have had as much to do with trying to assuage its wounded pride as with stamping out the terrorist acts of some Chechen warlords. The basic fact, however, is that Russia does not have the economic or technical wherewithal to return to its status as a military superpower.

Russia is still in the process of adjusting to its new diminished status. But its present weakened condition needs to be seen in proper perspective. As Rajan Menon has argued in discussing Russia's present status among the nations of the world, "power is dynamic and relational" (Menon 1998, 104). It is dynamic in the sense that it is subject to change. And Russia's recovery, whether a short-term or long-term matter, will make it a more important country. This is not subject to doubt. It is relational in that even in its present condition, Russia overshadows, in economic and military terms, not to mention population, territory and resource potential, the overwhelming majority of countries in the world. Even with the difficulties it presently faces, Russia is a country that can't be ignored. This observation is particularly relevant to the other former Soviet republics, the Near Abroad, which perforce are Russia's permanent neighbors.

References

"Accord on the Commonwealth of Independent States." 1991. *New York Times*, December 10, 1991, A10.

"A Ghost Lurks." 2000. *The Economist* 354 (8155): 60.

Barry, Donald, and Carol Barner-Barry. 1992. *Post-Soviet Politics: The Fall of the USSR and the Rise of the Successor States.* Englewood Cliffs, NJ: Prentice-Hall.

Braun, Aurel. 2000. "All Quiet on the Russian Front: Russia, Its Neighbors, and the Russian Diaspora." In *The New European Diasporas: National Minorities and Conflicts in Eastern Europe,* ed. Michael Mandelbaum. New York: Council on Foreign Relations.

"Charter of the Commonwealth of Independent States (22 January 1993)." 1997. In *Russia and the Commonwealth of Independent States: Documents, Data, and Analysis,* eds. Zbigniew Brzezinski and Page Sullivan. Armonk, NY: M. E. Sharpe.

Dunlop, John B. 1993. *The Rise of Russia and the Fall of the Soviet Union.* Princeton: Princeton University Press.

Grachev, Andrei S. 1995. *Final Days: The Inside Story of the Collapse of the Soviet Union.* Boulder, CO: Westview Press.

Kaiser, Robert G. 1992. *Why Gorbachev Happened: His Triumphs, His Failure, and His Fall.* New York: Simon and Schuster.

Kremenyuk, Victor A. 1994. *Conflicts In and Around Russia: Nation-Building in Difficult Times.* Westport, CT: Greenwood Press.

"The Military Evolution: Introductory Notes" 1997. In *Russia and the Commonwealth of Independent States: Documents, Data, and Analysis,* eds. Zbigniew Brzezinski and Page Sullivan. Armonk, NY: M.E. Sharpe.

Menon, Rajan 1998. "After Empire: Russia and the Southern 'Near Abroad'." In *The New Russian Foreign Policy*, ed. Michael Mandelbaum. New York: Council on Foreign Relations.

Olcott, Martha Brill, Anders Åslund and Sherman W. Garnett. 1999. *Getting it Wrong: Regional Cooperation and the Commonwealth of Independent States.* Washington, DC: Carnegie Endowment for International Peace.

Pikayev, Alexander A. 1998. "Russia and the Baltic States: Challenges and Opportunities." In *The Baltic States and World Politics*, eds. Birthe Hansen and Bertel Heurlin. New York: St. Martin's Press.

"Russia Slowly Moving to Recover 7 Billion Dollars of CIS Debt." 2000 (March 16). Dispatch of Deutsche Presse-Agentur; retrieved through Lexis-Nexis.

Sakwa, Richard and Mark Webber. 1999. "The Commonwealth of Independent States, 1991–1998: Stagnation and Survival." *Europe-Asia Studies* 51:379–415.

Simes, Dimitri K. 1999. *After the Collapse: Russia Seeks Its Place as a Great Power.* New York: Simon and Schuster.

Smolansky, Oles M. 1995. "Ukraine's Quest for Independence: The Fuel Factor." *Europe-Asia Studies* 47: 67–90.

Vavilov, Nikolai. 1999 (October 8). "Tikhoe umiranie SNG prodolzhaetsia," *Nezavisimaia gazeta.*

Chapter 4
Evolution of Russian Political Institutions: 1991–1993

Russia became an independent country at the end of 1991. At that time, it possessed Soviet-era political institutions, some of which had been created or substantially altered during the Gorbachev years. In many respects these structures resembled USSR-level institutions. Most important among them were:

- A substantially amended constitution adopted in 1978;
- A two-tier legislature, established in 1990, with a distribution of powers generally analogous to the USSR parliament, which had been created a year earlier;
- A presidency, created in 1991 and modeled on the USSR presidency, which had been established the previous year;
- A federal system in which central-federal relations were only vaguely spelled out;
- A Constitutional Court, created in 1990 but whose work did not commence until late 1991, around the time of the USSR's collapse.

These institutions played important roles in the operation of the Russian political system until the autumn of 1993, when a dramatic battle between the president and parliament resulted in a significant change in the basic political structures. This chapter discusses the operation of these institutions, and concludes with a description of the presidential-parliamentary confrontation of 1993 that led to significant institutional changes.

The 1978 Constitution

When the Soviet Union fell in 1991, Russia was referred to as the RSFSR (Russian Soviet Federated Socialist Republic). The constitution in place at that time had been adopted in 1978, the year after the so-called "Brezhnev Constitution" was promulgated for the Soviet Union as a whole. The RSFSR document was largely based on the USSR Constitution, and, in turn, served as a model for the soon-to-be adopted constitutions of the other

14 Soviet republics.

Between 1978 and 1993 the RSFSR Constitution was extensively amended. A number of the changes were of great importance, such as the creation of the presidency and the Constitutional Court, which had not existed theretofore, and the establishment of a new parliament to replace the traditional Soviet-era legislature. Other changes were more cosmetic in nature. For instance, in 1992 the Soviet-era designation RSFSR was dropped and the country was thereafter called the Russian Federation or simply Russia (both names were considered equally valid). In connection with this change, all constitutional references to RSFSR had to be replaced by the new terminology.

By the end of the 1980s there was general agreement that the 1978 constitution needed to be replaced by a completely new charter. Even though this would have required only a two-thirds vote of Parliament (the Congress of People's Deputies), it turned out to be a task of extraordinary difficulty. In the past, when political power was largely wielded by the Communist Party, scant attention was paid to the constitution. Now, however, the constitution was of fundamental importance to anyone interested in the distribution of political authority. From 1990 to early 1993, several official versions of draft constitutions were published. Each draft generated significant discussion as well as alternative proposals for many provisions. But basic disagreements prevented the reaching of consensus. Several factors explain the failure to achieve accord on this issue:

1. A divided legislature, in which a variety of forces, but particularly the new democrats and the representatives of the old structures, found it difficult to agree on basic issues. The lack of a system of political parties no doubt contributed to the inability to achieve consensus and compromise.

2. Conflicting views of the role of the state in Russian society. Traditionalists emphasized the need for strong central authority and a pervasive role in defining Russian interests, within and beyond the borders of the country; liberals stressed political and economic freedom, the development of social autonomy, and limited state authority. These differing conceptions to some extent cut across the normal lineup of

legislative forces.

3. Differences over the basic form of state organization to be provided for in the document. Should it be a presidential or a parliamentary system?

4. Controversy over the breadth of coverage of the document. Should it be a minimalist charter concentrating on state structure and individual rights, or a broader document embracing the whole social system? The drafts put forth the broader conception, but this approach drew criticism from numerous sources, including several notable jurists (Barry and Barner-Barry 1992, 49).

Beyond these more general considerations, there were numerous other differences on specific issues, such as the number of deputies needed to override a presidential veto and the role of parliament in appointing ministers. Frustrated by the inability to make progress on adopting a new constitution, President Yeltsin and some of his advisors hinted that they would consider submitting the constitutional issue to a popular referendum. But under the constitution the president had no role in the referendum process. This was just one of numerous areas in which Yeltsin believed that presidential power needed to be enhanced.

The Legislature

During the Gorbachev era, Russia followed the USSR lead in establishing a two-tier legislature. A popularly elected Congress of People's Deputies was designed to be the larger body, but one that would meet for only a few days each year. From its numbers a standing legislature, known as the Supreme Soviet, would be chosen. In the spring of 1990 (one year after the elections for the USSR Congress), voters in the RSFSR went to the polls to choose 1,068 members of the Congress. Voting was by the same single-member-district-majority system used on the USSR level. The 900 territorial districts overlapped with the 168 national-territorial districts, so that each voter had two votes. Contested elections took place in almost all districts, and an average of six to seven candidates ran for each seat. As in the national elections the year before, repeat elections or runoffs were required in a number of districts where majorities were not achieved in the first round of voting or where fewer than half of the electorate participated.

The elections were held when the monopoly position of the Communist Party was being challenged, but communists still held great influence in the country at large. It is not surprising, therefore, that the proportion of party members among deputies elected totaled over 86 percent. However, the Communist Party in the spring of 1990 was a much less disciplined organization than it had been earlier. Many members had stopped actively participating in the party, and a large number would leave the party in the near future. Boris Yeltsin, for instance, won election to the Russian Congress in March 1990 and resigned from the party in a dramatic gesture at the conclusion of the Twenty-Eighth Party Congress in July 1990. So the 86 percent figure is somewhat misleading. A large number of deputies, perhaps 20 percent of those elected, belonged to the Democratic Russia alliance (some while still simultaneously holding Communist Party membership). Thus, at this point in the evolution of the new Russian politics, the situation was too fluid and indefinite to draw firm conclusions. Some of the patterns of the past regarding parliamentary membership had clearly been broken, however. The number of women, workers and collective farmers dropped drastically (quotas for these categories had been established under the old system), while the proportion from the ranks of the intelligentsia grew (Mann 1990, 11–17).

The Supreme Soviet that the Congress chose was a two-house body of 252 total members. The powers of the Congress and the Supreme Soviet overlapped to some extent and blended in other ways. For instance, both had the power to adopt laws and resolutions, but the Congress had the right to rescind any act adopted by the Supreme Soviet. Only the Congress could amend the constitution or adopt a new one. The Supreme Soviet appointed the prime minister, subject to the approval of the Congress. On paper, the Congress was the more powerful body, but because it was designed to meet infrequently (for sessions of about ten days, one or two times a year), the Supreme Soviet was able to wield considerable authority on its own.

The chief official of the legislative branch was the chairman of the Supreme Soviet. Boris Yeltsin held this post during 1990 and 1991, and then he ran successfully for the new office of president. His place was taken by Ruslan Khasbulatov, an ethnic Chechen. Khasbulatov had been first deputy Supreme Soviet chairman under Yeltsin and was considered Yeltsin's protégé. But after achieving the post he became an ambitious and independent political actor who clashed with Yeltsin and his team.

The Executive

Like Gorbachev at the USSR level, Yeltsin found that the chairmanship of the RSFSR Supreme Soviet did not provide him with enough authority. And again like Gorbachev (but a little more than a year later), he engineered the creation of a separate presidency for Russia.

Yeltsin's path to the presidency was somewhat different from that of Gorbachev, who had rigged the arrangements for choosing the federal president so that the first incumbent would be chosen by parliament rather than the people. First, a referendum was held in March 1991 on creating a popularly elected presidency of the RSFSR (it accompanied the referendum held throughout most of the Soviet Union on whether the USSR as a renewed federation should be preserved). About 70 percent favored the presidency, and, after a campaign of nearly three months in which six candidates participated, Yeltsin won with 57 percent of the vote. By gaining an absolute majority Yeltsin avoided a runoff with the next closest candidate. Yeltsin's running mate, the new vice president, was Alexander Rutskoi, a hero of the war in Afghanistan and a reform communist. Rutskoi, like Khasbulatov, soon became one of Yeltsin's foremost adversaries.

Once in office, Yeltsin moved to the Kremlin and set up his headquarters near Gorbachev's residence. Even before the August coup attempt, Yeltsin was challenging Gorbachev's authority, as power appeared to be flowing to the republics. But the event that really cemented Yeltsin's ascendancy over Gorbachev was the failed coup. There were many reasons why the coup took place when it did, including the planned signing of the union treaty by the heads of several republics and the desire of the coup leaders to take advantage of Gorbachev's absence from Moscow during his vacation in the south of the country. But another development of considerable importance was Yeltsin's efforts to neutralize antireform structures in Russia. About two weeks before the coup, a Yeltsin decree went into effect banning all political structures and movements in the state sector. Although it did not mention the Communist Party by name, the decree was aimed directly at the party, as the vociferous condemnations of the move by party officials clearly showed.

When the coup came, Yeltsin was at the forefront of the opposition. And when it failed, he, not Gorbachev, was the beneficiary of the political fallout that followed. It was not immediately clear that Gorbachev's time in office was drawing to a close, but after the coup he had about 125 days left as president of the USSR. During that time, Yeltsin's stock as a political leader rose steadily. He moved quickly to consolidate his position, asserting control, at first with Gorbachev, over the defense and security forces, and suspending the activities of the Communist Party in Russia. Later Communist Party property was seized, and the party was effectively banned, setting the stage for a struggle before the Constitutional Court between the state authorities under Yeltsin and the remnants of the party.

Under the constitutional arrangements of the 1991–1993 period, the Russian president possessed considerable but by no means unlimited power. He could not be a member of the legislature or hold any other public or private position, but he was not prohibited from belonging to a political party (although Yeltsin chose not to affiliate with a party). The president could serve no more that two consecutive five-year terms. Regarding relations with the legislature, the president could propose legislation and had veto power over legislation adopted by the Supreme Soviet, which could be overridden by a majority vote of the full membership of both houses. But the president did not have the power to initiate a popular referendum, which could only be proposed by the Congress, or by one–third of the deputies on their own, or on the basis of a petition signed by at least one million citizens. The lack of presidential power to call referendums rankled Yeltsin, who wanted to be able to appeal to the people over the head of Parliament.

The president had the power to propose the prime minister, but, as indicated above, the actual appointment was done by the Supreme Soviet, with the approval of the Congress of People's Deputies. In practice, the president exercised the power to name and dismiss ministers and other cabinet-level officers. One of the president's most formidable powers was that of issuing decrees (*ukazy*). According to the constitution, such decrees could be adopted "on the basis of and in fulfillment of the Constitution and the laws of the Russian Federation and the decisions of the Russian Federation Congress of People's Deputies and the Russian Federation Supreme Soviet. The President's decrees may not run counter to the Constitution and the laws of the Russian Federation."

As this quotation indicates, the president's exercise of this power was to be "on the basis of and in fulfillment of" the constitution and laws adopted by Parliament. In spite of this provision, Yeltsin issued decrees on a wide variety of matters, often in apparent disregard of their relation to parliamentary action or inaction. This was a major source of friction between the executive and legislative branches. Yeltsin, an important *apparatchik* during the Soviet period, was accustomed to acting in this manner. A similar constitutional limitation on executive power during the Soviet period was routinely ignored. But the new legislature, in attempting to assert its authority, balked at the president's too broad use of the power to adopt decrees.

The constitution specifically provided that the president did not have the right to dissolve or suspend the activities of the Congress or the Supreme Soviet. On the other hand, the president could be dismissed (for violation of the constitution and laws or his oath of office) by the Congress of People's Deputies by a two-thirds vote of its total membership, on the basis of a ruling by the Constitutional Court.

In sum, then, the presidency was a reasonably powerful office. Popular election gave him a mandate separate from that of parliament, and he had some checks on parliamentary action, such as the veto power. But some of the limitations were equally clear: the inability to dissolve the legislature, limitations on his decree-making power (which began to be asserted as the 1991–1993 period proceeded), and the lack of a role in initiating popular referendums. These were among the matters that needed to be corrected, in Yeltsin's view, in any new constitution.

The Constitutional Court

The Russian Constitutional Court was created through a constitutional amendment in 1990. Political disagreements delayed the adoption of a detailed law on the Constitutional Court until August 1991, and it was only then that the members of the court were appointed. Although the court was intended to have 15 members, the Congress of People's Deputies was able to agree on only 13. This was the number that served on the Constitutional Court during the 1991–1993 period. Judges were appointed to the court for unlimited terms, but were required to retire at age 65.

The Constitutional Court was a separate institution from Russia's regular courts in that its sole purpose was to review constitutional issues. The law on the Constitutional Court prohibited it from reviewing political questions, but given its function as arbiter of the constitutionality of laws and other official acts, this prohibition had little meaning in practice. During the 1991–1993 period it issued a number of significant decisions, including rulings against both the president and parliament for overstepping their constitutionally mandated functions (Barry 1993, 30–31). Undoubtedly its most important decision in this period was in the so-called Communist Party case, involving the constitutionality of President Yeltsin's decrees in the autumn of 1991, suspending and then banning the RSFSR Communist Party and seizing its assets. The court's compromise ruling in this case satisfied few legal specialists, but it allowed the political system to extract itself from an exceedingly difficult situation, and it left the credibility of the Constitutional Court largely intact. A more troublesome aspect of Constitutional Court activity during this period was the habit of individual judges, particularly Constitutional Court Chairman Zorkin, of speaking out on legal and political issues, including matters before the court in cases that had not yet been decided. This practice brought considerable criticism to the court, particularly during the constitutional crisis experienced by the country during the autumn of 1993.

Federalism and Ethnic Problems

When the Soviet Union broke up, 25 million ethnic Russians were living in the countries of the Near Abroad. As indicated in the previous chapter, this has been one of several factors that have complicated relations between Russia and the republics of the former Soviet Union. Another significant issue is the 30 million non-Russians living within the Russian Federation. There is a considerable mixing of nationalities throughout the country, but there are also areas of substantial concentration of particular ethnic groups.

Soviet policy long favored recognizing these ethnic-territorial units and providing them with limited administrative autonomy within the overall framework of Communist Party and central government control. Thus, from well before the time Gorbachev took over, there were 31 political subdivisions in the RSFSR named after minority nationalities. Sixteen of these were Autonomous Soviet Socialist Republics (ASSRs), territories endowed with their own constitutions, capital cities, parliaments and other accouterments of sovereign states. They were similar to the union republics of the Soviet Union (such as Ukraine, Uzbekistan, Armenia, etc.), but generally smaller in population and not given the fictitious right to secede from the union that union republics had. Two more well-known of the ASSRs were the Tatar, located around the Volga River city of Kazan; and the Yakut Republic, covering a vast territory the size of India in Russia's northeast. Below the ASSRs were five autonomous oblasts, ethnic territories of smaller size that were granted a degree of administrative autonomy. At the bottom of the ethnic-territorial scale was the national okrug, generally sparsely populated areas of some ethnic concentration. There were ten of these in the RSFSR.

As little as Soviet policy over the years may have encouraged real autonomy in these regions, their sense of difference from regular territorial subdivisions and their language and cultural distinctiveness were kept alive, at least minimally. In a number of territories these characteristics were reawakened during the wave of nationalism that swept the USSR at the end of the 1980s. And even before the USSR had collapsed, some of the national regions in Russia showed stirrings of sentiments favoring more autonomy and even independence. Although these developments may have caused concern among many Russians, official policy, at least for a time, was more benign. Boris Yeltsin stated repeatedly on a trip through the RSFSR in 1990 that autonomous territories should take as much independence as they wanted (Barry and Barner-Barry 1992, 64). Clearly, he meant this autonomy to be exercised within the framework of the RSFSR, but some regions had other ideas. The Tatar Republic began asserting interest in greater control over its affairs in 1988, and adopted a declaration of sovereignty in 1990. Separatist rumblings began to be heard in the Chechen-Ingush Republic as early as 1991. While these republics seemed to be in the news the most, other parts of Russia were also stirring. For instance, the Republic of Yakutia proposed in 1990 to take control of the natural resources in its territory, including its significant holdings in diamonds, gold and timber.

In some ways it seemed that Yeltsin faced within Russia the same kind of challenge that confronted Gorbachev from the independence-minded parts of the USSR. But several factors made the situation within Russia significantly different. First, many of the territories in question were completely surrounded by Russian territory. Second, none could point to any recent experience with independence; they had long been a part of Russia. And third, the percentage of residents in many of the territories in question who belonged to the nationality for which the region was named was quite small. For instance, in the Tatar Republic at the beginning of the 1990s, 48 percent were Tatar and 43 percent were Russian; in Yakutia, 33 percent were Yakut and 50 percent were Russian. Thus, the claim to complete independence in these regions was less persuasive. However, this did not stop some territories from trying. In March 1992 Tatarstan held a referendum on state sovereignty, which passed handily, even though the Russian Federation Constitutional Court declared the action unconstitutional and President Yeltsin urged a no vote (Sheehy 1992, 3).

In the Chechen-Ingush Republic, Djokhar Dudaev, a former air force pilot, seized power after the August 1991 coup. He was elected president later in 1991, and hinted that he wanted to move the republic in a separatist direction. President Yeltsin sought to take control of the situation, declaring a state of emergency in the republic late in 1991. But the Russian Supreme Soviet rescinded the decree on the ground that it unnecessarily inflamed the situation. Shortly thereafter, the Chechen and Ingush territories were divided into separate republics. In brief, this is the background to the tension that has characterized relations between the Chechnya and the Russian central authorities up to the present time.

With regard to the other republics and regions in the Russian Federation, things have gone more smoothly. In March 1992 Yeltsin succeeded in getting a Federation Treaty signed by all subunits of the Russian Federation, except the Chechen-Ingush Republic and Tatarstan (Ingushetia associated with the Federation Treaty after its separation from

Chechnya and Tatarstan signed a bilateral treaty with Moscow in 1994). The Federation Treaty gave considerable autonomy to the members of the federation, which comprise more than 80 units, counting both the ethnic-territorial entities and the strictly territorial regions (the latter including the cities of Moscow and St. Petersburg). As a result of amendments to the Russian Federation Constitution, the word "autonomous" was deleted from the names of the republics. Most of the autonomous oblasts were raised to the status of republic, resulting in a total of 21 ethnic-territorial republics in the Russian Federation.

The 1993 Constitutional Crisis

After the euphoria following the collapse of the USSR and the emergence of Russia as an independent state, political divisions within Russia, theretofore somewhat muted, came to the fore. Since the main power structures were the Parliament and the presidency, it is not surprising that these institutions played major roles in a series of conflicts. Of great importance in the struggle was the natural institutional rivalry—which structure would dominate in the exercise of political power? In this regard, of course, constitutional provisions were of great importance. But the controversy also had policy and personality dimensions as well. There were genuine differences between the president's team and the Congress of People's Deputies over the programmatic actions that an independent Russia should pursue. This applied in particular to economic policy. The "price liberalization" launched by the Yeltsin Government in January 1992 brought an end to most price controls and the traditional Soviet system of central planning. This almost immediately resulted in substantial price increases for a wide range of goods, followed by harsh condemnation from the Congress. Other aspects of the president's program also drew criticism, such as privatization of the economy. A particular sticking point was Yeltsin's advocacy of land privatization, which a majority of the Congress consistently opposed.

Personal antipathy between the Yeltsin side and other ambitious politicians grew as time went on. As suggested above, chief among Yeltsin's adversaries were Vice President Rutskoi and parliament speaker Khasbulatov. Rutskoi, increasingly manifesting a nostalgia for policies of the past, promoted programs that had little in common with those of Yeltsin. The president in turn stripped Rutskoi of many of his duties, and largely cut off personal contact with him. Khasbulatov, reportedly resentful that he had not become Yeltsin's prime minister, turned from being a personal ally of the president to a strong opponent. (Murray 1995, 161–63). He ran sessions of parliament in an autocratic manner, and although not a particularly popular figure among his colleagues, he was able to use the considerable resources of his office to enhance his personal power.

As the government's move to reform the economy proceeded, relations with Parliament continued to deteriorate. The democratic movements in the congress, weak and divided, offered little support for the government. The anti-Yeltsin forces, meanwhile, gradually gained in cohesion. In the autumn of 1992 a new group emerged, a seemingly unlikely coalition of hard left communist and hard right nationalists. Known informally as the "red-brown" coalition, it took the name National Salvation Front (FNS) at its inaugural congress. The Front united a variety of parliamentary blocs as well as numerous extra-parliamentary movements and personages. What the leaders of the FNS had in common, in the words of one analyst, was "their hatred for Yeltsin and the democrats, and their nostalgia for the USSR" (Murrell 1997, 111). Although the National Salvation Front did not develop into an important parliamentary organization, it brought to public attention the magnitude of the extremist component in Russian politics. Some members of the FNS later participated in paramilitary action that almost toppled the government in October 1993.

Increasingly impatient with his inability to find accommodation with Parliament, Yeltsin hinted on several occasions that he might invoke presidential rule and run the country on his own. Posturing and threats from both sides characterized the political scene in late 1992 and early 1993, until an agreement was finally reached to hold a popular referendum in April 1993. The results on the four referendum items in large measure favored Yeltsin:

1. 57.8% of voters expressed confidence in the president;
2. 53% expressed approval of his social and economic policies;
3. 49.5% favored holding pre-term presidential elections;

4. 67.2% favored holding pre-term parliamentary elections.

Prior to the referendum, the Constitutional Court ruled, on its own initiative, that since the final two questions had constitutional implications, a two-thirds affirmative vote by all *eligible* voters would be necessary to make the results binding. Thus, in spite of the impressive percentage on question four, the Congress saw no need to call for early parliamentary elections (its normal term would have run until 1995).

Armed with these results, Yeltsin felt sufficiently empowered to move quickly toward constitutional reform. He created another constitutional assembly and tried to bypass Parliament in drafting a new document. Again he was stymied by a variety of forces, including regional elites, who feared a weakening of their leverage in the federal arrangements that might emerge from a new constitutional order (Urban 1997, 285). Finally, on September 21, 1993 Yeltsin at last moved decisively. He issued a decree dismissing Parliament and calling for elections for a new State Duma, to be held December 12. He acknowledged that under the present constitution he did not have the authority to dissolve parliament. But he asserted that the security of Russia and its people was a higher value that as president he was obligated to protect.

There ensued a standoff that lasted more than 10 days, as many members of Parliament refused to accept Yeltsin's decree. A number of anti-Yeltsin extremists made common cause with the parliamentary leaders, joining them in the parliament building (known as the White House), where a large cache of arms had gradually been accumulated. Encouraged by Rutskoi and Khasbulatov, armed demonstrators attacked the Moscow mayor's office and laid siege to the main television station. The rebellion was finally put down on October 4 when a somewhat reluctant minister of defense ordered tanks to shell the White House (this and much else in connection with the crisis was televised live by CNN). Rutskoi, Khasbulatov, and a number of other leaders on the parliamentary side were arrested and placed in prison.

A hastily arranged electoral campaign was then organized. On December 12 Russia's voters were presented with two tasks: to approve or reject a new constitution, drafted by the Yeltsin team; and to elect a new parliament, the two-chamber Federal Assembly. According to the official results (which some critics challenged), 55 percent of the electorate turned out to vote on the constitution, of whom 58 percent voted in favor. The parliamentary voting was another matter. If Yeltsin and his allies had been hoping for a compliant, cooperative legislature, their disappointment was considerable. The democratic forces fell far short of a majority in the State Duma, the more powerful lower house. The surprise of the voting was the strong performance of the Liberal Democratic Party of Russia, headed by the erratic nationalist Vladimir Zhirinovsky. The voting results for the Federation Council, the upper house, were more to Yeltsin's liking, but this body was decidedly inferior in power to the State Duma. The details of the election will be discussed in Chapter 6, in the context of an examination of the development of Russian political parties.

References

Barry, Donald. 1993. "Constitutional Politics: The Russian Constitutional Court as a New Kind of Institution." In *Russia and America: From Rivalry to Reconciliation*, eds. George Ginsburgs, Alvin Z. Rubinstein, and Oles M. Smolansky. Armonk, NY: M. E. Sharpe.

Barry, Donald, and Carol Barner-Barry. 1992. *Post-Soviet Politics: The Fall of the USSR and the Rise of the Successor States*. Englewood Cliffs, NJ: Prentice-Hall.

Mann, D. 1990. "The RSFSR elections: The Congress of People's Deputies." *Report on the USSR* 2(15) 11–17.

Murray, Donald. 1995. *A Democracy of Despots*. Boulder, CO: Westview Press.

Murrell, G.D.G. 1997. *Russia's Transition to Democracy: An Internal Political History, 1989–1996*. Brighton, UK: Sussex Academic Press.

Sheehy, Ann. 1992. "Tatarstan Asserts Its Sovereignty." *RFE/RL Research Report* 1 (14), 1–5.

Urban, Michael. 1997. *The Rebirth of Politics in Russia*. Cambridge: Cambridge University Press.

Chapter 5
The Constitution:
Foundation for the Rule of Law?

Thus, a new constitution came into being. It was the product of a confrontation between the executive and legislative branches of the old system (and the forces that supported or collaborated with them), a conflict that took on the dimensions of a rebellion. Although this new constitution was a document put forth by the winning side, it would not be completely accurate to say that it was *imposed* on the Russian people. An appropriate majority of the populace voted in favor if its adoption. It is likely, however, that a considerable number of those who supported the constitution did so to avoid the greater chaos that might have ensued had the document not been affirmed. In any case, most of the political forces in the country seemed prepared, at the end of 1993, to accept the constitution as the basis for organizing the exercise of political power. Since that time, a variety of provisions of the constitution have been criticized, and numerous amendments have been proposed. But after the upheaval of 1993, the first task was to get started again, and the new document at least provided a basis for that.

In examining the Russian constitution, or any constitution, the student needs to understand that the provisions of a country's basic law do not always reflect political reality. Some constitutions are wholly or largely ignored by the people in power in a country. Others, although adopted with sincere intentions, may have a number of provisions that have been more or less superseded by political events but no one has bothered to change the outmoded passages. In still other cases, the constitutional text may accurately depict the *formal* aspect of governing, but does not take into account *informal* considerations, based on such factors as a country's traditions, its political and legal culture, and the way in which the practice of politics has evolved since the document was adopted.

In general terms, the new Russian charter has a number of features in common with its predecessor. The two are of similar length (the 1978 document, as originally adopted, contained about 8,500 words, the 1993 constitution about 8,000). Both begin with general sections about the structure of the political-economic system, followed by long sets of provisions on the rights and obligations of citizens. Both then spell out the nature and functions of the main institutions of the state (legislature, executive, judiciary, the federal system and local structures), and conclude with procedures for amendment.

A number of provisions in the original 1978 constitution were clearly not meant to be taken seriously. The document contained an elaborate description of the organs of state operation, while the real locus of political power—the Communist Party—was scarcely mentioned. The guarantees of freedom of speech and assembly (Article 48) were regularly violated in the campaign against dissidents. The same could be said of the guarantees of confidentiality of mail, telephone and telegraph transmissions (Article 54) and other articles in the extensive section on rights and liberties. With regard to the constitution adopted in 1993, the situation was different: by this time, the country had evolved to the point where constitutional provisions were taken more seriously. The distribution of political power in the new document more closely reflected political reality. Political actors now felt some obligation to abide (or at least appear to abide) by the document's provisions, so the content of these provisions had become a matter of genuine political controversy. Still, a number of articles in the present constitution should be seen not so much as *guarantees* but rather as *promises* or *hopes*. They constitute programmatic goals that are seen as desirable, rather than pledges capable of immediate accomplishment. Thus, for instance, the guarantee of a right to a home for everyone, to be provided by the state if necessary (Article 40), is clearly beyond the state's means at the present time. The same applies to the guarantee that "[e]veryone shall have the right to work under conditions meeting the requirements of safety and hygiene" (Article 37), or that "[e]veryone shall have the right to a favorable environment" (Article 42). Some other provisions of the constitution remain unrealized not because they are beyond the capacity of the state to achieve them, but because some authorities work actively to prevent their implementation. Thus, the guarantee of free choice of place of residence (Article 27) has been thwarted by political leaders in some cities. And the right to own land as private property (Article 36) has consistently been opposed by those in control of Parliament.

The reader may examine the text of the 1993 constitution in Appendix A. In this chapter a general discussion of some of the document's more important provisions will be made.

Rights and Freedoms

A few of the rights provided for in the constitution have already been mentioned. But Chapter 2 of the Constitution, "Rights and Freedoms of the Person and Citizen," is much more extensive, comprising 48 articles, some with multiple provisions. For convenience, these rights may be divided into the following categories: personal, political, criminal justice and socioeconomic. Among a large number of personal guarantees are the right to privacy (Articles 23 and 24); to freedom of information (Article 24); and to freedom from torture or violence by the state and from being subjected involuntarily to medical, scientific or other experiments (Article 21). Political liberties include freedom of speech (conditioned by a prohibition against the propagation of utterances that arouse social, racial, national or religious hatred) (Article 29); freedom of assembly (Article 31); and freedom to determine one's nationality and language (Article 26). Criminal justice protections include the presumption of innocence (Article 49); the prohibition on double jeopardy (Article 50); the right against self-incrimination (Article 51); and the right to qualified legal counsel, provided free of charge in certain cases (Article 48). Among the more notable socioeconomic rights are: state protection of maternity, childhood and family (Article 38); security benefits for the elderly and others in need (Article 39); free medical care (Article 41); free education, including higher education available on a competitive basis (Article 43).

Along with the catalog of rights, the constitution imposes a number of obligations on citizens, including preserving the cultural heritage and protecting historical and cultural monuments (Article 44); paying taxes (Article 57); preserving nature (Article 58); and defending the fatherland (Article 59). In addition, able-bodied children over 18 are required to care for their parents who are unable to work (Article 38).

Given Russia's constitutional tradition, it is reasonable to ask whether the listing of all of these rights in the 1993 document makes much difference. American scholar Robert Ahdieh's view that these provisions amount "more to words than to substance" finds considerable acceptance both in Russia and abroad (Ahdieh 1997, 173). This reinforces a point made earlier—that the constitution is part aspiration, part legal reality. The drafters of the document hoped that the country could eventually come to live up to the constitution's noble words. It might also be pointed out that many of the constitutional rights discussed above are stated in clearly positivist law terms: entitlements are created by the state, and, therefore, they can be withdrawn by the state as well. The natural law view that human rights are higher than state authority, that they preexisted the establishment of state structures, has not found wide acceptance in Russian legal theory.

Also of importance is the attitude of Russians toward law, or their legal culture, as some analysts term it. A number of scholars assert that because of the country's long authoritarian past, Russians do not expect justice from the legal system and, therefore, have little respect for law themselves. Judicial and law-enforcement organs are seen as corrupt and arbitrary, so citizens seek to avoid and evade the law to the extent possible (Alekseeva 2000, 20). If this is an accurate picture, it bodes ill for the development and enforcement of constitutional rights. Some analysts detect signs, however faint, that greater respect for the guarantees in the basic law is beginning to develop (Juviler 1998, 147–52; Ahdieh 1997, 101–103). Of considerable importance in this context is the Russian Constitutional Court, which will be discussed later in this chapter. This institution is charged with ruling on the constitutionality of the acts of state organs, including those that are alleged to have violated constitutional guarantees. In exercising this power, it serves as a potential check on arbitrary state action, a function that went unperformed during the ages of authoritarian rule in Russia.

Central State Institutions

Russia's extensive catalog of rights is typical of many constitutions adopted in recent times. But this wasn't always the case. The Bill of Rights of the U.S. Constitution (Amendments 1–10) was added almost as an afterthought, and became effective several years after the adoption of the original document. A central part of any constitutional text involves the creation and distribution of political power. As Giovanni Sartori put it in his book *Comparative Constitutional Engineering*, "a constitution without a declaration of rights is still a constitution, whereas a constitution whose core and centerpiece is not a frame of government is not a constitution" (Sartori 1997, 196).

Russia's 1993 constitution contains four chapters, comprising about 50 articles, on the organs of central political authority: the president of the Russian Federation; the Federal Assembly (parliament); the government of the Russian Federation (prime minister and ministers); and the judicial authority.

The President
The president is popularly elected to a term of four years, and may not serve more than two consecutive terms. Any citizen 35 or over who has lived in Russia for at least ten years may be elected. The presidency is endowed with impressive power. The post's incumbent is identified as head of state and is charged with being guarantor of the constitution, with protecting individual rights and freedoms as well as the sovereignty of the Russian Federation, and with determining the basic objectives of domestic and foreign policy (Article 80). The president's power to nominate or appoint officials is extensive. As a rule, higher-level officials must be approved by one or the other house of parliament: the prime minister and chairman of the central bank by the State Duma (lower house); judges of the Constitutional Court, the Supreme Court, the Supreme Arbitration Court, as well as the prosecutor general (Procurator General) by the Federation Council (upper house) (Article 83). Other officials, such as ambassadors, commanders of the armed forces, and ministers below the prime minister, do not require parliamentary approval. The president has the right to call a referendum, to propose laws to parliament, and to sign or veto laws adopted by parliament (Article 84). A two-thirds majority of the total membership of both houses is required to override a presidential veto (Article 107).

Substantial powers are granted to the president in foreign and military affairs and in times of crisis. Article 86 charges him with directing the foreign policy of the country and with negotiating and signing international treaties (which must be approved by both houses of parliament—Article 106). He is commander-in-chief of the armed forces, and in the event of aggression against Russia or the threat thereof, has the right to introduce martial law in the country as a whole or in parts thereof (Article 87). If significant civil disorders take place, the president may decree a state of emergency for the whole country or portions of it (Article 88).

Lest the impression be given that the president's powers in the areas just mentioned are unlimited, two observations should be made. First, the introduction of both martial law and a state of emergency require approval by parliament's upper house, the Federation Council (Article 102). At least on paper, this might restrict the president from abusing his authority. Second, the constitution provides that the particulars regarding declaring either martial law or a state of emergency are to be spelled out in a "federal constitutional law" (Articles 87 and 88). Such a law, in providing the details on how a constitutional provision is to be implemented, is meant to guide (and thus potentially limit) the authorities in carrying out certain constitutionally mandated functions. A more detailed discussion of this type of legislation is in order.

Like its predecessor, the 1993 constitution contains some provisions that depend for their application on the existence or adoption of implementing legislation. Sometimes only a simple law adopted by parliament is required (for example, Article 36 provides that the conditions and procedure for the use of land are to be set down in regular legislation). But in a number of cases, the constitution requires that this supplementary legislation be a federal constitutional law. In essence, a federal constitutional law is a piece of legislation on an important topic that requires the support of an extraordinary majority in parliament. It occupies a position below the constitution but above regular laws. Article 108 states that federal constitutional laws are to be adopted on issues envisaged in the constitution and that their passage requires the support of three-fourths of the total membership of the Federation Council and two-thirds of all State Duma deputies. The president is barred from vetoing federal constitutional laws.

Although such laws did not exist earlier in Russia, they are not unknown in world constitutional practice. For example, "organic laws" in

France serve a purpose similar to Russia's federal constitutional laws, and also require an extraordinary majority for their passage (see Article 46 of the French Constitution). Among the more important federal constitutional laws envisaged by the Russian constitution (in addition to those covering martial law and states of emergency) are those on the government of the Russian Federation, the judicial system, the Constitutional Court, the Supreme Court, the Supreme Arbitration Court, referendums and the convening of a constitutional assembly for drafting a new constitution. In all, some 14 provisions of the Russian Constitution mandate the promulgation of federal constitutional laws. But so far only a few of them have been adopted. There is not yet a federal constitutional law on declaring either martial law or a state of emergency. On the other hand, the Russian president has not yet sought to invoke either of these provisions. Even during the first Chechen war (1994–1996), President Yeltsin did not seek to declare a state of emergency. It is widely believed, however, that he deliberately avoided such a move in order to keep the Federation Council from examining his actions (Nogee and Mitchell 1997, 126). Under the previous constitution, in 1991, Yeltsin had imposed a state of emergency after Chechnya declared independence from Russia, only to have his act overturned by Parliament (Sakwa 1993, 120).

Two other significant presidential powers remain to be discussed. First, Article 90 authorizes the president to issue binding decrees (the Russian word is *ukazy*). Article 90 goes on to state that such decrees "may not contravene the Constitution of the Russian Federation or federal laws." In practice, however, these words have not served as much of a limitation on presidential power. In the context of a Soviet and Russian tradition of executive dominance, political leaders have long made broad use of the power to issue decrees in areas where legislative action would be more appropriate. Russian legal scholars have not been reluctant to decry this practice, but their criticism has had little impact. A better organized and more assertive parliament is required in order to establish an appropriate balance between legislative and executive authority.

Finally, regarding the president's power to dissolve Parliament prior to the end of its term: such power exists in a number of countries with parliamentary or quasi-parliamentary systems (Great Britain and France are examples). When Parliament is dissolved, new elections are held in a short time. In systems with two houses, the power of dissolution usually applies only to the lower house. It may be employed for a number of reasons: to break a deadlock between the two branches, to allow the calling of legislative elections at an opportune time or to "punish" members of Parliament by making them run for reelection prematurely. In the previous Russian constitution, it will be recalled, no power of dissolution existed, and President Yeltsin violated the basic law when he dismissed the legislature in September 1993. However, the new constitution spells out the conditions for dissolving the legislature in reasonably precise terms. There are two basic circumstances when the president can dissolve the State Duma (lower house): in connection with his nomination for chairman of the government (prime minister), and in connection with the Duma expressing no confidence in the government. Under Article 111, if the Duma rejects the president's choice(s) for prime minister three times, the president appoints the prime minister, dissolves the Duma, and announces new elections. According to Article 117, dissolution can occur under two different but related circumstances. If the Duma expresses no confidence in the government, the president may either announce the resignation of the government or reject the Duma's decision. But if the Duma again votes no confidence within three months, the president must either announce the government's resignation or dissolve the Duma. Alternatively, the government may itself raise the issue of the Duma's confidence in it. If the Duma votes no confidence, the president must either announce the resignation of the government or dissolve the Duma. Thus far during the operation of the 1993 Constitution, no issues of dissolution have come up under Article 117. But in connection with appointing the prime minister, the Duma and the president have on more than one occasion come close to a dissolution crisis over the lower house's rejection of the president's candidate. Incidentally, Article 111 pretty clearly indicates that the president's successive nominations should be different people, but President Yeltsin made a practice of challenging the Duma by putting up the same person more than once (Luryi 1999, 585).

Parliament

The Parliament, known as the Federal Assembly, is made up of two houses. The lower house is the State Duma (often referred to simply as the Duma) and the upper house is the Federation Council. As is the case in most parliamentary systems, the lower house has decidedly more authority than the upper house.

The Duma is made up of 450 deputies, popularly elected for four-year terms. The Federation Council includes two representatives from each of the country's 89 constituent regional entities (*sub"ekty* or "subjects" in Russian), one from the legislative and one from the executive part of the regional power structure. The procedure for choosing representatives to the Federation Council is left to federal legislation. The actual mode of selecting Federation Council members has gone through several changes in the short period of the operation of the 1993 Constitution (details on this matter will be covered in the next chapter).

Each house names its own officers, the chair (often referred to as speaker) being the most important. Each establishes its committee structure and procedural rules. Each has its exclusive areas of jurisdiction, some of which have already been mentioned. Among the important Federation Council powers are passing on presidential nominees for a number of posts; approving or rejecting presidential decrees on martial law and a state of emergency; and judging impeachment charges brought against the president by the Duma. The Duma's exclusive functions include ruling on a number of presidential appointments, raising the issue of confidence in the government, exercising the power of amnesty, and bringing impeachment charges against the president.

Articles 105 and 106 show the dominant position of the Duma in lawmaking. Under Article 105, a piece of legislation is first adopted by the Duma and then sent to the Federation Council. For regular legislation (as opposed to federal constitutional laws), a majority of the total membership of the Duma is required for passage. The Federation Council is considered to have approved the legislation if either:

    a) over half of its membership votes in favor; or
    b) it does not consider the matter within 14 days.

If the Federation Council rejects the legislation, a conciliation commission made up of representatives of both chambers is established to resolve the differences. Then the piece of legislation is sent back to the Duma. If the Duma agrees with the conclusions of the conciliation commission, the new text may be approved by a regular Duma majority. But if the conciliation commission is unable to reach agreement or its recommendations don't satisfy the Duma, then the latter can adopt the original text of the law by a two-thirds vote of its total membership (interpretation of *Konstitutsiia*...1994, 322–23).

Even the language of this provision, in the original Russian, suggests the dominance of the Duma in the process. Article 105 states that "federal laws" (*federal'nye zakony*), not bills or proposed legislation, are "adopted" (*prinimaiutsiia*) by the Duma, and that these "federal laws" are then sent to the Federation Council. The latter's job is to "approve" or "reject" the "federal law." After this stage, of course, the law goes on to the president for either signing or veto.

The Federation Council's somewhat restricted participation in lawmaking, as described above, applies to all but a handful of categories of legislation. Article 106 *requires* Federation Council approval on a number of issues having to do with budget matters, ratification and denunciation of international agreements, and the security of the state. In addition, as explained above, the Federation Council is guaranteed a role in the adoption of federal constitutional laws.

As indicated above, only the Duma can express no confidence in the government. The Duma lacks authority to vote no confidence in the president, but may start the impeachment process by bringing charges against him. The grounds for removal are treason or "some other grave crime." The Duma's charges must be confirmed by a conclusion of the Supreme Court and by a resolution of the Constitutional Court asserting that the correct procedure has been followed. The Duma's decision to bring charges and the Federation Council's decision to remove the president have the same voting threshold: a two-thirds vote of each chamber's total membership (Article 93).

The Government

The word "government" (upper case G is sometimes used in this context) refers to that part of the executive branch headed by the prime minister and including the ministers (heads of the principal departments of the administrative hierarchy). This may seem somewhat unusual to a person living in the United States, where the term "government" is often employed to embrace the whole institutional apparatus, including the executive, legislative and judicial branches. An approximate equivalent in the American context of this "parliamentary" sense of government is the word "administration," as in the Bush administration or the Clinton administration.

The government of the Russian Federation is comprised of the chairman (the equivalent of the prime minister), the deputy chairmen, and ministers. In other countries this group is known collectively as the cabinet or the council of ministers, terms that are sometimes used in Russia as well. The chairman is appointed by the president and confirmed by the Duma. Deputy chairmen and ministers are appointed by the president, on the recommendation of the chairman, without parliamentary participation.

The chairman is charged with determining the basic objectives of the government and organizing its work. Specific duties of the government outlined in the constitution include drafting and implementing the budget (which is subject to Duma approval) and other financial and economic measures; and administering policies in a wide variety of fields, including culture, science, education, health, social security, ecology, law, defense, foreign policy and security (Article 114). In pursuing these objectives, the Government, operating under the constitution, laws and presidential decrees, is given the power to issue decrees and orders (*postanovleniia* and *rasporiazheniia*) having the force of law (Article 115).

Given the constitutional structure just described, it can be said that the Russian system has a *dual executive*: a president, with a substantial personnel apparatus attached to that office; and a government, headed by a chairman and deputy chairmen, but also including ministers, who preside over ministries composed of large bureaucracies (in such fields as foreign affairs, defense, health, education, justice, etc.). The activities of these two executive bodies are bound to overlap to some extent, but where conflicts might arise, the position of the president has so far been dominant. The president has the power to dismiss the government, including its chairman (Article 117). And indeed, President Yeltsin showed no reluctance to dispense with prime ministers, especially during his second term, 1996–1999. Moreover, a government resolution that is deemed to be in conflict with the constitution, a law, or a presidential decree may be rescinded by the president (Article 115).

The dual executive operating in Russia is modeled on the French system, which also features a powerful, popularly elected president along with a prime minister. In France, too, the president is the dominant figure. But the French president's power is somewhat diminished, with the prime minister gaining in authority, under conditions of *cohabitation*. Cohabitation comes about when parliament's lower house becomes controlled, as a result of an election, by political forces or parties different from the president's. When that happens, the French president feels bound to appoint a prime minister who represents the dominant forces in the lower house. At that point, the president yields at least part of the policy agenda to the opposition.

This is one of the *informal* aspects of constitutional operation that Russia has not yet embraced. It is fair to say that the president's supporters lacked a majority in the Duma during the whole of Yeltsin's tenure under the 1993 Constitution (the picture has been less clear since Vladimir Putin has been president). But Yeltsin continued to nominate (and have confirmed) prime ministers of his own personal choosing. Evidently the party system will need to mature, and coalition politics will need to become better established, before this convention of parliamentary operation takes root in Russia.

Judicial Authority

The section in the constitution on judicial authority contains 12 articles, covering a variety of aspects of judicial and procuraturial activity. Judges of the Russian Federation are required to be over 25 years of age, to have higher legal education, and to have worked in law for at least five years (Article 119). Several constitutional provisions seek to protect and insulate judges from outside influence. Article 121 states that "judges shall be unremovable." Article 122 asserts that "judges shall possess immunity." And Article 120 contains an old standby, a throwback to communist times: "Judges shall be independent and shall be subordinate only to the Constitution of the Russian Federation and to federal law." This formulation bears a close resemblance to Article 167 of the 1978 Constitution: "Judges and people's assessors are independent and are subordinate only to the law." True judicial independence, of course, depends on much more than constitutional exhortations. It requires, at a minimum, a support system for judges (including economic support) that allows them to do their jobs without fear, without interference, and with a level of economic security that diminishes the temptations of corruption. It also requires a sufficient cadre of trained legal professionals to serve on the bench, people with the kind of ethical grounding that the task requires. No doubt a number of Russian judges have these characteristics, but the consensus view seems to be that such jurists do not yet sufficiently dominate the profession.

A longish section of the constitution spells out the functions of the Constitutional Court. It is composed of 19 judges (15 were provided for under the previous constitution), and is assigned a wide variety of disputes for resolution. The common characteristic of these disputes is the issue of *constitutionality*: does the action being contemplated, or already accomplished, violate a provision of the constitution? Such disputes might pit two bodies of the federal state apparatus against each other (parliament versus the president, for instance); or the federal government against a regional government; or two regional authorities against each other. Other cases are brought by citizens, alleging that one or another of their constitutional rights have been infringed upon. The activity of the Constitutional Court is spelled out only in the barest terms in the constitution. A more detailed description of its functions and procedures is provided in a federal constitutional law on the Constitutional Court, adopted in 1994.

No constitutional court existed in Russia prior to 1991. As a new institution, it has the potential for mediating disputes among state institutions, as well as supporting constitutional rights, in a way that has not existed in Russia before this time.

Articles 126 and 127 outline the powers and duties of two other high courts, and the hierarchies of lower courts that they supervise. The

Supreme Court is at the apex of the regular judicial system, basically serving as the final appeal in civil, criminal and other cases handled by the ordinary courts. The Supreme Arbitration Court is the highest judicial body in a system of courts established for settling economic disputes.

A final institution covered in the chapter of the constitution on judicial authority is the Procurator General (Article 129). Sometimes referred to as the Prosecutor General, this office has a wider mandate than that of U.S. prosecutors. In addition to prosecuting accused criminals, the Procurator General (and subordinate procurators in a highly centralized structure) is responsible for seeing that the law is scrupulously observed in all parts of the legal system. Although the procuracy has long existed in the Russian legal system, some Russian observers doubt the wisdom of putting such far-reaching power in the prosecutorial arm of the state (Yakovlev 2000, 5).

The Federal System

The constitution provides considerable detail on the nature of federal relations in Russia. Fifteen articles, some with numerous provisions, are devoted to the subject. The federation is composed of 89 regional entities or subjects. The Russian Federation exercises exclusive jurisdiction over a number of functions, including foreign, defense and security policy; the federal budget, taxation policy, currency, credit and customs regulation; the country's energy system; the state borders, territorial waters, air space, and the continental shelf. A number of areas are shared by the federation and its constituent units, including law and order, natural resources, public health and education. Functions not under the exclusive jurisdiction of the federation or in the shared category are left to the constituent entities to administer (Articles 71–73).

Article 76 provides that federal law will prevail in the area of shared jurisdiction. Article 78 allows the federal executive to establish its own territorial organs to see that federal law is enforced. Article 85 gives the president the right to suspend acts by the executive organs of federal entities that conflict with the federal constitution, federal laws and "international obligations of the Russian Federation," as well as acts that violate human and civil rights and freedoms. Such suspensions remain in effect until the issues are resolved by the courts.

These provisions constitute an attempt by the federal authorities to reassert a measure of dominance over the regions, which had eroded considerably in the years prior to the adoption of the constitution. During the Soviet period, Russia, like the USSR as a whole, was a federation. Its constituent units were 31 ethnically based territories (autonomous republics, autonomous oblasts and national areas). When the traditional mechanisms of central political power (a dominant Communist Party directing a well-organized state apparatus, including a strong KGB) were in place, Moscow had little trouble controlling these regions. But as central authority weakened in the late 1980s and early 1990s, some of the ethnically-based territories began to call for greater autonomy. As the newly elected Russian president in 1991, Boris Yeltsin encouraged this development. As part of his effort to gain support in Russia in his competition with USSR president Gorbachev, he encouraged the regions to take "as much sovereignty as you can swallow" (Starovoitova 1997, 11; Tarr 1999, 707). A Federation Treaty was adopted in 1992. It was signed by all of the republics except Tatarstan and Chechnya. Describing the republics within the federation as "sovereign," the Federation Treaty allowed them to adopt their own constitutions and laws, to elect parliaments and heads of state, and to create other institutions associated with statehood. Although it said nothing about secession, use of the word sovereignty, in the context of the time, suggested to some that republics could exercise the right to secede (Lapidus and Walker 1995, 93).

The constitutional crisis of September-October 1993 led to the adoption of the new constitution. In this document the concept of republic sovereignty was almost completely ignored. Nor was the right to secede mentioned. But not all of the ambiguity regarding federal relations was resolved. Under article 65, the "subjects of the federation" now include 89 units. Thirty-two of them are named after particular ethnic groups (in 1992 the Chechen-Ingush Republic was divided into two separate entities, thus raising the number of ethnically-based regions to 32). The other 57 are strictly territorial units. Twenty-one of the ethnically based units are *republics*, this number including all of the autonomous republics and four of the five autonomous oblasts that existed during the Soviet period. These republics are accorded a somewhat grander status under the constitution than the other units. They have the right to establish their own state language, which may be used along with Russian, the state language of the Russian Federation as a whole (Article 68). And republics have *constitutions*, while the other units adopt *charters* as the fundamental law of their territories (Article 5). All subjects of the federation are declared to have equal status (Article 3), but this is hardly the case in practice (DeBardeleben 1997, 47).

Since the adoption of the 1993 Constitution, republic autonomy has continued to be an issue. Chechnya has fought two bloody wars against the Russian authorities since 1994 in an effort to gain its independence. To quiet the demands for further autonomy from Tatarstan, in 1994 President Yeltsin signed a power-sharing agreement with that republic, granting it tax breaks and allowing it a large measure of control over its natural resources. Several other republics obtained similar concessions. This provoked protests from non-ethnic regions, and prompted Yeltsin to sign dozens of further agreements, particularly during his presidential re-election campaign in 1996, when he was attempting to curry favor with the territories (Kjeldsen 1998, 385).

A number of the country's non-ethnically based territories have expressed resentment over what they consider to be the privileged treatment of the republics, some going so far as to seek republic status for themselves. A look at several demographic and economic indicators helps put the situation in perspective. Ethnically-based republics constitute a rather small portion of Russia's total population—only 15.7 percent. In only 5 of the 21 republics does the titular nationality constitute a majority. Even in Tatarstan, where such strong separatist sentiments have been expressed, Tatars make up only 48.5 percent of the population, versus 43 percent Russians. The republic of Karelia is only 10 percent Karelian and nearly 75 percent Russian. Several of the republics have considerable economic potential. For instance, the republic of Sakha (formerly Yakutia) possesses vast resources and is especially noted for producing gold and diamonds. Tatarstan, an important industrial region, is a large producer of petroleum and automobiles. But it is also true that a number of republics are economically underdeveloped and depend heavily on Moscow for subsidies. A telling statistic is that of the 15 subjects of the Russian Federation that receive more from the treasury in Moscow than they contribute, 14 are republics (Lapidus and Walker 1995, 104).

Thus, the authorities in Moscow face two major problems in federal relations. The first is the perception among many of the territories that the nationality-based units receive favored treatment. The second is the erosion of central control over the federal units. Of the two, the second is considerably more important. It is based on three interrelated factors: the decline of state power in Russia in general; the increased assertiveness of some of the regions; and concessions Moscow has granted to placate the restive territories. Basically, it is the richer regions, those with the most bargaining power, that have been able to extract the concessions. The weaker regions have little choice but to go along with what the central authorities prescribe. This has created what is widely described as "asymmetric federalism" in Russia (Smith 1998, 1393).

The 1993 Constitution made some modest steps in strengthening Moscow's hand in relation to the federal units. Vladimir Putin, soon after he was elected President in March 2000, moved to shift the balance more firmly in the direction of central authority. Several laws adopted by parliament at Putin's behest, as well as a number of presidential decrees, were aimed at strengthening central control. The most important of these was a law providing that regional governors would no longer be permitted to serve in the federal parliament's upper house, the Federation Council. They are to be replaced by appointed officials and, in the process, will lose their immunity from prosecution. These moves were achieved without constitutional amendment, although some critics complained that their effect was tantamount to constitutional change. Making actual changes in the constitutional text, however, is a considerably more challenging task, as the next section will explain.

Amending the Constitution

As constitutions go, the 1993 Russian charter is exceedingly difficult to amend. Under the 1978 Russian constitution, only the Parliament participated in the process. Although amendments required the support of two-thirds of the total membership of the Supreme Soviet, this was normally not difficult to achieve. As a result, literally hundreds of amendments were made to the 1978 Constitution. An indication of the relative difficulty of changing the 1993 document is that as of this writing, eight years after its promulgation, not one amendment has been adopted.

The provisions on constitutional amendment are contained in three articles, numbers 135–37. The following parties may propose amendments to the constitution: the president, either house of Parliament, groups within either house that constitute at least one-fifth of the membership, the government, and the legislatures of the subjects of the federation. In terms of the actual amending process, the procedure to be followed can take three basic forms, depending on the part of the constitution to be changed. For Chapters 3–8 of the constitution (covering the structure and operations of the basic state institutions), the process starts in Parliament, where amendments are adopted according to the procedure for adopting federal constitutional laws. As described above, this requires the support of three-fourths of the total membership of the Federation Council, and two-thirds of all Duma deputies. A proposed amendment that passes this stage comes into force only after approval by the legislatures of at least two-thirds of the subjects of the federation (Article 136).

With regard to Chapters 1, 2 and 9 of the constitution (fundamental principles of the constitutional order, rights and freedoms of the person and citizen, and constitutional amendments and constitutional revision, respectively), the procedure is different. Article 135 states flatly that the provisions of these chapters may not be amended by Parliament. What Parliament can do, if a proposal for amendment of any part of these chapters is put forward, is to start the process for drafting a new constitutional document. This requires the support of three-fifths of the total membership of both houses. If this is achieved, then Parliament adopts a federal constitutional law for convening a constitutional assembly. The constitutional assembly may either confirm the constitution as it is, or draft a new constitution. This new document can be adopted in one of two ways: by a two-thirds vote of the constitutional assembly, or by a referendum supported by over half the voters in which at least half of the electorate participates.

Article 137 provides for a narrow exception to the previous two procedures, and affects only article 65 of the constitution, on the constituent entities (subjects) of the federation. It provides that changes in article 65 (creation of new subjects, or other changes in the status of subjects), may be effected through the adoption of a federal constitutional law. This process, then, is the simplest of all, since it can be accomplished wholly by Parliament. Given this simplicity, it might be a tool for the authorities to achieve greater control over certain of the more restive federal units (by, for instance, the creative combining of certain entities into larger units). While this would be technically possible, one could safely predict that the political fallout from such a move would be considerable.

Article 137 aside, it is arguably easier to adopt a whole new constitution than to amend parts of it, since the latter process requires the approval of two-thirds of the legislatures of federal units. The option of drafting a completely new document seems to be increasingly favored by those who support President Putin's political agenda.

References

Ahdieh, Robert B. 1997. *Russia's Constitutional Revolution: Legal Consciousness and the Transition to Democracy 1985–1996.* University Park, PA: Pennsylvania State University Press.

Alekseeva, Ludmilla. 2000. "The Human Rights Situation in the Russian Federation, 1998." In *Human Rights in Russia.* Washington, DC: Commission on Security and Cooperation in Europe.

DeBardeleben, Joan. 1997. "The Development of Federalism in Russia." In *Beyond the Monolith: The Emergence of Regionalism in Post-Soviet Russia*, eds. Peter J. Stavrakis, Joan DeBardeleben, and Larry Black. Baltimore, MD: Johns Hopkins University Press.

Juviler, Peter. 1998. *Freedom's Ordeal: The Struggle for Human Rights and Democracy in Post-Soviet States.* Philadelphia, PA: University of Pennsylvania Press.

Kjeldsen, Stig. 1998. "The Treaty Process Evolves: Russian Bilateral Power-Sharing Treaties." *Review of Central and East European Law.* 24:363–385.

Konstitutsiia Rossiiskoi Federatsii: Kommentarii. 1994. Eds. B.N. Topornin, Iu. M. Baturin, and R. G. Orekhov. Moscow: Iuridicheskiia Literatura.

Lapidus, Gail W. and Edward W. Walker. 1995. "Nationalism, Regionalism, and Federalism: Center-Periphery Relations in Post-Communist Russia." In *The New Russia: Troubled Transformation*, ed. Gail W. Lapidus. Boulder, CO: Westview Press.

Luryi, Yuri. 1999. "The Appointment of a Prime Minister in Russia: The President, the Duma, the Constitutional Court." *Review of Central and East European Law.* 25:585–610.

Nogee, Joseph L. and R. Judson Mitchell. 1997. *Russian Politics: The Struggle for a New Order.* Boston, MA: Allyn and Bacon.

Sakwa, Richard. 1993. *Russian Politics and Society.* London: Routledge.

Sartori, Giovanni. 1997. *Comparative Constitutional Engineering: An Inquiry into Structures, Incentives and Outcomes.* 2nd ed. New York: New York University Press.

Smith, Graham .1998. "Russia, Multiculturalism and Federal Justice." *Europe-Asia Studies* 50:1393–1411.

Starovoitova, Galina. 1997. *Sovereignty After Empire: Self-Determination Movements in the Former Soviet Union.* Washington, DC: United States Institute of Peace.

Tarr, G. Alan. 1999. "Creating Federalism in Russia." *South Texas Law Review* 40: 689–713.

Yakovlev, Aleksandr. 2000. "Dikatura zakona zashchitit ot proizvola vlastei."*Rossiiskaia gazeta, July 28.*

Chapter 6
Political Parties and Elections: Underdeveloped Politics

General Features of the Russian Party System

A generally accepted maxim of politics is that the achievement of democracy is closely associated with the development of a rational system of political parties (Colton 2000, 103). Perhaps the most basic *political* failing in Russia since the USSR's demise (as opposed to problems in the economic or other spheres) involves the difficulties associated with building its party system. A constitution can be adopted with relative ease, a chief executive and parliament duly elected, and a judicial system put in place. But until parties can effectively perform their various roles, including most importantly aggregating the interests of the populace and acting as mediators between citizens and the state, political success in Russia is likely to prove elusive.

Before a workable party system can be created in Russia, a number of challenges need to be faced. Among many Russians there remains "allergy" to the idea of political parties, in part because of negative associations with the only party they ever knew, the Communist Party of the Soviet Union (Rudenshiold and Barnes 1994, 20). Because of this, there has been a tendency among some political groupings to identify themselves as movements, unions or associations rather than parties. The taint of the Communist Party may also explain in part Russians' lack of trust in parties, a fact confirmed by numerous surveys (Sedov 1998, 236; White, Rose and McAllister 1997, 132).

However, there has not been a shortage of parties in post-Soviet Russia. Hundreds of them have been established, although only a few have played significant roles in politics (Rudenshoild and Barnes 1994, 23; Colton 2000, 104). Many are short-lived entities, here today and if not gone tomorrow, then soon thereafter. A number of parties that have been in existence for some time follow the French practice of frequently changing their names. All of this adds up to a picture of considerable confusion, not only for the analyst trying to make sense of the party system, but for the voter as well. A 1997 Russian source summed up the situation with this ironic observation: "the political spectrum changes not daily but hourly" (Oleshchuk and Pavlenko 1997, 6).

A factor that is said to have a major influence on party and voter stability in the West is *party identification*, that is, a more or less consistent association with and support of particular parties by some portion of the citizenry. Although the data from surveys on party identification in Russia have not produced uniformly consistent results, all surveys show a lower level of party identification among Russian citizens than is the case with citizens in the West, particularly those in the United States (Colton 2000, 110–16; White, Rose and McAllister 1997, 134–36; Sedov 1998, 230–32). Given that Russia's is such a complicated party system, and that its parties have been in existence for only a few years, after more than seven decades of one-party rule, relatively low party identification is not surprising. Nor is the fact that the party with the highest level of party identification among Russia's voters is the one with the deepest roots in the Russian/Soviet past, the Communist Party of the Russian Federation.

Background on the Present Party System

As with many other aspects of contemporary Russian politics, the development of political parties traces its roots to the Gorbachev period. Until Gorbachev, the Communist Party of the Soviet Union was the only political party in existence. It monopolized political activity and directed the operation of the machinery of the state. Those who sought to influence political action outside the party, such as dissidents supporting one or another cause, did so at their peril, and could expect harsh treatment from the state. They were, in Walter Connor's apt phrase, "entering politics without a license" (Connor 1975, 24).

This was the system that Mikhail Gorbachev inherited when he came to power in March 1985. As his program for glasnost and perestroika unfolded, however, it produced a fundamental shift in the distribution of political power. As the authority of the Communist Party weakened, other interests organized to air grievances and push for the achievement of their goals. At first most of these organizations, called "informals" (*neformaly*) in Russian, tended to have rather specific interests. There were countless varieties of such associations, but among notable examples were groups aimed at combating deteriorating ecological conditions, or working for the restoration of historical monuments, or complaining about official graft and corruption. And, of course, many organizations were created specifically to represent the interests of one or another ethnic group (Petro 1991, 105–23).

Given their rather narrow orientation, many of these associations were more akin to the West's interest groups or single cause movements than to political parties. While there was some level of cooperation among such groups in the electoral campaigns of the late Gorbachev period, more formal interest aggregation aimed at the creation of real parties was yet to come. It will be recalled that Article 6 of the Soviet Constitution was changed only in March 1990. That change ended the Communist Party's monopoly on political power. Responsibility for running "state and public affairs" was given to the Communist Party "other political parties, as well as trade union, youth, and other public organizations and mass movements."

It is fair to say that this constitutional change amounted to little more than the recognition of an accomplished fact: that the Communist Party was no longer capable of maintaining a monopoly on legitimate political activity. Nevertheless, it is also clear that at this time, *organized political parties* worthy of the name had not yet developed. The 1989 election for the USSR Congress of People's Deputies, although a *relatively* open process, had no other parties participating in the campaign. Members of the Communist Party constituted 85 percent of those elected to the Congress. The same was true of the spring 1990 election of the RSFSR Congress (where over 86 percent of those elected were communists). By the time the USSR collapsed at the end of 1991, a party *system* in Russia was only beginning to take shape.

Russian Parties

Parties are created to gain political power. As Russia moved away from a single party system, elections became the most important political mechanism for distributing power, and thus stimulated the organization of political parties. When legislative elections were called for December 1993, soon after the constitutional crisis of September-October, a number of parties came into being virtually overnight. In somewhat similar fashion, successive elections have provided further impetus to party development. Some of this has involved the creation of new parties, while in other cases what has taken place has been merely the rearrangement of existing political forces.

Thus, elections can serve as important benchmarks in the evolution of the Russian party system. As elections are examined more closely, it will also become clear that the *electoral system*, that is, the basic voting rules, can have an important effect on parties. This is especially true in Russia of parliamentary elections, but it applies to some extent to presidential elections as well. For the 1993 Duma election, the old electoral system was abandoned. In both 1989 and 1990 (electing the USSR Congress of People's Deputies and the RSFSR Congress of People's Deputies, respectively), the single member district majority system was used. Fearing that this arrangement would retard the development of parties, the architects of the 1993 system decided that a portion of the deputies should be elected by proportional representation. Under the proportional representation part of the arrangement, voters would vote for parties rather than individual candidates, thus, it was reasoned, enhancing the importance of parties.

The 1993 electoral arrangements, which were adopted with very few changes for the 1995 and 1999 elections as well, shared a number of essential features with the system created by the Federal Republic of Germany after World War II. Under this system, half of the deputies are chosen by single member district plurality, and half by the proportional representation party list system. Each voter has two votes, one for a district representative and the other for a party. To discourage the proliferation of parties, the electoral law provides (as it does in Germany) that a party must receive at least 5 percent of the vote in order to get any of the party list seats. Although this system seems to work as intended in Germany (which had an established party system prior to the Nazi takeover), in Russia, the number of parties that contest Duma elections has remained large (although only a few of them have exceeded the crucial 5 percent threshold in any given election). This matter will be discussed in greater detail below, in connection with an analysis of the elections.

At the beginning of 1999, the year of the most recent Duma elections, 141 parties were listed as having registered with the Ministry of Justice ("Skol'ko v Rossii partii?" 1999, 2). It would obviously be impractical to discuss all of these political entities, nor would it make much sense, because "only" 26 of them were registered by the Central Election Commission to compete in the 1999 election. Rather, we will concentrate on a small number of parties that have shown a reasonable amount of electoral strength, as well as several others that have managed to survive through successive elections.

How should these parties be classified? We will employ here the classic left-right approach, which puts the communists on the left, the extreme nationalist parties on the right, and other parties arrayed somewhere between the poles. Two caveats should be mentioned in connection with this classification, however. First, because of the country's long one-party past, a sense of political left and right appears to have little meaning to a large proportion of Russian voters, although it is gaining acceptance among more sophisticated Russians (Colton 2000, 144–148). And second, a number of Russian parties (as well as individual politicians) embrace policies that would appear inconsistent with their presumed place in the political spectrum (for instance, the communists are quite nationalist on a number of issues, a stance usually associated with right-wing parties; and many Russian parties, regardless of their supposed left-right position, favor a significant increase in centralized governmental power, which is also often associated with the political right).

Leftist Parties
The major party of the left is the Communist Party of the Russian Federation (CPRF), founded in 1990 and headed since its inception by Gennadii Zyuganov. The CPRF is the best organized party in the country, with a large membership and a broad network of local organizations. Its considerable electoral success over the years continued in the 1999 Duma election, when it gained the largest percentage of the party vote (over 24 percent). While cautiously embracing the market system, the CPRF strongly opposed the privatization measures of the Yeltsin era. It favors the restoration of state ownership of a large segment of the economy, and a

significant role for the state in providing social welfare to Russian citizens. Several other communist splinter groups have been created during the post-Soviet period, most endorsing more militant programs than the CPRF. The electoral strength of these parties has been minimal.

The other main force on the left has been the Agrarian Party, a close ally of the CPRF on many issues, whose program has mainly emphasized agricultural issues. During the 1999 Duma election campaign, the leadership of the Agrarian Party decided to ally itself with the Fatherland-All Russia movement (discussed below under centrist parties). This caused a split in the Agrarian Party, with some of its members staying with the CPRF.

Democratic-Reformist Parties

Undoubtedly the best-known party in this category is Yabloko. "Yabloko" means apple in Russian, but the party name is an acronym derived from the surnames of several of its founders, most notably Grigory Yavlinsky. Yabloko favors a socially oriented market economy, but it has not been able to make common cause with other parties endorsing similar programs. Originally, the other principal party in this part of the political spectrum was Russia's Choice, headed by Yegor Gaidar, who, as Yeltsin's acting prime minister, initiated a vigorous program in 1992 aimed at introducing a market economy in Russia. Russia's Choice did well in the December 1993 Duma election, gaining the second highest party vote. But in 1995, as "Russia's Democratic Choice-United Democrats," this movement fell below the 5 percent threshold and won only a few seats in the territorial constituencies. In 1999 it disappeared from the ballot altogether. Many of its adherents, including Gaidar, were absorbed into a new bloc, the Union of Right Forces, whose party list was headed by former prime minister Sergei Kirienko and former first deputy prime minister Boris Nemtsov. The Union of Right Forces did surprisingly well in the election, finishing fourth in the party voting with over 8 percent of the vote, apparently in part because of its support for then-prime minister Putin during the last stages of the campaign.

Centrist Parties

The main centrist movement of the mid-1990s was Our Home is Russia, created in 1995 to support the government of Victor Chernomyrdin, who had succeeded Gaidar as prime minister. Because of its association with Chernomyrdin and other government ministers, Our Home is Russia was referred to for a time as "the party of power." It made a fairly strong showing in the 1995 Duma election, when it won the third largest number of total seats. But when Yeltsin dismissed Chernomyrdin in 1998, the party's fortunes went into decline. In the 1999 Duma election it got barely 1 percent of the party vote and ceased to be a major factor in Russian politics.

A centrist party that showed surprising electoral strength in 1993 was Women of Russia, which matched Yabloko in Duma seats (each gained 23). Women of Russia did not have a particularly feminist orientation, but advocated increased investment in social welfare programs and projected an image of a pragmatic force for consensus. Like a number of other parties, it has not been able to sustain its 1993 success, finishing below the 5 percent threshold in both 1995 and 1999. These results seem to support the conclusion of one close observer that "there is no future for a special women's party in Russia" (Belin 2000a, 10).

The party with perhaps the least well-articulated program is the Interregional Movement Unity. Yet at the end of the 1990s, Unity showed extraordinary electoral strength. Formed in September 1999, just two months before the Duma election, its only clearly expressed goal was to support the government of newly appointed prime minister Putin. The leader of the party, Sergei Shoigu, was one of Putin's ministers. Benefitting from favored treatment by state-run media outlets, Unity gained over 23 percent of the party vote in the election, just behind the leading communists. As a party with "no discernible ideology," in the words of one analyst, its success is indicative of the volatile nature of party politics in Russia (Belin 2000a, 6).

Another party with a considerable following at the end of the 1990s was Fatherland-All Russia. It combined a movement begun in 1998 by

Moscow mayor Yurii Luzhkov with several of other forces, including a number of regional leaders and a significant part of the Agrarian Party. When former premier (as well as former chief intelligence officer and former foreign minister) Yevgenii Primakov joined the movement, its chances in the 1999 Duma election appeared favorable. It was referred to for a time as the coming party of power. But the prospects for Fatherland-All Russia were eclipsed to some extent by the swift rise of Unity at the end of the 1999 campaign. Fatherland-All Russia entered the Duma with the third largest number of deputies, behind the communists and Unity. This is another party with a difficult-to-define program. A part of the party clearly favors patriotic themes and the strengthening of central control by the state. Yet some party leaders advocate greater regional authority and others espouse social democratic rhetoric as the main focus of the party's program (Makarenko 1999, 66–68). The prospects for keeping these diverse forces together in one political entity for very long seem doubtful at best.

Rightist Parties
Over the years, a number of rightist parties, some with extreme nationalist programs, have emerged in Russia. With one exception, these organizations have uniformly done poorly at the polls. The exception is Vladimir Zhirinovsky's Liberal Democratic Party of Russia (LDPR). Zhirinovsky is a colorful character, sometimes given to outrageous behavior, whose policy statements favoring a strong brand of Russian nationalism have won him considerable support among some segments of the electorate. However, his willingness to cooperate at times with presidential and governmental institutions somewhat contradicts the maverick image that Zhirinovsky has cultivated. Zhirinovsky first came to national and international attention when he received over six million votes in the 1991 Russian presidential election. Then, in the 1993 Duma election, the LDPR achieved the highest percentage of the party vote of any party (about 23 percent). Since that time, in two presidential elections and two further Duma elections, Zhirinovsky and his party have not performed nearly as strongly. But the LDPR is one of only three parties (the others are the CPRF and Yabloko) to have surpassed the 5 percent barrier in the 1993, 1995 and 1999

elections. In 1999 the LDPR was removed from the ballot because of registration irregularities. But the party was re-registered and participated in the election under the name Zhirinovsky Bloc.

The Russian Party System
To sum up, hundreds of political parties and movements have been created in Russia since the demise of the USSR. Only a fraction of these have been duly registered by the Ministry of Justice, as required by law. And many registered parties have not met the requirements for getting on the ballot (in 1999 this involved collecting 200,000 valid signatures or submitting a deposit to the Central Election Commission). Still, a sufficient number of these organizations have competed in Duma elections (13 in 1993, 43 in 1995, 26 in 1999) to allow one to characterize the Russian political landscape as complex. The erratic programmatic goals of a number of parties have already been mentioned. Another problem is that of long-term party stability. Suffice it to say that only about half of the parties that stood for the 1993 Duma election were on the ballot in 1995, and fewer than 20 percent of the 1995 parties competed in 1999. To a considerable extent, the party system has been reinvented for every Duma election.

In part this is related to the nature of a number of Russian political parties: rather than being institutionalized organizations that politicians join in order to pursue their ambitions and further their goals, some Russian parties are vehicles created primarily for particular individuals or a small group of politicians. Since the purpose of such entities is to support the ambitions of individuals, the incentive to cooperate and coalesce with other parties is diminished. When politicians in such parties hold political power or are in favor with a segment of the electorate, their parties are viable. But when they lose power or popularity, the party ceases to have a reason for being. In a more mature political system, parties are sufficiently institutionalized so as continue to function when the fortunes of individual politicians wane.

On the other hand, it is certainly premature to make a definitive judgment about the Russian party system. Party competition has been permitted in Russia for only a few years. Many European countries, at early stages of their party development, had similarly amorphous party systems

(Colton 2000, 136). And there are signs, however tentative, that the party system in Russia is beginning to develop in a more coherent fashion. As noted earlier, the sense of party identification among Russian voters appears to be growing. And if one can point to only a few parties that, under their present names, have been consistent presences on the political scene in recent years, one can identify numerous politicians with a continual record of activity throughout this period who have shifted alliances or joined renamed political movements.

The rules of party competition also seem to be enhancing party stability. The organization of factions in the Duma is one of these. Parliamentary rules require that party groupings have at least 35 deputies to participate in directing legislative work. This acts as an incentive for smaller groups to cooperate and coalesce. And there is some evidence that presidential elections, about which little has been said up to now, have the potential for increasing political cooperation (Remington 1999, 168–71). Finally, it appears that particularly in the 1999 Duma election, a number of voters cast their ballots more rationally, demonstrating their understanding that support for parties with little chance of breaking the 5 percent barrier amounted to wasting votes (Belin 2000a, 7). This was one of the objectives that the electoral system was designed to achieve, and it may be that that goal is beginning to be reached. For a better sense of this and other aspects of voting behavior in Russia, the discussion now turns to the elections themselves.

Elections

There are two types of national elections in Russia: parliamentary and presidential. The present discussion will concentrate on elections since 1993, when the new constitution was adopted. Since that time, there have been three parliamentary elections, in 1993, 1995, and 1999; and two presidential elections, in 1996 and 2000.

The 1993 Parliamentary Election

To review a number of points made in previous chapters: President Yeltsin dismissed the legislature in September 1993 and had the military put down an insurgency that centered on the parliament building in October. Plans were then hurriedly implemented for adopting a new constitution and electing a new parliament, both of which were voted on by the people in December. Voters were put in the ambiguous position of voting for deputies to a legislature that was being brought into being by a constitution that they were being asked to approve at the same time. Be that as it may, the constitution was adopted and the members of the new Federal Assembly were duly elected.

Because of the short time frame, members of both the lower house (Duma) and the upper house (Federation Council) were popularly elected in December 1993. Thereafter, national parliamentary elections have involved only the Duma. The electoral rules for the December election were set forth in edicts promulgated by President Yeltsin, based on drafts of an electoral law that had been prepared and discussed during the preceding months.

As mentioned, the electoral system for the Duma election combined single-member district plurality (SMDP) voting with party list proportional representation (PR). In the 450 member Duma, half of the deputies were to be elected by each method, with the voter having two votes, one for the district representative and the other for the party of choice. In order to get on the PR ballot, a party needed to collect 100,000 signatures, with no more than 15 percent of these from any one administrative district. Individual candidates for the single-member districts could qualify either by being nominated by a party that had been accepted on the ballot or by collecting the required number of signatures (one percent of the registered voters in the district).

These requirements, combined with the short time period available, limited the number of participants in the election. Still, about 1,400 candidates registered for the district seats; and 21 parties presented signatures to the Central Election Commission. Of these 21, eight were found ineligible, leaving 13 parties to contest the election.

Once the parties and individual candidates were on the ballot, further rules came into play. On the party list voting, a party could qualify to participate in the apportionment of seats only if it received at least 5 percent of the vote. In the single member races, participation by at least 25 percent of the electorate was required for a district race to be considered valid. No election was held in Chechnya, and in several districts in Tatarstan, turnout was below 25 percent, thus lowering the number of district seats filled at the time of the regular election.

As suggested earlier, the Russian system for electing the Duma parallels German Bundestag elections in key respects: half of the seats are elected by PR with a 5 percent threshold, and the other half are apportioned by single-member district plurality. There is one key difference between the two systems, however. In Germany, the plurality and PR systems are interconnected, so that a party's PR percentage is highly determinative of the total number of seats a party will receive. In Russia, with its underdeveloped party system, this link between the two parts does not exist. PR seats are apportioned independently of the district contests. As will be seen, there have been notable differences in the results produced by the two electoral methods.

Table 6.1 summarizes the 1993 Duma election results. Eight parties surpassed the 5 percent barrier and shared in the apportionment of PR seats. As the table shows, each of these parties received a somewhat higher percentage of seats than votes (column four compared with column two), since parties 9–13 each received less than 5 percent and therefore no PR seats. Thus, almost 9 percent of voters (those who voted for parties 9–13) received no PR representation.

The strong performance by Zhirinovsky's LDPR, with almost 23 percent of the PR vote, surprised many analysts, who had expected Russia's Choice to perform better. But the LDPR's strong showing on the party vote was considerably negated by its relatively poor results in the single-member constituencies. As a result, Russia's Choice, with 30 of its candidates elected in single-member districts, emerged as the party with the largest number of seats. There was a broad spread of electoral strength, with no single party getting even 16 percent of the seats. In a Duma with this kind of composition, it was not to be expected that a single party would dominate parliamentary activity.

Parties 9–12 received no PR representation, but won several seats in single-member races. Party 13, Cedar, was completely shut out, winning neither single member nor PR seats. Thus, 12 parties were represented in the Duma.

The big winners on the single-member district side were independents. They garnered nearly two-thirds of the districts seats, which translated to almost one-third of total Duma membership. These results serve to confirm the view of those who argued that to build a party system, voting for parties through PR arrangements was necessary.

Table 6.1
Results of the Duma Election, December 1993

Party	PR Party List			District Voting	Total Seats	
	% votes	seats	% seats	seats	N	%
1. Russia's Choice	16.0	40	18.0	30	70	15.6
2. LDPR	22.9	59	26.2	5	64	14.2
3. CPRF	12.4	32	14.2	16	48	10.7
4. Agrarian	7.9	21	9.3	12	33	7.3
5. Yabloko	7.9	20	8.9	3	23	5.1
6. Women of Russia	8.1	21	9.3	2	23	5.1
7. PRES	6.8	18	8.0	1	19	4.0
8. Dem. Party of Russia	5.5	14	6.2	1	15	3.3
9–12. Four Parties below 5%		0		8	8	1.7
13. Cedar	.8	0		0	0	0.0
Independents				141	141	31.3
Total		225		220	445	

Source: Adapted from White, Rose and McAllister 1997, 123.
Notes:
Party abbreviations: CPRF=Communist Party of the Russian Federation; LDPR=Liberal Democratic Party of Russia.
Parties 9–13 received a combined total of 8.73 percent of the party vote. The remainder of the party vote, 7.5 percent, was made up of invalid ballots or ballots cast "against all" parties.

In the territorial districts, more than six candidates, on average, ran in each race. Given that the winner needed only a *plurality* (i.e., more votes than anyone else) to win, seats often went to candidates who got considerably below a majority of the votes. In one notable race in St. Petersburg, an anti-reform television personality took a seat with barely a quarter of the vote, when four quarreling reformist candidates stayed in the race and divided the remainder of the ballots. The downside of PR voting, for the democrats and centrists, was the performance of the Zhirinovsky-led Liberal Democrats. His extremist rhetoric and charisma carried his party to the top position in the party vote. But for those who insist on the need for PR in order to build parties, this is one of the costs that a fledgling electoral system may have to incur. As shown, Zhirinovsky's party colleagues, when running as individuals in the district voting, did relatively poorly.

A note is in order here on the relationship between election results and the lineup of parties and blocs in the Duma. When the Duma is organized for business, some shifting in party membership and party alliances takes place. Moreover, the parliamentary rule that requires groupings of at least 35 deputies to participate in directing legislative work means that parliamentary alliances are bound to be struck, and that many deputies elected as independents find it prudent to abandon their independent position and join parliamentary factions once the work of the Duma begins. Thus, as will be discussed in Chapter 7, the party lineup within the Duma is likely to manifest considerable differences from apparent party strength immediately after the election.

As mentioned above, the upper house was also popularly elected in December 1993. Each of Russia's 89 regions was entitled to send two members to the Federation Council, one from the region's executive branch and one from the legislature. These elections were run strictly by the plurality method, with a lower number of candidates contesting seats than in the Duma (2–3 per seat in the Federation Council, as opposed to 6+ in the Duma). The results showed very low party affiliation among the Federation Council members elected: about 84 percent identified themselves as independent (Lentini 1995, 84).

The 1995 Parliamentary Election

By prior arrangement, the parliament chosen in 1993 was to serve for only two years, because of the haste with which the election was organized and conducted. The Duma election of 1995 was for a full four-year term, as provided in the constitution. Prior to the election, an intense amount of activity took place aimed at making changes in the electoral system. Among the more important of many proposals put forward, the Yeltsin team sought to increase single-member district representation to 300 seats and reduce those selected by PR to 150. But this was opposed by many in the Duma, and never came close to being achieved. In the end, the electoral law adopted in 1995 made only a few cosmetic changes to the procedures used in 1993 (Belin and Orttung 1997, 22–30).

The aim of the PR part of the 1995 law was the same as that of 1993: to encourage smaller parties either to drop out or to cooperate with other parties by offering combined lists of candidates that would have a chance of clearing the 5 percent barrier. This, it was hoped, would eventually result in fewer parties and a more rational party system. But reaching these objectives failed in the extreme in 1995. In the end, 43 parties qualified for the ballot, producing party lists that contained a total of 5,675 candidates, three times the number of 1993. About 2,700 candidates ran for single-member district seats, nearly double the 1993 figure. On average, 12 candidates ran for each district, and in one constituency the number was 27 ("Ryabov Gives Overview of Elections" 1995).

Given these numbers, the results were to some extent predictable. They are summarized in Table 6.2. Only a few of the 43 parties on the ballot had a realistic chance of surpassing the 5 percent threshold, but the actual results exceeded the predictions of some of the most pessimistic analysts. Four parties, the Communist Party of the Russian Federation, the Liberal Democrats, Our Home is Russia (the party of prime minister Chernomyrdin) and Yabloko qualified to receive PR seats. Taken together, these parties received 50.5 percent of the vote, but gained 100 percent of the seats. Thus, virtually half of the electorate, those who voted for parties other than the top four, got no PR representation. *Proportional* representation was so named because it was designed to bring about a relatively close relationship between votes and seats. The Russian election of 1995 showed how PR could produce extreme distortions of proportionality when certain conditions prevailed.

Complaints that the PR results "violated the rights of millions" were expressed vehemently in some quarters (e.g., Latsis 1995, 1), but to little effect. Help was even sought from the Russian Supreme Court by a disgruntled voter who claimed that the system had deprived him of representation. But the court rebuffed his suit ("Supreme Court Affirms Legitimacy of Electoral Law" 1997). Most analysts correctly ascribed the problem to the irrationality (and perhaps selfishness) of certain politicians, who preferred pursuing their own narrow agendas (which in some cases included victory for themselves in single-member district contests), rather than seeking to create larger political movements(Belin and Orttung 1997, 10; White, Rose and McAllister 1997, 223; 227).

Table 6.2 Results of the Duma Election, December 1995						
	PR Party List			District Voting	Total Seats	
Party	% vote	seats	% seats	seats	N	%
1.CPRF	22.0	99	44.0	58	157	35.0
2.LDPR	11.2	50	22.2	1	51	11.3
3.Our Home is Russia	10.1	45	20.0	10	55	12.2
4.Yabloko	6.9	31	13.8	14	45	10.0
5–22.Other-A (see below)		0		64	64	14.2
23–43.Other-B (see below)		0		0	0	0.0
Independents		0		78	78	17.3
Total		225		225	450	

Source: Adapted from White, Rose and McAllister 1997, 224–25.
Notes:
Party Abbreviations: CPRF=Communist Party of the Russian Federation; LDPR=Liberal Democratic Party of Russia.
Parties 5–22, "Other-A": Eighteen parties that failed to reach the 5 percent threshold but managed to win single-member seats. The number of such seats ranged from 20 for the Agrarians to one each for ten different parties, and the total number of seats for all 18 was 64. These parties received a combined total of 36.6 percent of the party vote.
Parties 23–43, "Other-B": Twenty-one parties that contested the election but failed to win either PR seats or district seats. These parties received a combined total of 8.2 percent of the party vote.
The remainder of the party vote, 4.7 percent, was made up of invalid ballots and votes cast "against all" parties.

In the single-member district races, independents again won the most seats, although their total was just over half the number elected in 1993. The communists also did well, winning 58 seats, and thereby becoming the largest Duma party by far, with about 35 percent of the deputies. The spectacular failure on the single-member district side was the LDPR, with only one winning mandate. As in 1993, Zhirinovsky's charisma did not extend to his party colleagues in the district races.

The overall results, then, continued the unclear picture of the Duma's composition that characterized the body after the 1993 election. The CPRF was by far the strongest party, but even with the support of other deputies sympathetic with the communists, it did not come close to commanding a parliamentary majority. There would be no chance that the strongly anti-communist president, Boris Yeltsin, would entertain the idea of appointing a communist prime minister. But the election results meant that the communists would be entitled to a fair share of leadership positions in the Duma.

The method of choosing the Federation Council was changed by law in 1994. Under the constitution (Article 96) the Duma is to be "elected" by a procedure to be established by federal law. But the same article refers to the "procedure for forming" (*poriadok formirovaniia*) the Federation Council, and also commits this to federal law. As indicated above, the Federation Council was popularly elected in 1993, by the plurality method. After considerable controversy, a law was adopted in 1994 providing that the two representatives to the Federation Council from each region would be that region's governor and head of the legislature. This arrangement has also proved to be controversial. In 2000, newly elected President Vladimir Putin succeeded in getting parliament to adopt new legislation, effective in 2002, to prevent governors and legislative speakers from also serving on the Federation Council.

The 1999 Parliamentary Election

The rules for the 1999 election remained essentially the same as in the past. The most important change allowed parties and individual candidates to submit money deposits as an alternative to collecting signatures. The deposit would be returned if a specified percentage of the vote was received. This option was offered because of the allegedly widespread practice of buying or forging signatures.

The election, held on December 19, followed a particularly turbulent period in national politics. President Yeltsin, weakened by health problems and with his popularity at an all-time low, was given to increasingly erratic behavior. He fired five prime ministers or acting prime ministers (Viktor Chernomyrdin twice) within a period of 17 months. His last appointee, Vladimir Putin, was chosen only in August, barely four months before the election. A new political movement, Unity, was quickly organized to support Putin. As Table 6.3 shows, Unity achieved a stunning success,

Table 6.3
Results of the Duma Election, December 1999

Party	PR Party List			District Voting	Total Seats	
	% votes	seats	% seats	seats	N	%
1. CPRF	24.3	67	30.0	56	123	28.0
2. Unity	23.6	64	28.4	8	72	16.3
3. Fatherland-All Russia	13.3	37	16.4	30	67	15.2
4. Union of Rt. Forces	8.52	24	10.7	5	29	6.6
5. Zhirinovsky Bloc	5.98	17	7.5	1	18	4.1
6. Yabloko	5.93	16	7.1	4	20	4.5
7–14. Other-A (see below)		0		19	19	4.2
15–26. Other-B (see below)		0		0	0	0.0
Independents		0		93	93	21.1
Total		225		216	441	100.0
Continued on the next page						

> *Sources*: "Spisok..." 18; Corwin 2000a; Corwin 2000b.
> Notes:
> Party abbreviation: CPRF=Communist Party of the Russian Federation.
> The Liberal Democratic Party of Russia was removed from the ballot for registration violations. Vladimir Zhirinovsky re-registered his party for the election as the Zhirinovsky Bloc.
> Reelections were required in eight single-member constituencies. The election for the single-member seat representing Chechnya was held later.
> Parties 7–14, "Other-A": Eight parties that failed to reach the 5 percent threshold but managed to win single-member seats. The number of such seats ranged from nine for Our Home is Russia to one each for four parties. These parties received a combined total of 5.45 percent of the vote.
> Parties 15–26, "Other-B": Twelve parties that contested the election but failed to win either PR seats or single-member seats. These parties received a combined total of 8.07 percent of the vote.
> Ballots cast "against all" candidates: 3.3 percent.

finishing second only to the CPRF and ahead of a number of established parties.

The performance of the CPRF was decidedly mixed. It remained the largest party in the Duma, and by winning many more single-member district seats than any other party, showed that its regional organization remained relatively strong. On the other hand, it lost about 35 seats from its 1995 total, which dropped its percentage in the Duma from 35 to 28. Since a considerable proportion of its support typically comes from older voters, the prospects for the party to expand its share of the vote in the future do not appear bright.

Zhirinovsky's LDPR was denied a place on the ballot in October because of registration irregularities. Its list of candidates was hastily re-registered as the "Zhirinovsky Bloc," which was the name listed on the ballot. The party continued to fall in support, barely passing the 5 percent barrier and gaining only one SMD seat. Yabloko came even closer to elimination from the PR apportionment. Like the Liberal Democrats, its percentage of the vote dropped for the third election in a row. Of the six parties that surpassed the 5 percent threshold, three were not on the 1995 ballot (four if the Zhirinovsky Bloc is counted). When one also considers that a majority of the 20 other parties that contested the 1999 election was not among the 1995 parties (at least under the same name), it is clear that the Russian party system still has not achieved a high degree of stability.

On the other hand, several aspects of the 1999 election can be read in a somewhat more optimistic light. The number of parties contesting the election dropped by almost 40 percent in comparison with 1995. Six parties passed the 5 percent barrier, as compared with four in 1995. And their percentage of the total vote was much higher (81.7 percent as against 50.5 percent). Thus, the percentage of wasted votes, when voters' choices resulted in no representation, was considerably diminished. If this can truly be attributed to "tactical voting," as one commentator has suggested, meaning a conscious unwillingness by voters to support parties with little chance of gaining representation, then an important gain in Russian voter sophistication has been achieved (Belin 2000a, 7–8).

The 1996 Presidential Election

Russian presidential elections require the winner to receive at least 50 percent of the vote. If not achieved in the initial balloting, a second round involving the top two candidates determines the winner. Boris Yeltsin had won the Russian presidency in 1991, about six months before the USSR's demise. Gaining nearly 59 percent of the vote in a contest that included five other candidates, Yeltsin easily avoided the need for a runoff. At that time, however, Yeltsin was near the height of his popularity. Since virtually all of his opponents had close ties with the communist regime, his easy win was not unexpected. The only somewhat surprising aspect of the contest was the performance of one little-known outsider. Vladimir Zhirinovsky, whom a Yeltsin biographer described as "the leader of an obscure Liberal Democratic Party," won nearly six million votes and achieved third place in the race (Aron 2000, 432). This was the beginning of Zhirinovsky's impressive career in Russian politics.

The situation was quite different for Yeltsin by the time of the 1996 election. His five years in office had not gone well for the country as a whole and for large numbers of its citizens. Consequently, his level of popularity had dropped considerably. As the election approached, some opinion (as well as polling data) suggested that Yeltsin could be beaten, particularly by a communist candidate who ran an effective campaign

(Hough, Davidheiser, and Lehmann 1996, 80–90).

As the election process took shape, the chaotic and undisciplined nature of Russian politics again manifested itself. Seventy-eight contenders signed up to run for president. Only 17 collected the requisite number of signatures. Of these, 6 were rejected because of signature fraud, leaving 11 candidates. Among the contenders, in addition to Yeltsin, were some familiar names: Gennady Zyuganov, the communist leader; Vladimir Zhirinovsky, the head of the Liberal Democratic Party; and Grigorii Yavlinsky, the founder of Yabloko. Also running were: Alexander Lebed, a well-known former general and Afghanistan war hero; a second communist candidate (who withdrew in favor of Zyuganov on the eve of the vote); a former champion weightlifter; a famous eye surgeon; and even former Soviet president Mikhail Gorbachev. In the end, however, only a few of the candidates had an impact on the election. Six of them got less than one percent of the vote (Gorbachev received one-half of one percent), and Yavlinsky and Zhirinovsky got well under 10 percent. The three leaders were Yeltsin with 35.5 percent, Zyuganov with 32 percent, and Lebed, with 14.5 percent. So the runoff would be between Yeltsin and Zyuganov, but Lebed would remain a factor.

In the 17-day period between the first and second round, Yeltsin made several important moves. He fired his unpopular minister of defense and a number of other hard-line advisors, including the chief of presidential security and the head of the successor organization to the KGB. But most importantly, he appointed Lebed as his national security advisor and secretary of the presidential Security Council. Although Lebed did not formally endorse Yeltsin, his appointment undoubtedly inclined a number of Lebed supporters to vote for the president.

In the end, Yeltsin's victory was an overwhelming one. The president received almost 54 percent of the vote to 40 percent for Zyuganov (the remainder consisted of "against all" votes and invalid ballots). The margin of victory was more than ten million votes. How was Yeltsin able to achieve success, when his prospects looked so dim some months before? In addition to the Lebed appointment and the impact of other endorsements between the two rounds of voting, the president and his advisors were able to divert the campaign from the negative aspects of Yeltsin's stewardship (the drop in the standard of living, crime and corruption, the war in Chechnya) by focusing attention on the evils of communism and presenting the president's team as the only alternative. When the contest was seen in these terms, a majority opted against communism (White, Rose and McAllister 1997, 248–49). American political scientist Michael McFaul saw the 1996 presidential election as "the last 'referendum' on communism" (McFaul 1997, xi).

It is also true that Yeltsin enjoyed the benefits of incumbency, including the ability to exert strong influence on the media. Particularly notable was the lopsided coverage that the Yeltsin campaign received on television (White, Rose and McAllister 1997, 251). As has been the case in all Russian elections so far, a number of charges of electoral fraud were made after the election. The Commission on Security and Cooperation in Europe judged the 1996 presidential election itself to have been "generally free and fair." But it also concluded that the *campaign* prior to the election, based largely on the incumbent's advantages just mentioned, was "clearly unfair" (Commission on Security and Cooperation in Europe 1996, 13; 16).

The 2000 Presidential Election

President Yeltsin did no campaigning between the two rounds of the 1996 presidential campaign. Not long after the election, the rumors about the perilous condition of his health were confirmed when it was announced that he would undergo heart bypass surgery. From that time on, although he was to serve more than three additional years, Yeltsin's grasp on the presidency seemed increasingly tenuous. During the economic meltdown of August 1998, when Russia defaulted on its domestic debt and underwent a currency devaluation, a fumbling Yeltsin, "whose intuition was extirpated by illness," according to the author of a major biography of the president, could find no way to cope with the crisis (Aron 2000, 684). Beset thereafter by further health problems, which led to several hospitalizations, Yeltsin finally resigned the presidency on the last day of 1999, turning over the reins to his prime minister of less than five months, Vladimir Putin. One of Putin's first moves as acting president was to issue an edict providing the former president with a generous pension, government housing, medical insurance and a number of other benefits. Perhaps most important, it guaranteed Yeltsin wide-ranging immunity from criminal liability and guaranteed the inviolability of the former president, his premises and his effects ("O garantiiakh Prezidentu..." 2000, 3).

Under the constitution (Article 92), the prime minister becomes acting president and the election of a new president must take place within three months. The constitution had reduced the presidential term of office from five to four years. Yeltsin served about three and one-half years of his second term. The election to replace him was set for March 26, 2000, about three months earlier than would have been the case if Yeltsin had finished his term.

With Yeltsin's surprise announcement, aspirants for the presidency hastened to complete registration requirements. As in 1996, 11 candidates ended up on the ballot, several of them well-known politicians. In addition to Putin, four who had contested the presidency in 1996 ran again: Zyuganov, Yavlinsky, Zhirinovsky and Aman Tuleev. The latter, a communist and governor of the Keremovo oblast, dropped out of the 1996 race at the last minute in favor of Zyuganov, but still received a small number of votes. In 2000 he stayed in the race. The other six candidates were given little chance of collecting many votes, but several of them were seen as having the potential to affect the prospects of leading contenders. Most prominent in this category was Yuri Skuratov, who had been fired as procurator-general by Yeltsin, and now threatened to speak about high-level corruption. In the event, however, these candidates had little effect on the race, collectively gaining barely 6 percent of the vote. The next three candidates—Yavlinsky, Zhirinovsky and Tuleev—also fared poorly, and had no impact on the outcome.

The presidential election of 2000 was basically a two-person race, with Putin winning on the first ballot with almost 53 percent of the vote. Zyuganov, who had been expected to do poorly, ran a strong second with 29 percent. Yavlinsky's 5.8 percent was considerably below his 1996 showing, and Zhirinovsky, with 2.7 percent, continued the slide to his lowest level in three presidential races. Putin's margin of victory was narrower than expected, leading to the conclusion that the new president did not come away from the election with a solid mandate (Goble 2000). But winning on the first ballot against ten other candidates is a considerable achievement. If not a mandate, it certainly put Putin in a strong position.

Election Fraud

As in 1996, the 2000 election was followed by charges of significant election fraud. Without the irregularities, some alleged, Putin might not have won on the first ballot (Belin 2000b, 3–5). In addition, biased coverage of Putin by state-dominated television and much of the other media certainly gave him an unfair advantage over other candidates (Belin 2000a, 11–15).

About six months after the election an English-language Moscow newspaper, *The Moscow Times*, published the results of an extensive investigation of the 2000 election. It alleged massive abuse of the electoral process ("Special Report/Election Fraud" 2000). The investigation was reported by a number of Western publications, but was mostly ignored in Russia. On the other side of the picture, the Organization for Security and Cooperation in Europe, which had observers at election sites, gave a positive evaluation of the election, although acknowledging some abuses (Borisova 2000, 1; Blasier 2000, 24).

It is fair to say that no election in post-Soviet Russia has avoided at least some allegations of fraud. Further, the feeling that the authorities have done little to curb abuses seems to be quite widespread. The precept often expressed by lawyers—that it is important to establish not only fairness, but also the appearance of fairness—seems applicable to the Russian election. Until the authorities can introduce changes that will put the allegations of campaign and voting irregularities to rest, the sense of legitimacy that is so crucial to the development of democracy will remain elusive.

Conclusion

If free elections are not the sole defining characteristic of a democracy, then it is certainly true that democracy cannot exist without them. They have been a central feature of politics in the West since at least the beginning of the twentieth century. Except for a limited period of time before the onset of Bolshevik rule, Russia's experience with competitive elections began only in the last years of the twentieth century, making it very much of a latecomer on the road to democracy (White, Rose and McAllister 1997, xi). Like several other European countries (Germany, Austria, the nations of Eastern Europe), Russia experienced a period of one-party rule during the twentieth century that eliminated its competitive party system. But unlike those other countries, Russia's authoritarian phase lasted so long that no links to the earlier party system survived. In building political organizations, Russia had to start from scratch.

In the ten years or so since the Soviet system collapsed, Russia's party system has manifested several notable characteristics:

- A multitude of parties, including many that fade quickly from the political scene, only to be replaced by other short-lived organizations;
- A number of "personality-based" parties, built around one or a few dominant individuals, who are often reluctant to cooperate with other politicians and political organizations (Belin and Orttung 1997, 160). Many such parties are rightly viewed as "irrational actors," in the words of Stephen White and his associates, since, by eschewing cooperation, they minimize their chances of surpassing the 5 percent hurdle and sharing in the allocation of PR seats (White, Rose and McAllister 1997, 198–200);
- Numerous parties that fail to develop an ideology or clear programmatic goals, thus depriving voters of the opportunity to make informed choices;
- The disinclination of many parties to make alliances in Parliament for the purpose of commanding a majority. Similarly, there is seldom much effort to establish a unified opposition, which could offer an alternative vision as to how the country should be run.

These are all characteristics of a party system in the early stages of development. Russian politicians need first to understand the benefits of cooperation, and then to practice the art of coalition-building, efforts that will undoubtedly take time. A part of the problem for Russian parties, however, also has to do with the limited function of parties in presidential elections and with the unusual nature of presidential-parliamentary relations. Neither President Yeltsin nor President Putin created a party to represent their positions in Parliament or before the public, though both have accepted the support of particular parties (Rose 2000, 53). Nor have parties been a force in presidential elections. With a few exceptions, candidates have run essentially as independents (Petrov 2000, 4–5).

Presidential-parliamentary relations are complicated both by Russia's inexperience in parliamentary government and by constitutional provisions. In the typical parliamentary system of Western Europe, the prime minister chosen by the head of state is the leader of the majority party in Parliament or the leader of the coalition that commands the majority. As indicated, however, Russian parties have not worked to create majority coalitions. Structurally, of course, Russia's constitutional system is not the pure parliamentary type, but a hybrid system based on the French model. France, like Russia, has a popularly elected president with significant constitutional powers. If the lower house of the French parliament is controlled by a party or coalition that supports the president, the president is free to choose the prime minister and to oversee the operation of the whole executive branch. But if the French lower house is controlled by a party or coalition that does not support the president, then the president is bound to appoint as prime minister the leader of that opposition group. Under these conditions, known as *cohabitation* in France, the power and authority of the president are considerably diminished, particularly in the sphere of domestic politics (Safran 1998, 185–90).

In post-communist Russia the concept of a majority coalition in support of the president has been slow to develop. But neither has a majority coalition been created in opposition to the president. Thus, the president has had a free hand in naming the prime minister. Under the constitution, the Duma must approve the president's choice, and there has been some struggle on occasion over presidential nominees. But no group of parties has coalesced to demand that its leader be named prime minister.

Thus, the French have developed an integration of presidential-parliamentary relations, based in part on organized party and coalition efforts. The Russians have designed the structure of presidential-parliamentary relations on the French model, but without a mature party system to facilitate the integration of the two institutions, they operate as independent entities with no established way to mediate their controversies.

Both President Putin and a number of leading legislators appear to be aware of the problems associated with parties in Russia. A government-sponsored law aimed at reducing the number of political parties was introduced in 2001. Its provisions so favored the established larger parties, however, that many saw it as basically undemocratic. An alternative scheme that appeared to be developing in mid-2001 involved the creation of a voting bloc of several centrist parties in the Duma that would support the president's program. Whether this arrangement will lead to a formal coalition, or perhaps even to the creation of a single ruling party, is unclear. Having fewer parties is certainly desirable in Russia's chaotic party system. But the means of reaching this end are important, too. What is most necessary is for Russian parties to develop to the point where they can assume what should be their principal roles: attracting sufficient support, as single parties or in cooperation with other groups, in order to take lawful control of government operations; and developing credible policies in opposition to make them potential governing parties.

References

Aron, Leon. 2000. *Yeltsin: A Revolutionary Life*. New York: St. Martin's Press.

Belin, Laura. 2000a. "RFE/RL Election Report," http://www.rferl.org. No. 8, January 7.

Belin, Laura. 2000b. "RFE/RL Election Report," http://www.rferl.org. No. 1 (9), March 3.

Belin, Laura. 2000c. "RFE/RL Election Report," http://www.rferl.org. No. 5 (13), April 7.

Belin, Laura and Robert W. Orttung. 1997. *The Russian Parliamentary Elections of 1995*. Armonk, NY: M. E. Sharpe.

Blasier, Cole. 2000. "Electing Putin Po-Tatarskii." *NewsNet: The Newsletter of the AAASS* 40:4, 24–5.

Borisova, Yevgenia. 2000. "OSCE Stands by Putin's Win." *The Moscow Times*, September 23.

Colton, Timothy J. 2000. *Transitional Citizens: Voters and What Influences Them in the New Russia*. Cambridge, MA: Harvard University Press.

Commission on Security and Cooperation in Europe. 1996. *Report on Russia's Presidential Election*. Washington, DC: Commission on Security and Cooperation in Europe.

Connor, Walter D. 1975. "Generations and Politics in the USSR." *Problems of Communism* 24:5, 20–31.

Corwin, Julie A. 2000a."Who's Who: Duma Deputies in Single-Mandate Districts." *Russian Federation Report* 2:1, January 5.

Corwin, Julie A. 2000b. "Who's Who in Russia's New State Duma." *RFE/RL Newsline* 4:4, Part I, January 6.

Goble, Paul. 2000. "End Note: A Victory Not a Mandate." *RFE/RL Newsline* 4:61, Part I, March 27.

Hough, Jerry F., Evelyn Davidheiser, and Susan Goodrich Lehmann. 1996. *The 1996 Russian Presidential Election*. Washington, DC: Brookings Institution Press.

Latsis, Otto. 1995. "Itogi vyborov podtverdili: narusheny prava millionov izbiratelei." *Izvestiia*, December 23.

Lentini, Peter. 1995. "Overview of the Campaign." In *Elections and the Political Order in Russia*, ed. Peter Lentini. Budapest: Central European University Press.

Makarenko, Boris. 1999. "Fatherland-All Russia (OVR)." In *Primer on Russia's 1999 Duma Elections*, eds. Michael McFaul, Nikolai Petrov, and Andrei Ryabov, with Elizabeth Reisch. Washington, DC: Carnegie Endowment for International Peace.

McFaul, Michael. 1997. *Russia's 1996 Presidential Election: The End of Polarized Politics*. Stanford, CA: Hoover Institution Press.

"O garantiiakh Prezidentu Rossiiskoi Federatsii, prekrativshemu ispolnenie svoikh polnomochii i chlenam ego sem'i." 2000. Edict of the President of the Russian Federation. *Rossiiskaia gazeta*, January 5.

Oleshchuk, V. A. and V. B. Pavlenko. 1997. *Politicheskaia Rossiia: Partii, Bloki, Lidery*. Moscow: Ves' Mir.

Petro, Nicolai N. 1991. "Perestroika from Below: Voluntary Sociopolitical Associations in the RSFSR." In *Perestroika at the Crossroads*, eds. Alfred J. Rieber and Alvin Z. Rubinstein. Armonk, NY: M. E. Sharpe.

Petrov, Nikolai. 2000. "The Year 2000 Presidential Elections: The End of Public Politics?" *Briefing Papers* (Carnegie Moscow Center) 2:3 (March).

Remington, Thomas F. 1999. *Politics in Russia*. New York: Addison Wesley.

Rose, Richard. 2000. "A Supply-Side View of Russia's Elections." *East European Constitutional Review* 9:1-2, 53-59.

Rudenshiold, Eric and N. Catherine Barnes. 1994. "Political Party Development in Russia: Integration and Disintegration." In *Russia's Future: Consolidation or Disintegration?*, ed. Douglas W. Blum. Boulder, CO: Westview Press.

"Ryabov Gives Overview of Elections." 1995. *OMRI Daily Digest* 1:231, November 29.

Safran, William. 1998. *The French Polity*. Fifth Edition. New York: Addison Wesley.

Sedov, Leonid. 1998. "Consistency and Change among Russian Voters." In *Elections and Voters in Post-communist Russia*, eds. Matthew

Wyman, Stephen White, and Sarah Oates. Cheltenham, UK: Edward Elgar.

"Skol'ko v Rossii partii?" 1999. *Rossiiskaia gazeta,* January 16.

"Special Report/Election Fraud." 2000. *The Moscow Times,* September 12.

"Spisok Izbrannykh Deputatov Gosudarstvennoi Dumy Federal'nogo Sobraniia Rossiiskoi Federatsii Tret'ego Sozyva." 1999. *Rossiiskaia Gazeta*, December 9.

"Supreme Court Affirms Legitimacy of Electoral Law." 1997. *RFE/RL Newsline* 1: 14 (Part I), April 18.

White, Stephen, Richard Rose, and Ian McAllister. 1997. *How Russia Votes*. Chatham, NJ: Chatham House.

Chapter 7
Operation of the Major Political Institutions

In Chapter 5 the constitutional bases of the principal political institutions—the executive, parliament and the judiciary—were outlined. In this chapter the operation of these structures will be discussed. The last section of the chapter deals with President Putin's efforts to reassert central control over the regions.

The Executive

In structural terms, the Russian executive follows the French model: both have a dual executive composed of a popularly elected president and an appointed prime minister. Differences between the two polities, however, in political tradition, political culture and the nature of their party systems, have led to divergent patterns of executive operation in the two countries.

As in France, the Russian presidency and government possess distinct administrative structures. But unlike France, where the president maintains a relatively small staff of advisors, the Russian presidency has grown into a truly enormous bureaucracy. This includes a large number of personal aides and political advisors, an administrative structure called the chancellery, and a presidential press service. In addition, the so-called Administration of Affairs operates within the presidency, handling a wide variety of business activities on behalf of the Kremlin (Jensen 1998, 1–2; Huskey 1999, 50–70). The Administration of Affairs runs a number of factories, maintains a network of country homes and hotels, and is responsible for the use and upkeep of thousands of motor vehicles. Not only do these activities produce significant revenues for the presidency, but they also provide its incumbent with important political leverage through the judicious distribution of the scarce goods and resources at its disposal.

Among the departments within the president's large advisory administration, clear lines of authority have not been well established. The result has often been overlapping jurisdiction, duplication of effort and interdepartmental controversy. As president, Yeltsin had little interest in the routine aspects of administration and was thus disinclined to work toward reform. In apparent response to Parliament's attack on the size of the presidential staff, he carried out limited downsizing on a couple of occasions. But many of those let go found positions in other parts of the executive apparatus. Eugene Huskey has likened this practice to the old *nomenklatura* system under communism, when incompetent officials often were quietly shifted to other positions rather than being fired (Huskey 1999, 92). In its size and the extensiveness of its reach, the presidential bureaucracy has been compared to the Communist Party apparatus during the Soviet period. This arrangement seemed to suit Yeltsin, a long-time Soviet *apparatchik*. Vladimir Putin, soon after his election as president in March 2000, asserted that Russia's bureaucratic structure was "choking" the country, and called for a considerable downsizing. But an even higher priority of Putin's is to strengthen the Russian state. Whether these two aims are compatible remains to be seen.

Partly separate from the presidency is the apparatus of the government. As explained in Chapter 5, the government consists of the chairman of the government (prime minister), deputy chairmen and ministers. Typically this group numbers about 30 individuals. The president appoints the prime minister, subject to the approval of the Duma. The prime minister then proposes candidates for deputy chairmen and ministers to the president, who makes the actual appointments.

Not only do the prime minister and his deputies have staffs of considerable size, but each of the ministers heads ministries, bureaucratic organizations of thousands and in some cases tens of thousands of employees. These include agencies that exist as ministries in most countries in the world (e.g., defense, foreign affairs, justice, education) as well as some that are less common and reflect particular issues or problems that Russia presently faces (e.g., the Ministry for Antimonopoly Policy and the Support of Entrepreneurship; the Ministry for Federation Affairs, Nationalities Policy and Migration Policy). In addition to the ministries, a large number of other "federal executive organs" exist. The prime minister is responsible (under Article 112 of the constitution) for proposing the composition of this set of organs to the president, who creates the corpus of federal executive bodies by decree. These agencies go by a number of designations, including "state committees," "federal services" and "Russian agencies." They typically number about 30. Thus, the executive branch, comprised of the presidency, the government, and other federal executive organs, is a large and complex body.

It was mentioned above that the government was "partly separate" from the presidency. There are several reasons for putting it this way. The president is responsible for appointing all members of the government (as well as the heads of other executive branch agencies) and has the power to remove them, including the prime minister. He has the right (under Article 83 of the constitution) to chair meetings of the government, although this function is normally left to the prime minister. Perhaps most important, a number of executive agencies, including several ministries, report directly to the president rather than the prime minister. After Vladimir Putin assumed the presidency in the spring of 2000, five ministries (including the so-called power ministries, defense, foreign affairs, and interior) and a number of other bodies were placed under his jurisdiction. Perhaps most important of these other agencies, which totaled ten, were the main security organs. After the August 1991 coup, the Committee for State Security (KGB) went through a number of reforms and name changes (Albats 1994, vii, 306–8). Its foreign intelligence and internal security functions were eventually separated. By the late 1990s these activities were performed by the Foreign Intelligence Service (SRV) and the Federal Security Service (FSB), respectively. Both of these organizations are under the direct control of the president ("O strukture federal'nykh organov ispolnitel'noi vlasti" 2000, 2).

Another important organization under the presidency is the Security Council. In addition to a full-time secretary who exercises considerable power, this body is comprised of the prime minister, the power ministers, the heads of the principal security organs, and other selected officials. It serves as an advisor to the president on security matters, both domestic and foreign.

A division of labor of sorts between the president and prime minister has gradually evolved, with the prime minister concentrating on economic management and the domestic social sphere and the president overseeing foreign and security policy, as well as relations with the country's regions.

But just as there is overlap and duplication withing the presidential apparatus, relations between the presidential and government bureaucracies are characterized by a high degree of what Huskey calls "institutional redundancy" (Huskey 1999, 41). So far, efforts to streamline the executive branch bureaucracy have largely failed. The presidential apparatus seeks to serve as the functional equivalent of the old Communist Party bureaucracy, managing and controlling the centrifugal pull of the country's diverse forces. Under Yeltsin, at least, this required a large network of officials with far-reaching authority.

President and Prime Minister: The Yeltsin Era
Boris Yeltsin dominated the Russian executive branch for nearly a decade, 1991–1999. A product of the Soviet one-party system, Yeltsin embraced the rhetoric of democratic government, but his style in exercising his duties tended toward the autocratic. Given at times to erratic and unpredictable behavior, his years in power saw him frequently at odds with Parliament. Nor were his relations particularly stable with his own government. High turnover among top aides, including prime ministers, characterized his period of rule, particularly the latter years. Stories about his behavior while under the influence of alcohol were legion (see, e.g., White 2000, 100–101). And his health problems, especially during his second term, certainly affected his capacity to run the country. Nevertheless, Yeltsin *was* Russia's president for virtually all of the 1990s, and during this period enormous changes took place in the country. For good or ill, the legacy of the Yeltsin era will long remain with Russia.

Yeltsin easily won election as the Russian Federation's first president in June 1991. As the hero of the resistance to the anti-Gorbachev putsch two months later, he reached the height of his popularity. By the end of the year he had led the effort, engineered with the leaders of Ukraine and Belarus, to bring down the USSR. Even before the fall of the Soviet Union, however, Yeltsin had set about to effect a radical change in Russia. He persuaded the legislature to allow him to rule by decree for a year in order to implement his reforms. Because of the grave condition of the economy, Yeltsin chose first to concentrate on economic reform rather than attempting to deepen political democratization, through new elections and adopting a new constitution. He selected as his chief strategist Yegor Gaidar, a young liberal economist from a prominent Soviet family. Although Gaidar was given the title of deputy prime minister (Yeltsin formally took the prime ministership), he was, for all intents and purposes, the head of government. With little in the way of specific ideas or an integrated reform program (Shevtsova 1999, 25), the Gaidar team moved quickly. Prices on most good were freed from the controls that had long prevailed, and a program to privatize the economy was initiated. From the outset, the results were unencouraging. Prices rose far faster than Gaidar had predicted, while the value of the ruble against Western currencies plummeted. Although goods became more available in the stores, the purchasing power of most families was badly eroded. This not only caused resentment among the populace, but it also contributed to the rise in opposition to Yeltsin from a variety of forces.

It quickly became clear that the president had made a grave mistake in choosing Alexander Rutskoi as his vice-presidential running mate. Rutskoi had been a combat pilot, a general and a veteran of the war in Afghanistan. This background undoubtedly appealed to an important portion of the electorate. But he was also a conservative with little use for radical economic change. He openly opposed the reform policies, referring derisively to Gaidar and his associates as "boys in pink shorts" (Remnick 1997, 47). When frozen out of decision-making activities, Rutskoi's obstructiveness increased. He gradually came to be seen (and to see himself) as a person around whom an anti-Yeltsin opposition could rally.

Another growing focus of hostility toward Yeltsin was Parliament, led by speaker and former Yeltsin ally Ruslan Khasbulatov. Although not a particularly popular politician, Khasbulatov skillfully used the power of his office to win adherents to his side. As early as March 1992 he demanded the removal of Gaidar and his chief lieutenants. Yeltsin for a time resisted the pressure, but he soon took measures to modify the reform. When, in December, parliament adopted constitutional amendments increasing the legislature's control over the executive branch, Yeltsin yielded and abandoned his support for Gaidar. Yeltsin then backed Victor Chernomyrdin, who had little difficulty winning parliamentary approval as the new prime minister.

Chernomyrdin was a solid member of the *nomenklatura*, having served both in the Communist Party apparatus and as minister of the gas industry during the Soviet period. Before joining Yeltsin's government he had been head of Gazprom, the state gas production industry. With considerably better conservative credentials than Gaidar, Chernomyrdin was seen by the opposition in Parliament as a potential ally. In fact, he turned out to be a pragmatic politician who worked effectively with both Yeltsin and his opponents. Although the pace of economic reform slackened during his years in power, his centrist approach permitted both relative stability and the gradual continuation of market reforms. Moreover, as a somewhat plodding figure lacking in charisma, Chernomyrdin posed little threat of overshadowing Yeltsin. His tenure as prime minister lasted over five years, and in this sense has to be considered the most stable period of Yeltsin's presidency.

Chernomyrdin and his whole cabinet were abruptly discharged in March 1998. The reasons offered for the dismissal differed, depending on the source. Yeltsin himself said the move was made "to make reforms more energetic and effective" (Aron 2000, 679). Others saw it as an effort to appease Parliament, many of whose deputies felt that the cabinet contained too many liberals. But much evidence suggests that Chernomyrdin was getting too strong, taking more initiative than Yeltsin, whose health continued to deteriorate, was comfortable with. As biographer Lilia Shevtsova put it, Yeltsin "tolerated neither rivals nor overly strong collaborators." Chernomyrdin's dismissal represented Yeltsin's decision "to assert himself and to affirm his exclusive right to power" (Shevtsova 1999, 239, 240).

Under Chernomyrdin, few signs of substantial improvements in Russian economic performance were to be seen. But a number of changes in the country's economic landscape were evident. The ambitious privatization program that had been launched under Gaidar was essentially completed under Chernomyrdin. This included the notorious loan-for-shares privatization of 1995–1996, which many saw essentially as a vast giveaway of valuable state assets. Allegations of corruption by government officials, including Chernomyrdin, also soared during this period. Incidentally, the person who had managed the whole course of privatization, Anatoly Chubais, was fired as first deputy prime minister at the same time that Chernomyrdin was dismissed. If there was anyone more intensely disliked than Yeltsin by the parliamentary opposition, it was Chubais. Sacking him and other unpopular politicians was designed to smooth the way for Chernomyrdin's successor, Sergei Kirienko.

The nomination of 35-year-old Kirienko was a considerable surprise. Almost unknown in Moscow, the former *komsomol* official had been fuel and energy minister under Chernomyrdin for five months. He had no political base, thus offering no threat to Yeltsin. This also meant, however, that he was fully dependent on Yeltsin's support and had no independent resources to deal with adversaries.

Kirienko's first battle was over confirmation. Voting by a show of hands, the Duma rejected him twice, thus setting up a direct constitutional confrontation. Under Article 111 of the constitution, if the president's nomination is rejected a third time, the Duma is dissolved and new elections are called. On this occasion the Duma yielded, and the president had his way. On the third vote, using a secret ballot, Kirienko was confirmed easily.

The new prime minister's more serious challenge was running the country, particularly with the economy still in a parlous state. He had taken the reins at a particularly inauspicious time. World oil prices were dropping, cutting Russia's hard currency income and increasing the budget deficit. The country's continued deficiencies in collecting taxes and other economic problems produced a crisis in mid-1998 that led, in August, to Russia's defaulting on its debt and devaluing its currency. Kirienko was not alone responsible for these failings, but he was their principal victim. Yeltsin fired him in late August, five months after his appointment, and attempted to bring back Chernomyrdin as prime minister. This time, however, the Duma would not cooperate, as most major factions expressed their disapproval of the former premier in advance. When Chernomyrdin was soundly defeated on the first two ballots, it was Yeltsin's turn to back down. He nominated Yevgeny Primakov as prime minister, and his choice was quickly confirmed.

Primakov was a vastly different person from his predecessor. More than 30 years older than Kirienko, Primakov had had an impressive and varied career during the Soviet period as journalist, academic, legislator, presidential emissary and (it was widely alleged) KGB employee. On the eve of the USSR's collapse he became the head of Russia's Foreign Intelligence Service, one of the successor agencies to the KGB when its functions were divided after the August 1991 coup. He later served as Russia's foreign minister. Primakov had good relations with many in the Duma and brought a number of communists into the government. It was suggested at the time that by his conciliatory stance toward the Duma, Primakov had made his government responsible to parliament, giving rise to a Russian version of the French cohabitation (Aron 2000, 684, 717). Certainly Yeltsin did not want to appoint Primakov prime minister. And his grip on the presidency was weakened during this period, both by his failing health and by his continuing drop in popularity. But Yeltsin was not yet ready to yield to Parliament. Under Primakov the economy showed signs of stabilizing somewhat. But relations between Yeltsin and the prime minister, which were never easy, became further strained as Primakov was increasingly mentioned as a possible successor to Yeltsin. In April 1999 Yeltsin went so far as to criticize the prime minister publicly, saying that "today Primakov is useful, tomorrow we'll see" ("Primakov Defends Government Against Yeltsin Criticism" 1999). A month later Primakov was fired.

Several days after Primakov's dismissal, the Duma brought to a vote five articles of impeachment against President Yeltsin. The two most important of these charged him with unconstitutionally dispersing Parliament in 1993 and conducting an illegal war in Chechnya. All five charges were supported by a majority of the vote, but none reached the required two-thirds. The president had won another battle against Parliament, although this time only barely.

Yeltsin's next nomination for prime minister was Sergei Stepashin, long a Yeltsin loyalist. He was confirmed by the Duma within a week. Stepashin also had an impressive resumé. A longtime official of the interior ministry, he served as counter-espionage chief, minister of justice, and minister of interior prior to becoming prime minister. But Stepashin hardly had a chance to get used to his new position. In less than three months he was dismissed. The principal reason, apparently, was that he had failed to consolidate pro-Yeltsin forces in preparation for the December 1999 parliamentary elections (Dikun 1999, 4).

To replace Stepashin the president named Vladimir Putin. In announcing his choice Yeltsin made it clear that he wanted Putin to succeed him as president. Occupying the position of prime minister, Yeltsin suggested, would allow voters to know him prior to the presidential election in 2000. If successful, it would also give him a considerable advantage over other candidates.

Putin's career prior to becoming prime minister raised questions among many commentators as to his democratic credentials. Immediately after graduation from the law faculty of Leningrad University, he joined the KGB, where he worked for about 16 years. His most notable assignment was to East Germany, for a period of several years in the 1980s. He returned to Leningrad, soon to be renamed St. Petersburg, in 1990. After working briefly at his old university, he joined the staff of the reform democratic mayor Anatoly Sobchak, quickly rising to the position of deputy mayor. Sobchak called him "my most reliable, responsible and hard-working assistant" (Wines 2000, 1). When Sobchak lost his race for reelection in 1996, Putin moved to Moscow to work in the Kremlin, where he also made a strikingly swift rise. Yeltsin named him head of the FSB, the recently strengthened successor to the KGB, in 1998. The following year he became secretary of the Security Council, an important advisory body to the president. Putin held these two positions when he was nominated for prime minister in August 1999 at the age of 46.

Putin was quickly able to consolidate his position. After being confirmed on the first ballot, he set about to carry out his pledge to strengthen the Russian state, both internally and as an international actor. In response to military incursions by Chechen rebels in the neighboring Russian territory of Dagestan, and to terrorist attacks in Moscow and elsewhere, for which Chechens were widely believed responsible, Putin ordered large military operations against the Chechen military, commencing, in effect, another war with Chechnya. The 1994–1996 war had become highly unpopular with the Russian public. Somewhat surprisingly, this time the populace largely backed the military operation. Humiliated by the previous debacle in Chechnya, most Russians saw the present military action as a completely justified response to terrorism. Support for Putin in the polls rose quickly, and he soon became the favorite in the coming presidential election. As discussed in the previous chapter, Yeltsin's surprise announcement of his retirement at the end of 1999, a half-year before the end of his term, pushed forward the election by several months. In March 2000 Putin won on the first ballot to become Russia's second president.

President and Prime Minister: The Putin Era
Putin moved ahead quickly on a reform agenda. The main objective of his program was to strengthen the authority of the Russian state, both to allow the government to deal more effectively with domestic problems in general and to counter divisive activities in some of the regions. To pursue these goals involved changes in policy that were not universally popular. Regional leaders objected to restrictions on their authority; democrats and others feared a weakening of media freedoms and personal rights; and there seemed to be a more general concern that Putin's "KGB persona" might prevail, allowing a brand of authoritarianism to replace the relative political pluralism that had existed in recent years. Putin also made it clear that he hope to restore Russia's prestige as a world leader, and to pursue a more assertive foreign policy. To run his first government Putin named Mikhail Kasyanov, a 42-year-old economist who was serving as first deputy prime minister and minister of finance at the time of his appointment. Kasyanov won resounding approval from a much less assertive Duma, which, for the moment at least, was providing broad-based support for Putin.

Parliament

Each house of Parliament organizes its own proceedings, based on the adoption of standing orders (*reglament* in Russian). Both chambers choose a chairman, who acts as presiding officer, as well as deputy chairmen. In order to carry out its work each establishes a structure of standing committees as well as other bodies (commissions, working groups), the latter to handle special problems or matters relating to internal parliamentary operations. Standing committees are organized by subject matter (e.g., budget and other economic matters, defense, international affairs, etc.). As is the case with parliamentary standing committees in other countries, they hold hearings and consider legislative proposals in their functional areas. Federation Council members and Duma deputies are limited to membership on one standing committee.

Another part of the Duma structure is the Duma Council. Made up of the chamber's chairman and the heads of the party fractions in the Duma, it is responsible for the organization of Duma business. The makeup of the Duma Council points to one of the important differences between the two houses. The Duma, the more powerful body, is organized on the basis of party affiliation. Although many members of the Federation Council belong to political parties, the upper house is not organized on a party basis. As representatives of the regions, Federation Council members are expected to reflect regional rather than party interests (*Parlamentskoe Pravo Rossii* 1999, 55).

As shown in Chapter 6, the Duma seats assigned by the proportional representation portion of the ballot are party seats. But the winners of some portion of the other half of the seats, those decided by district voting, may not be initially identified with a particular party. In past elections between one-third and two-thirds of districts seats have been won by independents. The rules of Duma operation work to the disadvantage of independent legislators. As a result, many independents, as well as members of parties with small representations in the Duma, join larger party groups. Thus, the political composition of the Duma in operation is quite different from the apparent lineup of party forces as the result of an election.

To participate in the organization of Duma business, as well as in the distribution of privileges, such as office space and choice legislative assignments, party groups need a minimum of 35 members. This leads to considerable maneuvering among Duma members. A large party such as the communists may "loan" members to a group sympathetic with it in order to allow the group to reach the level of 35 members. Moreover, wholly new party fractions, which didn't even contest the election, often appear when the Duma is organized and prepared to commence business. The creation of such "convenience parties" leads to what Richard Rose has termed a "floating party system," an aggregation of party groups quite different from the set of parties that contested the election (Rose 2000,

55–56). So far, such Duma-only parties have contributed little to the stability of the party system, since they have not become sufficiently institutionalized to contest future elections. They exist only for the convenience of the Duma politicians who have created them.

Besides the weakness of party organization, another factor that diminishes the effectiveness of Parliament is corruption. Allegations of dishonesty among legislators, including outright vote selling, are widespread ("Buying Duma Votes–A Price List" 2000). Over the years, a number of members of Parliament have been subjected to criminal investigation by the procurator's office. But the immunity protection for deputies is exceedingly broad, and attempts to change the law in order to limit immunity have regularly failed. Efforts at influencing members of Parliament come from a variety of sources, including the executive branch. As indicated earlier, the resources of the president's Administration of Affairs are available for such purposes. According to the *Moscow News*, for instance, a large number of Duma deputies were promised new luxury apartments in connection with the adoption of the government's budget in 2000 (Skorobogatko 2000, 1).

Parliament and the Executive

As discussed in Chapter 5, Parliament under the new constitution became a decidedly weaker institution than it had been prior to 1993, especially in relation to the president. But this does not mean that it has been deprived of all power and authority. Russia's parliament performs a number of functions, the most important of which is adopting laws. The president can to some extent trump law-making by Parliament through the use of his decree power. However, many important policy actions cannot be implemented by means of decrees, but require legislation adopted by Parliament. These include, among other subjects, budget and tax legislation; the procedures for electing the Duma and forming the Federation Council; rules for judicial appointment and removal; treaty ratification; the basic codes of law; and federal constitutional laws. As presidential-parliamentary relations have evolved under the constitution, it appears that presidential decrees increasingly address narrow, more routine matters, while major policy issues are left to Parliament (Remington 2000, 507) It should be noted that under the constitution the president and the government (as well as members of Parliament and the legislatures of the regional bodies) have the power of legislative initiative: they can propose laws for consideration by Parliament. As Thomas Remington has shown, bills proposed by the president and the government have the highest probability of becoming law (Remington 2000, 518–19). This indicates a higher level of cooperation between the two branches than might have been expected, given the number of clashes between the executive and Parliament that have made the headlines over the years.

There is, of course, considerable evidence of conflict. Parliament has a number of powers at its disposal to thwart the president's will, which have been used on occasion, particularly during Yeltsin's tenure as president. Attempts to override the president's veto, although requiring extraordinary majorities in both houses, have been successful a few times. The president's clashes with the Duma over prime ministerial choices have already been discussed. The Duma's 1998 vote to impeach Yeltsin missed succeeding by just a few votes. It voted no confidence in Yeltsin's government in 1995, and came close to doing so on other occasions. Under the Russian constitution, the Duma can force the government's dismissal only by voting no confidence a second time within three months. If that happens, however, the Duma is also dissolved. So far, Duma members have been disinclined to take this step and thereby risk their seats by submitting themselves for reelection. But the threat of voting no confidence seems to have helped on occasion in gaining concessions from the president (Huskey 1999, 175, 268, note 34).

Federation Council approval of the president's nominees for major judicial posts is required. By rejecting a number of Yeltsin's choices for the Constitutional Court, the Federation Council was able to expose the president's weakness and force the naming of candidates more to its liking (Huskey 1999, 169). And the Federation Council repeatedly refused to confirm Yeltsin's dismissal of Procurator General Yuri Skuratov. It wasn't until Putin had been elected president that the upper house agreed to remove Skuratov.

The power to grant amnesty under the constitution belongs to the Duma. In February 1994, little more than two months after the adoption of the constitution, the Duma adopted an amnesty decree freeing two sets of staunch opponents of Yeltsin: members of the State Committee for the State of Emergency (the August 1991 coup plotters); and those involved in the October 1993 uprising against Yeltsin's dispersal of Parliament, most notably former vice president Rutskoi and former Parliament speaker Khasbulatov. All of those amnestied were incarcerated at the time of their release but had not been tried. Yeltsin and his aides were furious at the Duma's action, but were powerless to reverse it. A large number of Duma members backed the amnesty in order to embarrass the president. But others, some of them supporters of Yeltsin, were motivated by "civic reconciliation," hoping that the amnesty would help to put to rest two painful episodes of recent Russian history (Barry 1994, 437).

The distribution of power under the 1993 constitution has led a number of commentators to describe the system as "superpresidential" (Holmes 1994, 123; Jensen 1998, 1; Shevtsova 1999, 277). And it is unquestionably true that the balance of authority in the document leans heavily in the direction of the executive. But the years of operation under the constitution have shown that parliament is not completely lacking in weapons in its dealings with the president. As Remington has put it, "the president was neither so strong nor parliament so weak as first appeared" (Remington 2000, 504; accord Huskey 1999, 180). Moreover, President Yeltsin eventually came to see that bargaining and compromise could sometimes be more effective than confrontation in managing executive-legislative relations. Since assuming the presidency, Putin has had more success in getting along with Parliament. Several factors appear to account for this. As a result of the 1999 Duma elections, he has a stronger base of support in Parliament than Yeltsin had. Moreover, he does not have the history of hostile relations with the legislature, and with powerful forces therein such as the communists, that so characterized the former president's rule. Finally, many of the more contentious issues that marked the Yeltsin period, such as decommunization of the country and privatization of the economy, had been largely accomplished by the time Putin came to power. Putin's major goals, including strengthening the state and restoring Russia's international status, are objectives that much of the Parliament willingly supports.

In sum, the presidency still dominates the Russian political system. And with an incumbent less controversial than Yeltsin, who is willing to use the considerable constitutional resources and material incentives available to him, management of Parliament is likely to be an easier task. Many will continue to argue, therefore, that the Russian presidency is too powerful. But the country's short experience with its new constitution has shown that there is more balance to executive-legislative relations than appeared to be the case when the document was adopted in 1993.

The Judiciary

In addition to setting forth the basic features of court structure, several constitutional provisions assert the independence of judges and their insulation from factors that might influence the judicial process. Unfortunately, such declarations, by themselves, cannot guarantee judicial independence. A widely held consensus is that the dependence of judges on other parts of state authority, as well as the susceptibility of some of them to the temptations of corruption, are among the factors hindering the development of the rule of law in Russia.

The regular court system in Russia consists of three levels: district courts, the country's basic courts of general jurisdiction; regional and republic supreme courts; and the Russian Federation Supreme Court. Judges at the first two levels are, under the constitution, appointed by the president for unlimited terms. In practice, however, a number of other institutions pass on candidates prior to the president's action. These include judicial qualification commissions, legislatures of the regions where particular judgeships are located; and the Supreme Court. As discussed earlier, judges of the country's three top courts, the Constitutional Court, the Supreme Court, and the Supreme Arbitration Court, are appointed by the Federation Council, on the basis of nominations submitted by the president.

The Russian populace does not have a particularly high regard for courts. This is in part a carryover from the Soviet period, when the judiciary was under heavy regime control. But it also reflects the present reality that legal reform has not proceeded sufficiently to permit the courts to become truly autonomous and effective institutions. There are numerous reasons for this state of affairs, including staffing difficulties, low pay, less than ideal working conditions, the judiciary's dependence on other institutions, and the slowness of law reform itself (Huskey 1999, 150).

The profession of judge often does not attract the best or most ambitious lawyers. As two close observers of Russian courts have noted (citing a Russian Supreme Court report), the typical judge "is now a middle-aged woman with a correspondence or night school law degree" (Solomon and Foglesong 2000, 97). These authors go on to explain that professions dominated by women traditionally possess little prestige. The pay of judges is not high, although it has improved in recent years. But like other state employees, members of the judiciary have known times when salaries have been delayed. Moreover, judges are dependent on federal and local authorities for all manner of support, from adequate housing to court facilities and supplies. This dependence is hardly conducive to a truly effective judiciary. So far, a chronic lack of funds has slowed the realization of measures adopted to make courts more autonomous.

Under current conditions, Russian judges face considerable pressures in performing their duties. Among these are large caseloads and increasingly complex litigation. A new level of justice of the peace courts, below the district court level, was promised in a 1996 law. These courts are intended to handle simpler cases and should reduce the burden on district court judges. But again, a lack of funding has slowed this development.

A promising innovation introduced in the early 1990s was the use of jury trials in criminal cases. The right to trial by jury ("in cases stipulated by federal law") was provided for in the 1993 constitution (Article 47). But juries have not been used extensively so far. They have been introduced in only 9 of Russia's 89 regions, and support for the institution now seems to be diminishing. Not only have juries proved expensive, but they have been criticized in some quarters for their liberal bias, as seen in their relatively high acquittal rates (Huskey 1999, 155–59; Solomon and Foglesong 2000, 132–33).

The jury system is just one area where legal reform has been slow. Since court decisions are not self-executing, the judiciary is dependent on help from other state authorities for implementing judicial orders. New legislation aimed at strengthening the institution of the bailiff (both for maintaining order in courts and for enforcing judicial decisions) was adopted in 1997. But like other innovations in support of the judiciary, this too has been underfunded (Solomon and Foglesong 2000, 167).

A considerable amount of legislation that bears on judicial reform has been adopted in recent years, including new criminal and civil codes that replaced Soviet-era laws. Potentially an even bigger step, in terms of strengthening the judiciary, will be a new criminal procedural code, to replace the one adopted in 1960. Criminal procedural law has great bearing on the reciprocal rights of suspects and accused persons on the one hand and the state authorities on the other. It will also clarify the role of the courts in criminal proceedings. A number of provisions of the 1993 constitution involve criminal procedure, including article 22, which states that "no person may be detained for more than 48 hours without a court order." However, one of the interim provisions of the constitution reads as follows: "Until the criminal-procedural legislation of the Russian Federation has been brought into line with the provisions of this Constitution, the previous procedure for the arrest, detention and custody of persons suspected of committing a crime shall apply." Drafts of new criminal procedural legislation have been stalled for years, as friends and foes of a more liberal procedural code try to carry the day.

Much of the serious opposition to judicial reform comes from certain government ministries, principally the ministries of justice and internal affairs (which includes the police), as well as the procuracy (Huskey 1999, 152–53). These agencies see both a loss of prestige and a weakened ability to fight crime in some of the reform proposals. At present, for instance, the procuracy performs the dual function of sanctioning arrest in criminal cases and prosecuting persons charged with crimes. Some Russian jurists see this combination of functions as a blatant conflict of interest, but the procuracy has resisted the notion that its role should be reduced solely to prosecution (Yakovlev 2000, 5). As described above, the new constitution gives the duty of sanctioning arrest to the court. This is just one of the crucial issues that has delayed the adoption of criminal procedural legislation.

Of Russia's three high courts, the only completely new institution is the Constitutional Court. After performing creditably during the early phase of its existence, the Constitutional Court became embroiled in the

1993 constitutional crisis, in considerable part through the partisanship of its then chairman, Valery Zorkin. The court's operation was suspended by President Yeltsin late in 1993, and it did not begin issuing decisions again until 1995. When it resumed activity, the scope of its jurisdiction had been narrowed somewhat. And its claim to a monopoly on constitutional judicial review was challenged by the Supreme Court (Krug 1997, 725; Krug 2000, 129; Sharlet 2001, 64). As reconstituted after the 1993 crisis, therefore, the Constitutional Court appears to be a somewhat weakened institution.

Its recent performance has received mixed reviews. In the "Chechen Case" (1995) it upheld the constitutionality of President Yeltsin's use of military force in Chechnya. This was seen by many as an example of the court yielding to executive pressure. But the decision was not a clear-cut one. An unprecedented 8 of the 18 participating judges dissented in the case. For this and other cases where it has appeared too timid in checking official authority, the Constitutional Court has been accused of "exaggerated prudence" and "impotence" (Seagull 1996). Others see the court, though handicapped by difficulties growing out of the 1993 crisis, as an institution that has contributed to Russia's recent political stability by steering a judicious course through difficult political and legal terrain, and by enhancing the constitutional rights of Russian citizens (Sharlet 2001, 70–72; Di Gregorio 1998/1999, 387, 418–19). The relative openness of the Constitutional Court, and its willingness to air differences through published dissenting opinions, are also seen as positive characteristics, particularly in comparison with the closed practices of Soviet-era judicial tribunals (Barry 2001, 1).

Like other Russian courts, but to a smaller degree, the Constitutional Court has a dependence problem. Judges rely on the state for a range of privileges that go with the office but can seemingly be arbitrarily withdrawn (Sharlet 2001, 73; Schwartz 2000, 146, 161). Boris Yeltsin was not above using the largess of the presidential office to try to influence members of the court. The most important judicial reform, therefore, remains what it has always been in Russian law: the adoption and enforcement of concrete measures that will guarantee genuinely independent courts.

The Center and the Regions:
Putin's Efforts to Create "Power Vertical"

One of Vladimir Putin's major objectives in strengthening the Russian state has been to reassert central control in the country's regions. The erosion of Moscow's dominance over its territories began well before the USSR's demise, but the Yeltsin presidency did little to check the process. The 89 "subjects of the federation" are named in the constitution. Thus, changing the federal makeup of the country involves changing the constitution. As noted in Chapter 5, however, amending article 65, where the subjects of the federation are named, is relatively easy. It requires the adoption of a federal constitutional law, which can be passed with the assent of two-thirds of the Duma and three-quarters of the Federation Council. The subjects are not involved in the amending process, as they are in amending other parts of the charter. Still, the political risk of attempting to amend article 65 could be considerable. In the short run, at least, Putin and his cohorts are likely to adopt measures that leave the 89 territorial subdivisions intact.

In attempting to enhance central authority, Putin moved swiftly. Less than a week after his inauguration he adopted a decree grouping the federal units into seven large administrative regions. In place of the presidential representatives in each of the subjects, who had demonstrated little ability to assert Moscow's interests in their respective territories, more powerful presidential representatives were appointed for each of the new administrative regions. To strengthen the hand of these officials, a procurator's corps, a branch of the audit chamber, and other key administrative offices were established in the seven regions. In effect, a whole new bureaucratic layer was created. Chief among the presidential representatives' duties is to oversee the activities of the federal units and to guarantee their compliance with the constitution and with national law. Putin's choices for representatives followed what was fast becoming a pattern in his personnel policy: most appointees had a background in either military or security work (Corwin 2000a).

This administrative reform seemed to meet with substantial approval, although there was some criticism of Putin's use of his decree power for such an important matter. The chairman of the Federation Council, for instance, urged the adoption of a law defining the powers of presidential representatives, but to no avail. Putin's next moves clearly required legislative action, which was surprisingly fast in coming. He sent a package of bills to the Duma, which passed them in quick order. The most important of these barred territorial governors and heads of territorial legislatures from serving in the Federation Council, the nation's upper house. The constitution merely states that each subject of the federation sends two representatives to the Federation Council, one from its legislative branch and the other from its executive branch. But in practice, from 1995 on, the governors and legislative heads in each of the federal units served in the Federation Council. At first there was considerable resistance in the Federation Council to passing this legislation. In addition to giving up their seats in the national parliament, the incumbents stood to lose the broad immunity granted to legislators as well. But the Duma's strong endorsement of the measure made it clear that it could override the upper house's veto. In the end the Federation Council passed the measure easily. Another law adopted at about the same time further strengthened the president's hand by allowing him to initiate the process of dismissing regional leaders and dissolving regional legislatures that break the law.

To keep a better eye on lawmaking in the federal units, so as to prevent the territories from adopting measures contrary to national law, Putin adopted a decree in August 2000 creating a federal register of regional legislation. This measure requires the top official in each federation subject to send copies of all normative acts to the Russian Federation Ministry of Justice within seven days of their adoption ("O dopolnitel'nykh merakh po obespecheniiu edinstva pravovogo prostranstva Rossiiskoi Federatsii" 2000). Since federal units have often been charged with adopting laws that contradict national legislation, the need for such a register is obvious. In line with this initiative, renewed efforts to strengthen federal control over the courts and police in the regions were also made (Petrov 2000).

As a concession to the regional governors, a new body called the State Council was created in September 2000. Designated as strictly an "advisory organ," the State Council is chaired by the president and is comprised of the governors of the 89 federation subjects. It meets once every three months. Given its vague mandate and the fact that it owes its existence to a presidential decree rather than the constitution or even a law, it is difficult to imagine that the State Council will play a substantial role in policy-making. But it does provide the governors direct contact with the president, somewhat compensating for their loss of seats on the Federation Council.

The creation of the State Council has brought into question the future of the Federation Council. Without the top regional officials among its members, the Federation Council's significance will likely diminish. In the longer term, constitutional amendments to create a new set of federal relationships may be in the offing.

Taken together, the measures just discussed are designed to strengthen what the Russians call the "power vertical" (*vlastnaia vertikal'*) between the center and the regions. Whether this strategy will ultimately succeed remains unclear. Putin's approach is seen by some as a typical Soviet-era reaction, involving a set of top-down directives utilizing new structures and the massive commitment of personnel (Corwin 2000b). If these measures harden regional resolve and strengthen national-separatist sentiment, then the problems they are designed to address will only be exacerbated (Pain 2000). Putin's strategy with regard to Russia's regions demonstrates that he has brought a different political style to the presidency from that of his predecessor, one more direct and action-oriented, less aimed at consensus and accommodation.

References

Albats, Yevgenia. 1994. *The State Within a State.* New York: Farrar, Straus and Giroux.

Aron, Leon. 2000. *Yeltsin: A Revolutionary Life.* New York: St. Martin's Press.

Barry, Donald D. 1994. "Amnesty Under the Russian Constitution: Evolution of the Provision and Its Use in February 1994." *The Parker School Journal of East European Law* 1:437–461.

Barry, Donald D. 2001. "Decision-Making and Dissent in the Russian Federation Constitutional Court." In *International and National Law in Russia and Eastern Europe*, eds. Roger Clark, Stanislaw Pomorski, and F.J.M. Feldbrugge. Dordrecht, The Netherlands: Kluwer International.

"Buying Duma Votes—A Price List." 2000. *RFE/RL Security Watch* 1:2.

Corwin, Julie A. 2000a. "The New Centralizer." *RFE/RL Newsline* 4:120, Part I, June 21.

Corwin, Julie A. 2000b. "Putin's Regional Policy: An Emerging Consensus?" *RFE/RL Russian Federation Report* 43, November 22.

Di Gregorio, Angela. 1998/1999. "The Evolution of Constitutional Justice in Russia: Normative Imprecision and the Conflicting Positions of Legal Doctrine and Case-Law in Light of the Constitutional Court Decision of 16 June 1998." *Review of Central and East European Law,* 24:387–419.

Dikun, Yelena. 1999. "Heir By An Indirect Route." *Obshchaya gazeta* No. 32, August 12–18, in *The Current Digest of the Post-Soviet Press* 51:32, 4.

Holmes, Stephen. 1994. "Superpresidentialism and its Problems." *East European Constitutional Review* 2:4 and 3:1, 123–126.

Huskey, Eugene. 1999. *Presidential Power in Russia.* Armonk. New York: M.E. Sharpe.

Jensen, Donald N. 1998. "How Russia is Ruled—1998: IV. Institutions of Government." *Radio Free Europe/Radio Liberty*, http://www.rferl.org/nca/special/ruwhorules/institutions-4.

Krug, Peter. 1997. "Departure from the Centralized Model: The Russian Supreme Court and Constitutional Control of Legislation."

Virginia Journal of International Law, 37:725–87.

Krug, Peter. 2000. "The Russian Federation Supreme Court and Constitutional Practice in the Courts of General Jurisdiction: Recent Developments." *Review of Central and East European Law,* 26: 129-46.

"O dopolnitel'nykh merakh po obespecheniiu edinstva pravovogo prostranstva Rossiiskoi Federatsii." 2000. Edict of the President of the Russian Federation. August 10, No. 1486. *Rossiiskaia gazeta* August 16, 4.

"O strukture federal'nykh organov ispolnitel'noi vlasti." 2000. Edict of the President of the Russian Federation. May 17, No. 867. *Rossiiskaia gazeta* May 20, 1–2.

Pain, Emil. 2000. "The Changing Nature of Ethnic Politics under President Putin." *Meeting Report* (Russian and Eurasian Program, Carnegie Endowment for International Peace), 2:7, October 30.

Parlamentskoe Pravo Rossii. 1999, eds I. M. Stepanov and T. Ya. Khabrieva. Moscow: Iurist.

Petrov, Nikolai. 2000. "Decentralization and Recentralization in Russia." *Meeting Report* (Russian and Eurasian Program, Carnegie Endowment for International Peace), 2:7, October 25.

"Primakov Defends Government Against Yeltsin Criticism." 1999. *RFE/RL Newsline* 3:71, Part 1, 13 April.

Remington, Thomas F. 2000. "The Evolution of Executive-Legislative Relations in Russia Since 1993." *Slavic Review* 59:499–520.

Remnick, David. 1997. *Resurrection: The Struggle for a New Russia.* New York: Random House.

Rose, Richard. 2000. "A Supply-Side View of Russia's Elections." *East European Constitutional Review* 9:53-9.

Schwartz, Herman. 2000. *The Struggle for Constitutional Justice in Post-Communist Europe.* Chicago, IL: University of Chicago Press.

Seagull, Lev. 1996. "Court Gets Out Of Harm's Way." *Obshchaya gazeta,* November 7, 8 (available on LEXIS-NEXIS).

Sharlet, Robert. 2001. "Russia's Second Constitutional Court: Politics,

Law, and Stability." In *Russia in the New Century: Stability or Disorder?*, eds. Victoria E. Bonnell and George W. Breslauer. Boulder, CO: Westview Press.

Shevtsova, Lilia. 1999. *Yeltsin's Russia: Myths and Reality*. Washington, DC: Carnegie Endowment for International Peace.

Skorobogatko, Tatyana. 2000. "Housewarming on First Reading: Will the Government Manage to Trade in Budget Approval for Elite Apartments for Duma Deputies?" *Moscow News* September 20, 1.

Solomon, Peter H. Jr. and Todd S. Foglesong. 2000. *Courts and Transition in Russia: The Challenge of Judicial Reform*. Boulder, CO: Westview Press.

White, Stephen. 2000. *Russia's New Politics*. Cambridge: Cambridge University Press.

Wines, Michael. 2000. "Putin Retains Soviet Discipline While Steering Toward Reform." *The New York Times* February 20, 1.

Yakovlev, Aleksandr. 2000. "Diktatura zakona zashchitit ot proizvola vlastei." *Rossiiskaia gazeta* July 28, 5.

Chapter 8
Social Problems and the New Russian Economy

By some measures, the objectives of the Russian economic reform have been substantially achieved during the post-Soviet period. By the late 1990s nearly 90 percent of industrial enterprises were in private hands, although these firms provided only a quarter of total output (White 2000,127). Many of the larger enterprises remained fully or dominantly state-owned. A growing portion of the population was engaged in private commercial activity, as a market economy increasingly became a reality. And an entrepreneurial spirit had taken hold of many Russians, particularly among the younger age groups.

By other calculations, however, the economic moves of the reformers had produced almost unrelievedly discouraging results. In the period from 1992 through 1996 gross domestic product dropped every year, declining by a total of close to 40 percent. The decrease in industrial production during this period was even greater (Hedlund 1999, 345–46). The rate of inflation, which reached over 2,500 percent in 1992, dropped considerably over the following years, but still totaled about 125 percent in 1996. Such success as there was in controlling inflation was due in part to the widespread practice of nonpayment or late payment of wages to Russian workers.

In 1997 some improvements in economic indicators suggested that the economy might finally be turning around. But as discussed in Chapter 7, the August 1998 crash sent the economy tumbling again. Several factors combined to produce an upturn at the end of the 1990s. The ruble devaluation in 1998 made the cost of imported products prohibitively expensive for many Russians, increasing demand for domestically produced goods. At the same time, less expensive Russian goods became more attractive in foreign markets. Just as important was the tripling of world oil prices at the end of the decade, producing large revenues for Russia from its export of oil and gas. These improvements have undoubtedly helped to maintain a high approval rating for President Putin, but it is unclear whether the developments of 1999 and 2000 can be sustained.

World oil prices have a history of rather wide fluctuations. And the Russian economy faces so many basic problems, including a chronic shortage of investment funds, that true economic health is unquestionably years away (Dunlap 2000, 4).

This recital of basic economic facts tells little about the impact of economic reform on ordinary citizens, however. A reduction of inflation to a level that would still be incredibly high in Western countries has proved scant comfort to those millions of Russian citizens whose savings were wiped out by the loss of the ruble's value. Savings accounts have not been indexed to inflation, and small payments in recent years to senior citizens who have accounts in state savings banks have done little to compensate for the enormous inflation-based losses that the country's citizens have suffered. But the plight of ordinary Russians is hardly limited to savings account losses. Millions of Russians, including many holding full-time jobs, find themselves in dire economic straits. They were left behind in the economic revolution that took place during the 1990s, and found that the social safety net, not generous during the Soviet period but at least dependable enough to guarantee a minimal level of support, has become badly underfunded and inadequate to society's needs. Many Russians feel betrayed by the events of the 1990s, seeing unfairness in the way the state's wealth was distributed during the process of privatization.

With these considerations in mind, this chapter will address several matters associated with the lives of the country's ordinary citizens that bear on Russia's economic transformation: crime and corruption; economic inequality and poverty; and a variety of public health problems.

Crime and Corruption

Ordinary crime grew rapidly in Russia after the fall of the Soviet Union (White 2000, 160). Freeing the economy from the control of the state enormously increased the potential for private economic gain. It quickly became clear, however, that the state authorities were not up to the task of policing this vigorous new economic activity (in part because large numbers of officials were illegally benefitting from the new arrangements by accepting bribes and through other forms of corruption).

Organized crime has taken on particularly significant dimensions during this period. Thousands of criminal gangs, many of them operating internationally, exist in Russia. In the late 1990s Russia's minister of internal affairs estimated that 40 percent of the country's private businesses and an even higher proportion of state enterprises were controlled by organized crime (Jensen 1998, 2; Dakhlin, Makarychev and Sergounin 2000). Businesses not directed by criminal organizations find it necessary to pay protection money (a "roof," in Russian parlance) to criminal gangs. The gangs then protect the businesses from the depredations of other gangs and, if necessary, pay off the police. The practice amounts to simple extortion.

Organized crime in Russia runs the gamut of illegal activities, from black market operations and smuggling to prostitution, drug trafficking and car theft. High levels of violence also characterize the new Russian crime culture, most notably the wide use of contract killings. The main targets of such murders, according to one study, are the following:

> [B]osses of the criminal world who are killed as part of the struggle for power among criminal organizations—and whose death may result from business rivalries, personal animosities, or even such motives as revenge or professional jealousy; businessmen or bankers who resist hostile take-overs by criminal organizations; and journalists, law enforcement officers, officials, and politicians who are serious about exposing and eliminating corruption. (Williams 1997, 18–19)

In describing these developments as "the new Russian crime culture," it is not meant to imply that a clear break with the Soviet past has taken place. Many analysts trace the present structure of Russian organized crime to roots that developed during the last decades of the Soviet period (Handelman 1995, 93; Jensen 1998, 3). The word "mafia," used to describe Soviet organized crime groups, came into the Russian language before the fall of the USSR (Vaksberg 1991). But the machinery of repression of the Soviet state limited both the scope of operation of the criminal groups and the public awareness of their existence. After the fall of the USSR both of these limitations were swept away. Also notable in the last part of the Soviet period was the link, documented by several insiders, between important political personages and criminal gangs. In the words of one analyst, this amounted to a "direct alliance between organized criminal groups as suppliers of commodities and services to the political elite and the patronage offered in return" (Rawlinson 1997, 44).

As privatization got under way, certain segments of the population were able to use their positions and/or experience to emerge as principal players. Participants in illegal underground economic activity during the Soviet period provided one strand of new entrepreneurs, as did representatives from the technical and scientific intelligentsia, whose skills proved useful in the new private economy. But the dominant strain of the privatization elite consisted of the *nomenklatura*, both communist party officials and managerial personnel from former state enterprises (Silverman and Yanowitch 2000, 113–27).

Workers were very poorly represented among the new business owners. In 1992 the Russian state issued vouchers worth 10,000 rubles to every citizen of the country, which the owners could dispose of as they saw fit. The government's hope was that citizens would invest in the privatizing economy, thus helping to create a kind of people's capitalism. But rampant inflation quickly cut into the worth of the vouchers. Moreover, even when invested in a firm, vouchers owned by individuals provided no voice in a company's operation. Large numbers of vouchers were bought on the street at cut-rate prices by criminal and commercial groups and used to gain control of some of the most desirable firms.

Evidence abounds to demonstrate that privatization deals were often rigged so as to give insiders great advantages in gaining ownership of enterprises. Before the process was completed, many analysts, both inside Russia and abroad, had come to the conclusion that as a result of privatization, a considerable proportion of the state's assets had been, in effect, hijacked. "*Nomenklatura* privatization" gained wide currency as a descriptor of Russia's experience (Silverman and Yanowitch 2000, 125). To one author, privatization was "to put it plainly... the seizure of state property" (Sergeyev 1998, 165).

On a comparative basis, Russia's level of corruption appears to be quite high. Transparency International, a Berlin-based organization, publishes an annual "corruption perceptions index." In the 2000 edition Russia was rated 82nd of the 90 countries surveyed (i.e., among the most corrupt). The country analyses bring together the results of multiple surveys of businesspeople, the general public, and country specialists. They concentrate on "the misuse of public power for private gain," focusing on bribe taking and receiving kickbacks by officials and politicians ("Transparency International Releases the Year 2000 Corruption Perceptions Index" 2000).

A World Bank study published in 2000 sought to make a somewhat broader analysis of corruption in the CIS countries and the states of Central Europe and Eastern Europe. It looked at both "administrative corruption" (individual cases of bribe taking and receiving kickbacks) and "state capture," meaning "actions of individuals, groups, or firms in both the public and private sectors to *influence the formation* of laws, regulations, decrees, and other government policies (i.e., the basic rules of the game) by means of the illicit and non-transparent provision [of] private benefits to public officials" ("Anticorruption in Transition: A Contribution to the Policy Debate" 2000, 1). On both of these measures Russia ranked high in corruption, but not quite at the level of several other former Soviet republics.

Undoubtedly part of Vladimir Putin's much publicized strategy of strengthening the state is aimed at changing public perceptions about corruption in Russia. His advocacy of a "dictatorship of law" was first advanced during the 2000 presidential campaign. In repeating that call in his "state of the nation" address later that year, he linked the weakness of the state to the pernicious effects of corruption (Putin 2000).

In the short run, at least, some of Putin's state-strengthening moves seem to be aimed at reducing corruption. The campaign against certain wealthy business tycoons, often referred to as oligarchs, appears to have limited their political role. Many fear, however, that in advocating a dictatorship of law, Putin really has in mind creating a more authoritarian state. The attempt to place greater controls on the media and the apparent resurgence in the authority of the security apparatus are seen as evidence of this development. These matters will be revisited in the discussion of democracy in the concluding chapter.

Economic Inequality and Poverty

When the salaries of top party and state officials in the Soviet Union finally began to be disclosed in the late 1980s, the figures confirmed what had long been assumed: that there was a considerable gap between the country's highest and lowest income earners. Gorbachev's salary as a Politburo member, for instance, was nearly 20 times the minimum wage (Barry and Barner-Barry 1991, 199–201). In addition to basic salaries, many members of the elite also received extra cash payments (for being members of the national or republic legislature, for instance). And for the truly privileged, salaries were only the beginning of material benefits. Food stores restricted to certain categories of people, paid vacations at exclusive sites, special medical facilities, preferred housing, automobiles, country homes, pensions, special educational advantages for children—these were perquisites that went along with status in Soviet society.

With the demise of the Soviet Union, the structure of economic inequality changed, but not its essence. With the Communist Party's loss of its monopoly on political power, party leaders were denied not only the relatively high salaries that they enjoyed but also the material advantages that accompanied party office. As noted, however, many of the former *nomenklatura* were among several groups, including organized crime gangs, that flourished in the new economy. Among those whose condition worsened under the new circumstances were workers and salaried employees, including large numbers of professionals who had been compensated relatively generously under the old system.

Two measures that provide some insight into the new conditions are the distribution of money income and the poverty level. As of mid-2000, the top 10 percent of income earners received more than one-third of all income, while the bottom 10 percent received about 2.5 percent ("Ten % of Richest Russians Hold 1/3 of Population's Income" 2000). Although these numbers describe a level of inequality that is considerably more extreme than that at the end of the Soviet period (White 2000, 147–48), they don't present a complete picture. The previously discussed problem of wage arrears means that many of the income earners were owed at least part of the money included in these calculations. On the other hand, wages from regular jobs are often supplemented by income from second jobs or from such activities as part-time trading. And a 1998 survey indicated that nearly 75 percent of Russians grow at least some of their own food (Goble 1999). Thus, a variety of coping strategies employed by Russians means that official figures can be somewhat misleading.

Poverty in Russia is also a somewhat difficult concept to deal with. The Russian government regularly establishes a subsistence level for the country and calculates the proportion of the population receiving income below this level. At the end of the 1990s and into the beginning of the next century this figure typically amounted to more than one-third of Russian citizens, or close to 50 million people.

Even if accurate, however, these numbers mask a considerably more complex picture. For instance, there is significant regional variation in both income and the cost of goods and services in Russia, which produces higher levels of poverty in some areas than in others. In general, rural regions have a higher proportion of the poor than cities. Rising unemployment has pushed more women into poverty than men. Another notable consideration has to do with the *degree* of poverty of individual Russians. Many of them—and this applies particularly to pensioners—fall far below the minimum subsistence level (Remington 1999, 200–201; Hedlund 1999, 353–57). On the other hand, unreported income from work in the informal sector may cushion the effects of poverty-level "normal" income.

Some analyses of poverty approach the subject differently. Rather than accepting the government's determination of subsistence, they examine popular feelings of impoverishment as determined by opinion surveys. By this measurement the poverty level can range as high as 60 percent or even 80 percent of the population (Silverman and Yanowitch 2000, 156–57; White 2000, 147, 158). Looked at from either of these perspectives, there is not much room at present for a healthy middle class in Russia. Many who seemed to have reached that status were pushed toward poverty by the economic meltdown of 1998. It is said that the middle class in Russia amounted to 20 to 25 percent of the population in 2001 (Balzer 2001; Malkova 2001). If, as one Russian sociologist has put it, the middle class is "the mainstay of market relations and democratic government" in Russia, then this is yet a further reason why a "war on poverty" should be high on the agenda of Russia's economic planners (Khamrayev 2000).

Public Health Problems

The Soviet system provided free medical care to all citizens, a considerable achievement, even if the quality of care to the favored segments of society was vastly superior to that available to the masses. Even before the USSR's demise, however, it was clear that the health care system was seriously underfunded and beginning to break down (Twigg 2000, 43–44).

With independence, Russia had little choice but to embark on health care reform. The changes put into effect had two main components: decentralization, to give the regions some discretion and responsibility in the operation of the system; and compulsory medical insurance, funded by employers and local governments, to supplement allocations from the state budget (World Health Organization 1999, 23). In practice, however, these innovations have failed to come close to providing the necessary level of funding. Neither employers nor local governments have been able to meet the contribution levels assigned to them. And state budget allocations, especially after cuts resulting from the 1998 economic crisis, have done little to ease the funding situation. As one analyst described the situation as of the year 2000, funds from all sources "do not even approach the level necessary to cover the Russian constitution's promise of free health care to all citizens" (Twigg 2000, 47). The World Health Organization put Russia's health care spending in comparative perspective in a 1999 analysis. It reported that the country's expenditures amounted to just over 2 percent of its Gross Domestic Product, as against more than 8 percent for the countries of the European Union. Russia's figure put it behind all of the other former Soviet republics except Azerbaijan and Tajikistan (World Health Organization 1999, 23–24).

With spending at this level, it is not surprising that Russia faces a variety of serious health care issues. As funds for preventative health care have been cut, the incidence of a number of illnesses has soared. These include infectious diseases such as HIV/AIDS, syphilis, tuberculosis and hepatitis C. The same is true of health problems related to environmental factors. High levels of illness and birth defects associated with chemical pollution have been documented by Russian and American researchers (Feshbach 2001, 20).

Many Russian hospitals lack not only medicines and modern

equipment, but are housed in primitive physical plants as well. An astonishing 40 percent of the country's hospitals and clinics function without hot water or sewage disposal systems. Alongside these wretched institutions, a number of modern, well-equipped hospitals have been opened for well-off paying patients. Their prices are far beyond the capacity of most Russians, however, who must content themselves with under-the-table payments in the regular clinics in order to secure needed drugs and special attention from physicians (Wines 2000).

High levels of smoking, drug use and alcohol abuse also contribute to the general deterioration of health among Russians. Demographer Murray Feshbach reported in 2001 that an estimated 20 million Russians are alcoholics. This figure amounts to about one-seventh of the population. He put the death toll from alcohol poisoning in Russia in 2000 at 35,000, as compared with about one percent of that figure in the United States (Feshbach 2001, 19).

The conditions described have had important effects on the Russian population as a whole. Infant mortality in Russia remains at a high level compared with Western Europe (although it is somewhat lower than the average for the newly independent states as a whole). The birth rate has fallen consistently in Russia in recent years. Abortion remains, as it has been for decades, the primary means of birth control. About two thirds of all pregnancies are terminated by abortion (Field 2000, 13–14). At the same time, life expectancy in Russia is comparatively short. This is particularly the case with Russian men, whose lifestyle habits are thought to contribute significantly to mortality. Male life expectancy among Russian men was 61.4 years in 1998, which was lower than the average for the newly independent states as a whole. It had been as low as 57.6 years in 1994, a level that the World Health Organization attributed to an increase in alcohol consumption at that time (the WHO also noted that the highest level of male life expectancy in Russia in the past two decades coincided with Gorbachev's anti-alcohol campaign of the mid-1980s). A further point worth noting, and this applies to much of the information that one can cite regarding a large country like Russia, is that there are significant regional variations with respect to health data. For instance, male life expectancy for the Siberian republic of Tyva for 1998 was 56.4 years, much lower than in some of the European parts of Russia (World Health Organization 1999, 5).

The confluence of these two major factors—low birth rate and low life expectancy—has produced what Russian leaders have feared for some time: a declining population, which has only been partly offset by the considerable number of ethnic Russians (and other Russian speakers) who have migrated to Russia from other former Soviet republics in recent years. As of the year 2000, Russia's total population had fallen to 145 million, a drop of over three million since the Soviet Union's collapse. The Russian State Statistics Committee has predicted a decline of another 11 million by 2015 (Gentleman 2000, 19).

It is no wonder, then, that population dynamics are considered one of the more serious problems facing the country. President Putin, in his 2000 "state of the nation" address to the federal parliament, listed Russia's "alarming demographic situation" first among "the most acute problems facing our country." Citing an even more dire forecast than that given above, he asserted that "there may be 22 million fewer Russians" in 15 years. This, he said would be "a threat to the survival of the nation" (Putin 2000). Analysts may disagree to some extent about the numbers in the projections. But no one doubts the seriousness of the country's "population meltdown" (Feshbach 2001, 15). Among the major tasks facing the Russian state, the commitment of resources and personnel to the development of enlightened public health measures must rank near the top of the priority list.

References

"Anticorruption in Transition: A Contribution to the Policy Debate." 2000. Washington, DC: The World Bank. http://wb1noo18.worldbank.org/eca/eca.nsf/General.

Balzer, Harley. 2001. "Russia's Self-Denying Middle Class in the Global Age." In *Explaining Post-Soviet Patchworks: Volume I Actors and Sectors between Accommodation and Resistance to Globalization*, ed. Klaus Segbers. Aldershot, UK: Ashgate Publishing.

Barry, Donald D. and Carol Barner-Barry. 1991. *Contemporary Soviet Politics*. Fourth Edition. Englewood Cliffs, NJ: Prentice-Hall.

Dakhin, Andrei, Andrei Makarychev, and Alexander Sergounin. 2000. "Corruption in Russia: Political, Legal, Social and International Aspects." Analytical Report, Nizhny Novgorod Linguistic University, www.egroups.com/files/traccc.

Dunlap, Ben. 2000. "Russia's Economy: Rising from the Ashes?" *Russia Watch* 3, www.ksg.harvard.edu/bcsia/sdi.

Feshbach, Murray. 2001. "Russia's Population Meltdown." *The Wilson Quarterly* XXV:1, 15 21.

Field, Mark G. 2000. "The Health and Demographic Crisis in Post-Soviet Russia: A Two-Phase Development." In *Russia's Torn Safety Net: Health and Social Welfare during the Transition*, eds. Mark G. Field and Judyth L. Twigg. New York: St. Martin's Press.

Gentleman, Amelia. 2000. "Wanted: More Russian Babies to Rescue a Fast-dying Nation." *The Observer*, December 31, 19.

Goble, Paul. 1999. "Down to Subsistence." *RFE/RL Newsline* 3:28, Part I, February 10.

Handelman, Stephen. 1995. *Comrade Criminal: Russia's New Mafiya*. New Haven, CT: Yale University Press.

Hedlund, Stefan. 1999. *Russia's "Market" Economy: A Bad Case of Predatory Capitalism."* London: UCL Press.

Jensen, Donald N. 1998. "Crime Integral to System." Part II of *How Russia Is Ruled–1998*, www.rferl.org/nca/special/ruwhorules/index.html.

Khamrayev, Viktor. 2000. "No One to Lend Me a Hand." *Vremya novostei*, August 8. *Current Digest of the Post-Soviet Press* 52:32, 7.

Malkova, Vlada. 2001. "Russian middle class hits 25%." *The Russia Journal* (February 3–9).

Putin, Vladimir. 2000. "Russian President Putin's Address to the Federal Assembly July 8 2000." 2000, http://ksgnotes1.harvard.edu/BCSIA/SDI.nsf/web/Putinspeech.

Rawlinson, Patricia. 1997. "Russian Organized Crime: A Brief History." In *Russian Organized Crime: A New Threat?*, ed. Phil Williams. London: Frank Cass.

Remington, Thomas F. 1999. *Politics in Russia.* New York: Longman.

Sergeyev, Victor M. 1998. *The Wild East: Crime and Lawlessness in Post-Communist Russia.* Armonk, NY: M. E. Sharpe.

Silverman, Bertram and Murray Yanowitch. 2000. *New Rich, New Poor, New Russia: Winners and Losers on the Russian Road to Capitalism.* Expanded Edition. Armonk, NY: M. E. Sharpe.

"Ten % of Richest Russians Hold 1/3 of Population's Income." 2000. *ITAR-TASS* dispatch, May 3.

"Transparency International Releases the Year 2000 Corruption Perceptions Index." 2000, http://www.transparency.de/documents/cpi2000 cpi2000.html.

Twigg, Judyth L. 2000. "Unfulfilled Hopes: The Struggle to Reform Russian Health Care and Its Financing." In *Russia's Torn Safety Net: Health and Social Welfare during the Transition*, eds. Mark G. Field and Judyth L. Twigg. New York: St. Martin's Press.

Vaksberg, Arkady. 1991. *The Soviet Mafia.* New York: St. Martin's Press.

White, Stephen. 2000. *Russia's New Politics.* Cambridge: Cambridge University Press.

Williams, Phil. 1997. "Introduction: How Serious a Threat is Russian Organized Crime?" In *Russian Organized Crime: The New Threat?*, ed. Phil Williams. London: Frank Cass.

Wines, Michael. 2000. "Capitalism Comes to Russian Health Care." *The New York Times on the Web,* December 22.

World Health Organization. 1999. *Highlights on Health in the Russian Federation.* Copenhagen, Denmark: Epidemiology, Statistics and Health Information Unit, WHO Regional Office for Europe.

Chapter 9
Russia's Hard Road Toward Democracy

"You cannot find any perfect young democracies." These are the words of Yegor Gaidar, Russian Duma member and former acting prime minister. Speaking to an American audience in January 2001, he declared that his country had unquestionably achieved the status of a democracy, albeit one with imperfections (Gaidar 2001, 6). For numerous other commentators on the Russian scene, however, Gaidar's assertion surely goes too far. Flaws of one kind or another have led such writers to employ terms like "controlled democracy," "managed democracy," "incomplete democracy," and "delegative democracy" to describe the Russian system, circa the year 2000. And there are many of a more pessimistic bent who believe that Russia abandoned the democratic road in the early 1990s (Reddaway and Glinski 2000, 56) or somewhat later ("Summary" 2000, 6).

An examination of such writings makes at least two things clear: that there is a considerable range of opinion concerning the state of democracy in Russia; and that the authors of these assessments are not necessarily working with the same view of what democracy means. Rather than providing yet another pronouncement on the status of Russian democracy, this chapter has another aim: to compile a kind of balance sheet, in part based on information set forth in the preceding chapters, of the factors present in the Russian political system that enhance or impede the development of democracy. To do this, it will be necessary to examine two other matters first: major conceptions of democracy, in the view of a number of writers who have examined the subject in recent years; and the question of whether Russia as a country is characterized by such uniqueness, as some maintain, that democracy in Russia should be seen as a qualitatively different phenomenon.

What Democracy Means

It is no exaggeration to say that scores of definitions of democracy have been offered in print in recent years. It is also reasonable to assert that in broad terms, these definitions can be divided into two basic groups: those that see democracy as essentially involving a method or set of procedural mechanisms that provide people with the wherewithal to take part in the political process; and those that insist that democracy, to be worthy of its basic meaning (rule by the people), must involve more than mere procedures (Sørensen 1998, 9).

Adherents of the first concept usually assume that the democracy they envisage will be representative rather than direct democracy (Lijphart 1984, 1). Thus, a fairly typical definition of democracy of this type is the following:

> Modern political democracy is a system of governance in which the rulers are held accountable for their actions in the public realm by citizens, acting indirectly through the competition and cooperation of their elected representatives. (Schmitter and Karl 1996, 50)

Some who support this narrow conception assert that to qualify as a democracy, a country's democratic practices need to have been in operation over a considerable period of time (Lijphart 1984, 2, 38). Sometimes it is also said that the alternation in power of opposing political forces or parties is essential (Adelman 1995, 312). Pushing this concept further, achieving a *consolidated* democracy, some say, is determined by the "two-turnover test." This occurs, according to Huntington, if "the party or group that takes power in the initial election...loses a subsequent election and turns over power to those election winners, and if those election winners then peacefully turn over power to winners of a later election" (Huntington 1991, 266–67). The problem with this test is that some countries long acknowledged as democratic, such as postwar Italy and Japan, would fail, since they experienced what amounted to long periods of one-party or one-coalition rule without turnover. Other definitions assert that democratic consolidation is achieved when a country's political institutions are seen as "profoundly legitimate" by the citizenry, or when it can be taken as a given that contenders for power will act only within the established institutional framework (Diamond 1996, 238; Przeworski 1991, 26).

All of the considerations just discussed relate to the narrow or procedural conception of democracy. Advocates of the broader view insist that democracy involves more than simply providing a method for choosing leaders. What more? They speak of participation that goes beyond the mere act of voting for politicians to serve as representatives, and of a greater measure of equality in society, so that there can be true equality of opportunity to participate in the political process (Barber 1998, 74, 109–110, 127–29; Green 1998, 52–55). This suggests a system in which citizens enjoy not just political rights, but also social and economic rights that allow them to pursue the procedural guarantees that formal democracy provides (Sørensen 1998, 10).

It may be that these contesting views merely represent different points on the same continuum, "disputes," as David Beetham has called them, "about how much democracy is either desirable or practicable" (Beetham 1993, 55). Whether this is the case or not, it surely shows that there is room for disagreement in the West about conceptions of democracy.

Russian Uniqueness and Its Impact on Democracy

President Yeltsin called in 1996 for the formulation of a "national idea" for Russia, which he apparently hoped would unite the nation. Although the public comment on the subject that followed, in the press, open meetings, and round table discussions proved inconclusive, it suggested that the age-old debate in Russia about the country's uniqueness, and the relationship between Russian and Western culture, was being revived. There has long been a part of the Russian population that rejects the values of the West and proclaims Russian particularity, asserting, in effect, the superiority of its cultural and historical traditions. A benign form of the Russian idea emphasizes national consciousness and what Nicolai Petro calls "enlightened patriotism" (Petro 1995, 109). Its more extreme form manifests anti-democratic characteristics and virulent nationalism, including hatred toward other ethnic groups (McDaniel 1996, 51; Kelly 1998, 11). In its most recent version, hostility toward the West, particularly the United States, appears to be a major feature. This is an understandable enough reaction. The decline in Russia's status, from the dominant component of a major superpower to a weakened giant with a vastly reduced sphere of influence, has been a humiliating experience, particularly for more nationalistically minded Russians. Moreover, many Russians see the West, and particularly the United States, as largely responsible for economic measures that resulted in their impoverishment of the country. Some Russians go further, claiming that Western efforts are aimed deliberately at weakening Russia (Zinovyev, 2000; Fedorov 2000, 9–10). Nor are these views limited to extremists and rabid nationalists: a number of intellectuals and members of the Russian political elite are said to share such feelings as well (Piontkovsky 2001). To some extent, at least, democracy has been given a bad name in Russia in the process, because of its association both with the West and with the failed reform measures and corruption of the Yeltsin period.

The foregoing does not mean that all Russians have become anti-Western. Many influential Russians publicly embrace Western values and reject extreme forms of the national idea. And according to recent opinion surveys, a considerable proportion of the country's elite from various walks of life believes that Russia's development path should be that of the "civilized" West ("Russian Elite..." 2000). But there also seems to be considerable feeling in the country that Russia's democracy should and will reflect features peculiar to Russia, and will differ in important respects from that of the West.

For Western analysts of Russian politics, the implied standard against which democracy in Russia is measured is typically the narrow conception discussed above, although this is seldom spelled out in so many words (but see Dawisha 1997, 40, whose basis for analysis is "a procedural or minimalist conception of democracy"). For many Russians, however, democracy means something different. Some Russians express opposition to Western democracy merely because it is Western. Aleksei Podberiozkin, former leader of Spiritual Heritage, answered as follows to a question about democracy from a Western reporter: "What is best for you is not best for Russia" (Black 1999, 22A). Recent Russian opinion polls seem to buttress this view: a 1998 survey indicated that fewer than 20 percent favored "Western type democracy," compared with over 70 percent in the early 1990s (Fedorov 2000, 3).

But there are more thoughtful analyses that attempt to explain how and why many Russians look upon democracy differently. Russian political scientist Alexey Kara-Murza states that in the "classic model" of democratic development, economic liberalization precedes political democratization. Russia, he believes, is in a unique position in having developed political democracy without having achieved a sufficient level of "social democracy" (basic economic and social guarantees for the population) to sustain it. Because of the "economic degradation" that characterizes a large portion of the population, the democratic rights that exist cannot be fully appreciated. For Kara-Murza, then, providing the population with a higher measure of "social democracy" is necessary before real democracy in Russia can be achieved (Kara-Murza 2000, 16).

Perhaps the most thorough analysis of the uniqueness of Russian views on democracy is that of political scientist Alexander Lukin, in his 2000 book, *The Political Culture of the Russian "Democrats."* Lukin accuses most analysts of Russian political culture, Western and Russian alike, of "Eurocentrism" in their approach to the Russian system. In applying strictly Western standards, they have misunderstood the roots of Russian attitudes toward democracy. In his view (and here he purports to describe the opinions of many of Russia's true democrats as well), democracy is "based on a far broader equality than just equality before the law." This endorsement of substantive equality is founded on two factors rooted in the Soviet past: the opposition of large numbers of Russians to the inequality of Soviet society, which granted vast privileges to the *nomenklatura* class; and the broad endorsement of comprehensive welfare state measures of the Soviet period. In support of these assertions Lukin cites numerous surveys of Russian citizens, including polls of Russian emigres from the 1950s and 1980s as well as questionnaire results from the 1980s from inside the USSR. Although respondents from the emigre surveys overwhelmingly expressed hostility to the *political regime* in the Soviet Union, they strongly supported public medical care, housing, and other social amenities provided by the state. According to Lukin, the prevailing view was that the oppressive Soviet system needed to be destroyed, but the social justice provisions of the old system needed to be preserved. And how would the latter be maintained? Many Russians looked (and look) to a strong state to perform this function.

In sum, then, in the minds of many Russians, true democracy means guaranteeing substantial social support to the population, as well as providing the procedural mechanisms to make formal democracy work.

According to Lukin, when the Gaidar government endeavored to "make Russia 'like the West'" by introducing the market and reducing the state's role, "inequalities unheard of in the USSR" were the result (Lukin 2000, 35, 262, 264, 280–86).

Two elements that stand out in Lukin's depiction of a Russian conception of democracy are the emphasis on substantive equality and the reliance on the state to provide for the needs of the populace. Although Lukin does not cite Vladimir Putin, the latter's view on the role of the state has relevance to the present discussion. At the end of 1999, on the eve of his assumption of the acting presidency, prime minister Putin stated his views on a variety of issues. He embraced democracy, the rule of law, and political freedom, but he didn't see Russia becoming a democracy of the U.S. or British type. He envisaged a strong state for Russia, not only because it was consonant with Russia's traditional values, but also because it was absolutely necessary at Russia's present stage:

> Our state and its institutes and structures have always played an exceptionally strong role in the life of the country and its people. For Russians a strong state is not an anomaly which should be got rid of. Quite the contrary, ... [it is] a source and guarantor of order and the initiator and main driving force of any change. . . [P]eople are alarmed by the obvious weakening of state power. The public looks forward to the restoration of the guiding and regulating role of the state to a degree which is necessary, proceeding from the traditions of the present state of the country. (Putin 1999)

As shown above, some Western analysts believe that a minimalist conception of democracy is deficient in not emphasizing the need for a measure of substantive equality. In this they are in accord with Lukin and other Russians of a like mind. But strong state authority is not central to most Western ideas of democracy, because of the presumed difficulty of holding the state accountable for its actions (Sørensen 1998, 10; Held 1995, 146–47). Moreover, an overly assertive state is thought likely to restrict the development of a *civil society*, a healthy network of autonomous groups that pursue their interests independent of the state. Most Western analysts consider civil society to be a vital part of a working democratic system. Thus, the role proposed for the state in Russia must figure in any analysis of its progress toward democracy.

Russian Democracy: A Balance Sheet

It is important to consider a number of aspects of Russian political operations that bear on its democratic development. Since Russia has not yet achieved, to any significant degree, the substantive democracy described by Lukin and others, it will not be necessary to examine that broader conception of the term. Instead, the following analysis will concentrate on the procedural aspects of democracy, and the effects that strong state operations, so important to Lukin and Putin, have on its development.

Popular Elections

As one contemporary source has put it, "elections are a central, if not *the* central, institution of democratic governance" (LeDuc, Niemi and Norris 1996, 4; also Powell 2000, 4). Our examination of elections in Chapter 6 established that Russia has experienced several rounds of competitive elections during the post-Soviet period. Multiple parties and large numbers of individual candidates have participated in contests in which the results were far from foregone conclusions, as was the case through decades of Soviet elections. There have been serious criticisms of recent elections, however. Some level of electoral fraud has usually been alleged, although the Organization for Security and Cooperation in Europe, which has had observers at elections sites, has given Russian elections generally satisfactory marks. Moreover, none of the political parties has mounted major challenges to electoral results. At least as substantial, however, is the charge that government control of significant portions of the media has unfairly influenced election outcomes. Many neutral observers endorse this view. The issue of media control and its effect on democracy will be discussed below.

The popular vote on the 1993 constitution, while not an election, still represented an opportunity for Russians to express their views. The circumstances that brought about the vote, following President Yeltsin's unconstitutional dissolution of Parliament, were certainly anything but democratic. Recognizing this, it also seems clear, after nearly a decade of operation of the constitution, that the major political forces in Russia decided to accept the constitutional text, and the reported popular vote on it, as the basis for the country's political operations.

Political Parties

The weakness of Russia's party system has contributed to retarding democratic development in the country. A large number of parties, some short-lived and others inclined to frequent name changes, provides a confusing picture for the voter. This lack of stability also makes it difficult for parties to find common ground as a basis for cooperation. Moreover, for those parties that are vehicles to promote the political fortunes of individuals or small groups of politicians, there is further disincentive to seek cooperation. As a result, many Russian parties fail in what ought to be their primary goals: gaining control of the government and influencing policy. The concept of a ruling coalition of parties countered by opposition parties that envisage themselves as an alternative government has not yet taken hold in Russia. This has allowed the executive to dominate the legislature to a greater extent than would otherwise be the case.

When Vladimir Putin assumed the presidency, he expressed the view that there were too many parties in Russia. He supported a law aimed at creating a system of a few large parties. The law would require that a party, to be registered, have at least 10,000 members countrywide, with branch organizations of at least 100 people in no less than half of Russia's 89 regions. Certainly a law of this kind would result in fewer parties contesting elections, which many analysts and ordinary citizens see as necessary. But is this top-down dictation the way to achieve the goal? And can it help to create an institutionalized system of ruling coalition and opposition that Russia needs? For those in Russia who doubt Putin's intentions, believing that his aim is really the creation of a one-party state, such a law would be an unwelcome development. The better route would be a reduction in the number of parties through the enlightened cooperation of like-minded politicians.

The Role of the Media

The campaign for glasnost, initiated early in Mikhail Gorbachev's period as Soviet leader, was discussed in Chapter 1. Glasnost permitted the open discussion of many subjects formerly considered taboo, and ushered in a new phase in the development of the USSR. If the Kremlin leaders believed that they could control the process, however, they were quickly proven wrong. As journalists, historians, members of disaffected ethnic groups and others came to see the possibilities that glasnost offered, the regime's level of control was gradually subverted. The centrifugal force of glasnost, and the upheaval that it created across a number of facets of the Soviet system, were major factors in the USSR's demise.

In Richard Sakwa's view, the developments of the glasnost period "blossomed into genuine freedom of speech and press" in the early post-Soviet period (Sakwa 1993, 273). But the conditions that prevailed during this period were relatively short-lived. At many newspapers, senior staff were able to take over and run their papers as independent entities, while still receiving subsidies and other services from the state. But as privatization proceeded, and subsidies became less certain, many newspapers quickly found themselves in economic difficulty. A number of them ceased to exist, while others came under control of the government or that of financial or industrial groups. Thus, the print media were rather quickly subjected to new threats to their autonomy. In the case of television, the government maintained controlling interest in a number of stations, while a few of them managed to operate independently, albeit under the ownership of powerful financial interests (Belin 1997).

In connection with national elections, the media have not demonstrated a balanced record of coverage. This was particularly evident during the 1996 presidential election, when many business interests with media holdings sided strongly with Yeltsin. And there is agreement that regional media are generally even less free, as provincial authorities have utilized a variety of resources at their disposal to control the press (Andrusenko 2001, 1).

Vladimir Putin also enjoyed lopsided media support in his 2000 election victory. Since Putin assumed the presidency, moves against selected media oligarchs for alleged law violations have been made. The primary object of the authorities' recent attention has been Vladimir Gusinskii, whose major media outlet was NTV, Russia's only country-wide independent channel. In the spring of 2001 Gazprom, a state-owned gas company, succeeded in wresting control over NTV from Gusinskii, who had fled Russia for Spain to avoid criminal prosecution. The Gusinskii case caused a considerable public uproar, not because there was widespread sympathy for the oligarch but rather because the move against him was seen by many as a further effort at state control of the media.

A 2001 report on human rights practices in Russia, by the U.S. State Department, made a number of points about the state of press freedom. Here are some excerpts from that report:

> [During the year 2000] federal, regional and local governments continued to exert pressure on journalists by: initiating investigations...of media companies such as independent Media-Most; selectively denying access to information (including, for example, statistics theoretically available to the public) and filming opportunities; demanding the right to approve certain stories prior to publication; prohibiting the tape recording of public trials and hearings; withholding financial support from government media operations that exercised independent judgment; attempting to influence unduly the appointment of senior editors at regional and local newspapers and broadcast media organizations; and removing reporters from their jobs and bringing libel suits against them. The disappearance and subsequent arrest and prosecution of Radio Liberty reporter Andrei Babitskiy caused great concern, since there was credible evidence that the Babitsky case was politically motivated and that units of the Federal Government were involved in trying to silence critical reporting about the Chechen conflict. (U.S. Department of State, 2001)

In sum, pressure on the media has restricted its ability to speak with an independent voice. But the press and other communications outlets have not been forced into completely subservient roles. Newspapers have not been closed by the government, nor has formal censorship been imposed on print publications. And many journalists continue to criticize the government on a variety of issues. The open question appears to be about the ultimate intentions of the political leadership: how far will it go in attempting to impose its will? This applies both to the issue of press freedom and to the larger question of Russian democracy.

Political Leadership and Democracy
This section will examine political leadership narrowly defined, by concentrating on Russia's two presidents during the post-Soviet period, Boris Yeltsin and Vladimir Putin. The background and behavior in office of these two leaders will give insight into important aspects of Russia's

democratic development.

Boris Yeltsin unquestionably was, for a time, the most popular politician in Russia. The fact that he captured 89 percent of the vote when he won election to the USSR Congress of People's Deputies in 1989, and his easy first-round victory in Russia's first presidential election two years later, demonstrate the high level of public support that he enjoyed. And his courageous leadership of the anti-putsch forces in August 1991 only added to his stature. But this success in democratic (or at least semi-democratic) politics could hardly be expected to result in Yeltsin's automatic transformation into a democrat. The greater part of his political career was as an *apparatchik* in the Communist Party of the Soviet Union, a party that he did not leave until he was nearly 60. As a result, he was accustomed to the habits of bureaucratic-authoritarian politics, and less comfortable when operating in the milieu of electoral and parliamentary politics. His dealings with Parliament showed little appreciation of the importance of compromise and accommodation. He resorted extensively to executive decrees when parliamentary legislation would have been more appropriate. And, as pointed out more than once in this book, he violated the constitution in finally dismissing parliament, and called out the military to put down an uprising led by parliamentary and other opposition leaders. It is also true, of course, that many of Yeltsin's opponents, parliamentary and otherwise, were not models of democratic rectitude either. By and large they came from the same authoritarian mold as the president. Thus, when Yeltsin asserted that higher motives, namely, to save Russia from the imposition of a truly oppressive system, led him to resort to unconstitutional measures, a considerable number of Russians sided with him.

Yeltsin came to use the language of democracy, and on occasion spoke passionately in favor of freedom of the press (Aron 2000, 719–720). But behind the democratic rhetoric he often engaged in autocratic behavior. He never established a normal relationship with Parliament. Particularly during his second term in office, his effectiveness as a leader plummeted, along with his popularity. He was plagued by a variety of health problems that kept him from his duties for long periods of time. Yet he engaged in an irrational musical-chairs changing of prime ministers and other officials, in part to prevent any of them from gaining too much power. When he finally resigned at the end of 1999 he was a pathetic, sometimes clownish figure, far removed from the courageous and robust image that he had projected just a few years earlier.

Boris Yeltsin, then, was a true transition leader, who held a position near the top of the Soviet communist hierarchy before his time as president of an independent Russia. His built-in authoritarian impulses limited his ability to embrace democratic practices. Given these considerations, it would be unreasonable to expect a great deal more from him in advancing Russia's democratic development.

Vladimir Putin is literally of a different generation from Boris Yeltsin, having been born more than 20 years after the former president. He joined the Communist Party of the Soviet Union during his days as a law student at Leningrad State University, but never held an important party position. What sets Putin apart from most Russian politicians, and engenders suspicion about the prospect of his pursuing genuine democratic goals, is the career path he chose as a young man. Putin sought employment in the Soviet secret police, the KGB, while still in his teens, and joined the organization upon completion of law school. He served 16 years in "the organs," including about five years in East Germany. Putin resigned from the KGB at age 39, in 1991, the year the USSR fell. Eight years later Yeltsin named him prime minister, and barely four months after that Putin took over as acting president upon Yeltsin's resignation.

Peter Rutland believes that in spite of their age difference, Putin shares with Yeltsin (and others who spent years in the Soviet-era apparatus) an important element of political style, a style more characteristic of the bureaucrat than the democrat. This is an inclination to use "informal political networks" or, less kindly, "backroom deals," in handling affairs of state. Rutland asserts that one of Putin's main tasks as president will be to overcome this tendency by emphasizing formal institutional practices, not only in managing the presidency but in state administration in general (Rutland 2000, 317).

In a revealing self-portrait published in 2000, based on a series of interviews by three Russian journalists, Putin makes a number of comments about his career. The chapter on his years in East Germany is entitled "The Spy." But the next chapter, about his turn to politics in 1991, first in St.

Petersburg and then in Moscow, is called "The Democrat," which is the image that he now seeks to cultivate.

But how credible are Putin's democratic declarations? In his last interview, Anatolii Sobchak, Putin's mentor in St. Petersburg and the late former mayor of the city, affirmed Putin's strongly held democratic convictions (Sobchak 2000, 93–94). And Putin himself has repeatedly asserted his support for democracy. When asked in 2000, for instance, whether Russia was destined to pursue a "special path," he replied that Russia's course had already been charted: "It's the path of democratic development. Of course, Russia is a very diverse country, but we are part of Western European culture. No matter where our people live, in the Far East or in the south, we are Europeans" (Putin 2000, 169).

Like Yeltsin, Putin has become adept at employing the rhetoric of democracy. Whether his actions will confirm his words is a matter that remains to be seen, as Putin proceeds through his presidency. As already suggested, his election as president in March 2000 was to some extent discredited by allegations of fraud and media manipulation. These problems aside, to say that Putin's accession to the presidency amounted to a "democratic transfer of power" akin to what regularly takes place in the West, as some have suggested, surely overstates the case. Putin was the hand-picked successor of the incumbent president, and gained a significant advantage over rivals by having served as prime minister and then acting president just prior to his election.

In the presidency, Putin's record has been a mixed one. While professing interest in media freedom, many of his statements suggest a belief that the journalist's role is to support the state. The restrictions contained in his proposed new law on political parties were matched by a government policy adopted in 2000 that required all nongovernmental organizations (NGOs) to re-register. The effect of this measure was to limit the number of such bodies given government approval ("Russian Democracy Under Threat" 2000). This is one of the ways that the government has employed superficially lawful means to achieve questionable ends, in this case restricting the activities of human rights and other organizations and limiting the development of civil society.

Putin's efforts to reassert firmer control over the country's regions were discussed in Chapter 7. Fewer objections have been made to these measures than to some of the other Putin initiatives, since there is a widespread feeling in the country that central authority was badly eroded in the 1990s. Again, however, much depends upon how far Moscow intends to go in reining in the regions. A proposed move to replace elected governors with administrators appointed by the president could not only greatly weaken Russian federalism, but could also create a system of control somewhat akin to Communist Party administration during the Soviet period.

Does the renewed war in Chechnya, a centerpiece of Putin's domestic policy, reflect negatively on Russian democracy? This is a complicated question. Do messy and brutal military actions by established democracies (the United States in Vietnam or France in Algeria, for instance) render these countries undemocratic? The Russian government claims that it is carrying out a fight against terrorism, in response to acts committed outside of Chechnya by Chechen warlords. Moreover, public support for the government's actions since the resumption of fighting in 1999 has remained high. International criticism of Russia's operations in Chechnya has grown, however. And it is likely that Elena Bonner, the widow of Andrei Sakharov, speaks for many in Russia in asserting that "Russia has lost its new-born democracy" as a result of the Chechnya wars (Bonner 2001, 5).

Conclusion

This chapter began with a discussion of the Russian system as a "democracy with a qualifier" ("controlled democracy," "incomplete democracy," "delegative democracy," etc.). As the chapter's subsequent analysis demonstrated, there is much to support a conditional view of what Russia has accomplished in moving toward popular rule: the country is not there yet, and there is concern that it may slide back toward some more authoritarian form of government. A central factor in the picture is the role of the state. Those who advocate its strengthening see a powerful state as necessary to combat the chaos and lack of order that has characterized Russia in recent years. Critics assert that the machinery of state is responsible for many of the anti-democratic features now found in Russia, and that a more powerful state will only magnify these problems.

What of the view of the Russian people? Survey after survey has shown that Russians crave order for their society. To suggest, however, that this means they opt for dictatorship over democracy is what Rutland calls "a false polarity." A close look at the polls shows that order means respect for law, and complements high popular support for human rights and elections. The order that rates high with the people is not necessarily inimical to democratic values (Rutland 2000, 345). To be responsive to the popular will, Russian leaders will need to remain accountable to the people while achieving the order in society that they demand. It is a good bet that this goal will not be easily or quickly accomplished.

Which brings up two final points, about the appropriate time frame for assessing Russia's democratic development and the effect of Russia's supposed uniqueness on that process. Is it reasonable to judge the present state of Russian democracy against that which has long existed in the leading democracies of the West? If it is, then Russia should have a full-blown democracy by now. Or is it fairer to evaluate Russia at present against the background of the Russia of 10 or 15 years ago? In my mind the latter framework yields a more reasonable perspective for calculating Russia's democratic prospects. Rational judgments require reasonable expectations, and surely Russia deserves a longer time perspective than a decade to get its political house in order. As the late Alexander Dallin commented, it is common for countries in transition to go through extended periods of unconsolidated democracy, during which time authoritarian setbacks often take place (Dallin 1995, 261). As for Russia's uniqueness, and its supposed effects on the country's development, my view concurs with that of Martin Malia: Russia is not "somehow apart from modern history—it is merely a variant of certain general European phenomena" (Malia 1991, 95). As the post-World War II history of several European countries, including France, Italy and Spain, well demonstrates, the road to stable democracy is neither straight nor without occasional reversals. Russia in transition is likely to face further challenges to its incomplete democracy for some time to come.

References

Adelman, Jonathan R. 1995. *Torrents of Spring: Soviet and Post-Soviet Politics*. New York: McGraw-Hill.

Andrusenko, Lidiia. 2001. "Pechat' vsegda prazdnuet svoi den' vmeste s vlast'iu." *Nezavisimaia gazeta* (January 13, 1).

Aron, Leon. 2000. *Yeltsin: A Revolutionary Life*. New York: St. Martin's Press.

Barber, Benjamin R. 1998. *A Passion for Democracy: American Essays*. Princeton, NJ: Princeton University Press.

Beetham, David. 1993. "Liberal Democracy and the Limits of Democratization." In *Prospects for Democracy: North, South, East, West*, ed. David Held. Stanford, CA: Stanford University Press.

Belin, Laura. 1997. "Politicization And Self-Censorship In The Russian Media."Paper published by Radio Free Europe/Radio Liberty, http://www. rferl.org/nca/special/rumediapaper/index.html.

Black, Eric. 1999. "Russia's Heritage Sets It Apart; 'Not For Us' Are Western ways." *Star Tribune* (Minneapolis, MN), October 29.

Bonner, Elena. 2001. "The Remains of Totalitarianism." *New York Review of Books*, 48: 4, March 8.

Dallin, Alexander. 1995. "Where Have All the Flowers Gone?" In *The New Russia: Troubled Transformation*, ed. Gail W. Lapidus. Boulder, CO: Westview Press.

Dawisha, Karen. 1997. "Democratization and Political Participation: Research Concepts and Methodologies." In *Democratic Changes and Authoritarian Reactions in Russia, Ukraine, Belarus, and Moldova*, eds. Karen Dawisha and Bruce Parrott. Cambridge: Cambridge University Press.

Diamond, Larry. 1996. "Toward Democratic Consolidation." In *The Global Resurgence of Democracy*, Second Edition, eds. Larry Diamond and Marc F. Plattner. Baltimore, MD: Johns Hopkins University Press.

Fedorov, Yuri. 2000. *Democratization and Globalization: The Case of Russia* (Working Paper Number 13, Democracy and Rule of Law Project). Washington, DC: Carnegie Endowment for International Peace.

Gaidar, Yegor. 2001. "The Political and Economic Situation in

Russia." (Remarks at the Carnegie Endowment for International Peace, January 29, 2001), http://www.ceip.org/files/events/gaidar.asp.

Green, Philip. 1998. *Equality and Democracy*. New York: The New Press.

Held, David. 1995. *Democracy and the Global Order*. Stanford, CA: Stanford University Press.

Huntington, Samuel P. 1991. *The Third Wave: Democratization in the Late Twentieth Century*. Norman, OK: University of Oklahoma Press.

Kara-Murza, Alexey A. 2000. "Russian Democracy versus Russian Barbarism." *Russia Watch*, 4:16–17, www.ksg.harvard.edu/bcsia/sdi.

Kelly, Aileen. 1998. "When Russians Look Inward." *The New York Times*, September 6, 11.

LeDuc, Lawrence, Richard G. Niemi, and Pippa Norris. 1996. "Introduction: The Present and Future of Democratic Elections." In *Comparing Democracies: Elections and Voting in Global Perspective*, eds. Lawrence LeDuc, Richard G. Niemi, and Pippa Norris. Thousand Oaks, CA: Sage Publications.

Lijphart, Arend. 1984. *Democracies: Patterns of Majoritarian and Consensus Government in Twenty-One Countries*. New Haven, CT: Yale University Press.

Lukin, Alexander 2000. *The Political Culture of the Russian "Democrats"*. Oxford: Oxford University Press.

Malia, Martin. 1991. "Soviet Democracy and Soviet History." In *After Perestroika: Democracy in the Soviet Union*, eds. Brad Roberts and Nina Belyaeva. Washington, DC: The Center for Strategic and International Studies.

McDaniel, Tim. 1996. *The Agony of the Russian Idea*. Princeton, NJ: Princeton University Press.

Petro, Nicolai. 1995. *The Rebirth of Russian Democracy*. Cambridge, MA: Harvard University Press.

Piontkovsky, Andrei. 2001. "Letter from a German Friend." *The Russia Journal* (January 20–26), http://www.russiajournal.com.

Powell, G. Bingham, Jr. 2000. *Elections as Instruments of Democracy*. New Haven, CT: Yale University Press.

Przeworski, Adam. 1991. *Democracy and the Market: Political and*

Economic Reforms in Eastern Europe and Latin America. Cambridge: Cambridge University Press.

Putin, Vladimir. 1999. "Russia at the Turn of the Millennium." (The Government of the Russian Federation web site), http://www.pravitelstvo.gov.ru/english/statVP-engl-1.html.

Putin, Vladimir. 2000. *First Person.* New York: Public Affairs.

Reddaway, Peter and Dmitri Glinski. 2000. *The Tragedy of Russia's Reforms: Market Bolshevism Against Democracy.* Herndon, VA: United States Institute of Peace.

"Russian Democracy Under Threat." 2000. *News Release* (Radio Free Europe/Radio Liberty), October 24, http://www.rferl.org/welcome/english/releases//2000/10/6-241000.html.

"Russian 'Elite' Nearly Evenly Split as to How Russia Should Develop–Poll." 2000. Interfax release, October 27. *Johnson's Russia List*, 4625, October 28.

Rutland, Peter. 2000. "Putin's Rise to Power." *Post-Soviet Affairs* 16: 313–354.

Sakwa, Richard. 1993. *Russian Politics and Society.* London: Routledge.

Schmitter, Philippe C. and Terry Lynn Karl. 1996. "What Democracy Is…and Is Not." In *The Global Resurgence of Democracy,* Second Edition, eds. Larry Diamond and Marc F. Plattner. Baltimore, MD: Johns Hopkins University Press.

Sobchak, Anatolii. 2000. "He Knew How to Make Himself Replaceable." *Literaturnaia gazeta* (23–29 February, 3), published in *Russian Politics and Law*, 38:5.

Sørensen, Georg. 1998. *Democracy and Democratization: Processes and Prospects in a Changing World.* Boulder, CO: Westview Press.

"Summary." 2000. In *Russia in the Course of 1999–2000 Election Cycle,* eds. M. McFaul, N. Petrov, A. Riabov, http://pubs.carnegie.ru/english/books/2999/09np/toc.asp.

U.S. Department of State. 2001. "Russia: Country Reports on Human Rights Practices–2000." *Johnson's Russia List*, 5119, February 27.

Zinovyev, A. 2000. "President: Mission Impossible." *Vek*, 30. *Johnson's Russia List*, 4441 August 6.

Appendix A
The Constitution of the Russian Federation

(Adopted December 12, 1993 by national referendum)

We, the multinational people of the Russian Federation, united by a common destiny on our land, asserting human rights and liberties, civil peace and accord, preserving the historic unity of the state, proceeding from the commonly recognized principles of equality and self-determination of the peoples honoring the memory of our ancestors, who have passed on to us love of and respect for our homeland and faith in good and justice, reviving the sovereign statehood of Russia and asserting the firmness of its democratic foundation, striving to secure the well-being and prosperity of Russia and proceeding from a sense of responsibility for our homeland before present and future generations, and being aware of ourselves as part of the world community, hereby adopt the Constitution of the Russian Federation.

SECTION ONE

Chapter 1. The Fundamentals of the Constitutional System

Article 1.
The Russian Federation–Russia shall be a democratic federal rule-of-law state with a republican form of government. The names "Russian Federation" and "Russia" shall be equivalent.

Article 2.
The person, his rights and freedoms shall be the supreme value. It shall be a duty of the state to recognize, respect and protect the rights and freedoms of the person and citizen.

Article 3.
1. The multinational people of the Russian Federation shall be the vehicle of sovereignty and the only source of power in the Russian Federation.

2. The people of the Russian Federation shall exercise their power directly, and also through organs of state power and local self-government.
3. The referendum and free elections shall be the supreme direct manifestation of the power of the people.
4. No one may usurp power in the Russian Federation. The seizure of power or the misappropriation of authority shall be prosecuted under federal law.

Article 4.
1. The sovereignty of the Russian Federation shall apply to its entire territory.
2. The Constitution of the Russian Federation and federal laws shall have supremacy throughout the entire territory of the Russian Federation.
3. The Russian Federation shall ensure the integrity and inviolability of its territory.

Article 5.
1. The Russian Federation shall consist of republics, territories, regions, federal cities, an autonomous region and autonomous areas, which shall be equal subjects of the Russian Federation.
2. A republic (state) shall have its own constitution and legislation. A territory, region, federal city, autonomous region or autonomous area shall have its own charter and legislation.
3. The federated structure of the Russian Federation shall be based on its state integrity, a uniform system of state power, a division of the scope of authority and power between the bodies of state power of the Russian Federation and the bodies of state power of the subjects of the Russian Federation, and the equality and self-determination of the peoples in the Russian Federation.
4. All the subjects of the Russian Federation shall be equal in relations with the federal bodies of state power.

Article 6.
1. Citizenship of the Russian Federation shall be acquired and terminated in accordance with federal law, and shall be one and equal irrespective of

the grounds on which it has been acquired.
2. Every citizen of the Russian Federation shall enjoy all rights and freedoms on its territory and perform equal duties, as provided for by the Constitution of the Russian Federation.
3. A citizen of the Russian Federation may not be deprived of citizenship or of the right to change it.

Article 7.
1. The Russian Federation shall be a social state, whose policies shall be aimed at creating conditions that ensure a dignified life and free development of the person.
2. The Russian Federation shall protect the work and health of its people, establish a guaranteed minimum wage, provide state support for family, motherhood, fatherhood and childhood, and also for the disabled and for elderly citizens, develop a system of social services and establish government pensions, benefits and other social security guarantees.

Article 8.
1. Unity of economic space, free movement of goods, services and financial resources, support for competition and freedom of any economic activity shall be guaranteed in the Russian Federation.
2. Private, state, municipal and other forms of ownership shall be recognized and shall enjoy equal protection in the Russian Federation.

Article 9.
1. The land and other natural resources shall be used and protected in the Russian Federation as the basis of the life and activity of the peoples living on their respective territories.
2. The land and other natural resources may be in private, state, municipal and other forms of ownership.

Article 10.
State power in the Russian Federation shall be exercised on the basis of the separation of the legislative, executive and judicial branches. The bodies

of legislative, executive and judicial power shall be independent.

Article 11.
1. State power in the Russian Federation shall be exercised by the President of the Russian Federation, the Federal Assembly (Federation Council and State Duma), the Government of the Russian Federation and courts of the Russian Federation.
2. State power in the subjects of the Russian Federation shall be exercised by the organs of state authority formed by them.
3. The division of authority and power between the bodies of state authority of the Russian Federation and the bodies of state authority of the subjects of the Russian Federation shall be established by this Constitution, and Federal and other treaties on the division of authority and power.

Article 12.
Local self-government shall be recognized and guaranteed in the Russian Federation. Local self-government shall operate independently within the bounds of its authority. The bodies of local self-government shall not be part of the state power bodies.

Article 13.
1. Ideological diversity shall be recognized in the Russian Federation.
2. No ideology may be instituted as a state-sponsored or mandatory ideology.
3. Political diversity and a multiparty system shall be recognized in the Russian Federation.
4. Public associations shall be equal before the law.
5. The establishment and the activities of public associations, whose aims and actions are directed at the forcible alteration of the fundamentals of constitutional governance and the violation of the integrity of the Russian Federation, the undermining of the security of the state, the forming of armed units, the incitement of social, racial, national and religious strife shall be prohibited.

Article 14.
1. The Russian Federation shall be a secular state. No religion may be

instituted as a state-sponsored or mandatory religion.

2. Religious associations shall be separated from the state, and shall be equal before the law.

Article 15.

1. The Constitution of the Russian Federation shall have supreme legal force and direct effect, and shall be applicable throughout the entire territory of the Russian Federation. Laws and other legal acts adopted by the Russian Federation may not contravene the Constitution of the Russian Federation.

2. Organs of state power, organs of local self-government, officials, citizens and their associations must comply with the Constitution and laws of the Russian Federation.

3. Laws shall be officially published. Unpublished laws shall not be applicable. No regulatory legal act affecting the rights, freedoms or duties of the person and citizen may apply unless it has been published officially for the information of the general public.

4. The commonly recognized principles and norms of international law and international treaties of the Russian Federation shall be component parts of its legal system. If an international treaty of the Russian Federation establishes rules that differ from those stipulated by a law, the rules of the international treaty shall apply.

Article 16.

1. The provisions of the present chapter of the Constitution shall be the foundations of the constitutional system of the Russian Federation and may not be changed except as provided for in this Constitution.

2. No other provisions of this Constitution may contravene the foundations of the constitutional system of the Russian Federation.

CHAPTER 2. Rights and Freedoms of the Person and Citizen

Article 17.

1. In the Russian Federation the rights and freedoms of the person and citizen are recognized and guaranteed according to the universally recognized principles and norms of international law and this Constitution.

2. The basic rights and freedoms of a person shall be inalienable and shall belong to everyone from birth.

3. The exercise of rights and freedoms of a person and citizen may not violate the rights and freedoms of other persons.

Article 18.

The rights and freedoms of a person and citizen shall have direct effect. They shall determine the meaning, content and application of the laws, and the activities of the legislative and executive branches and local self-government, and shall be secured by the judiciary.

Article 19.

1. All people shall be equal before the law and in a court.

2. The state shall guarantee the equality of rights and freedoms regardless of sex, race, nationality, language, origin, property or employment status, residence, attitude toward religion, opinions, membership in public associations, or any other circumstance. Any restrictions of the rights of citizens on social, racial, national, linguistic or religious grounds shall be forbidden.

3. Man and woman shall have equal rights and freedoms and equal opportunities to exercise them.

Article 20.

1. Everyone shall have the right to life.

2. Capital punishment may, until its abolition, be instituted by the federal law as exceptional punishment for especially grave crimes against life, with the accused having the right to have his case considered in a court with the participation of a jury.

Article 21.

1. The dignity of the person shall be protected by the state. No circumstance may be used as a pretext for demeaning it.

2. No one may be subjected to torture, violence or any other harsh or humiliating treatment or punishment. No one may be subjected to medical, scientific or other experiments without his or her free consent.

Article 22.
1. Everyone shall have the right to freedom and personal inviolability.
2. Arrest, detention and keeping in custody shall be allowed only by an order of a court. No person may be detained for more than 48 hours without an order of a court.

Article 23.
1. Everyone shall have the right to privacy, to personal and family secrets, and to the protection of one's honor and good name.
2. Everyone shall have the right to privacy of correspondence, telephone communications, mail, cables and other communications. Any restriction of this right shall be allowed only by an order of a court.

Article 24.
1. It shall be forbidden to gather, store, use and disseminate information on the private life of any person without his/her consent.
2. The bodies of state authority and the bodies of local self-government and the officials thereof shall provide to each citizen access to any documents and materials directly affecting his/her rights and freedoms unless otherwise stipulated by law.

Article 25.
The home shall be inviolable. No one shall have the right to enter the home against the will of persons residing in it except in cases provided for by federal law or under an order of a court.

Article 26.
Everyone shall have the right to determine and state his national identity. No one can be forced to determine and state his national identity. Everyone shall have the right to use his (her) native language, and to a free choice of the language of communication, education, training and creative work.

Article 27.
1. Everyone who is legally staying on the territory of the Russian Federation shall have the right to freedom of movement and to choose a place to stay and reside.

2. Everyone shall be free to leave the boundaries of the Russian Federation. The citizens of the Russian Federation shall have the right freely to return to the Russian Federation.

Article 28.
Everyone shall be guaranteed the right to freedom of conscience, to freedom of religious worship, including the right to profess, individually or jointly with others, any religion, or to profess no religion, to freely choose, possess and disseminate religious or other beliefs, and to act in conformity with them.

Article 29.
1. Everyone shall have the right to freedom of thought and speech.
2. Propaganda or campaigning inciting social, racial, national or religious hatred and strife is impermissible. The propaganda of social, racial, national, religious or language superiority is forbidden.
3. No one may be coerced into expressing one's views and convictions or into renouncing them.
4. Everyone shall have the right to seek, get, transfer, produce and disseminate information by any lawful means. A list of information constituting state secrets shall be established by federal law.
5. Freedom of mass media shall be guaranteed. Censorship shall be prohibited.

Article 30.
1. Everyone shall have the right to association, including the right to create trade unions in order to protect one's interests. Freedom of action for public associations shall be guaranteed.
2. No one may be forced either to join or to remain in any association.

Article 31.
Citizens of the Russian Federation shall have the right to gather peacefully, without weapons, and to conduct meetings, rallies, demonstrations, marches and picketing.

Article 32.
1. Citizens of the Russian Federation shall have the right to participate in

the administration of the affairs of state, both directly and through their representatives.

2. Citizens of the Russian Federation shall have the right to elect and to be elected to bodies of state governance and to organs of local self-government, as well as take part in referendums.

3. Citizens who have been found by a court to be incompetent, and also citizens placed in detention under a court verdict, shall not have the right to elect or to be elected.

4. Citizens of the Russian Federation shall have equal access to state service.

5. Citizens of the Russian Federation shall have the right to participate in administering justice.

Article 33.

Citizens of the Russian Federation shall have the right to turn personally to, and send individual and collective petitions to, state bodies and bodies of local self-government.

Article 34.

1. Everyone shall have the right freely to use his or her abilities and property for entrepreneurial or any other economic activity not prohibited by the law.

2. No economic activity aimed at monopolization or unfair competition shall be allowed.

Article 35.

1. The right of private property shall be protected by law.

2. Everyone shall have the right to have property in his or her ownership, to possess, use and manage it either individually or jointly with other persons.

3. No one may be arbitrarily deprived of his or her property except on the basis of a decision by a court. Property can be forcibly taken for state needs only on the basis of prior and just compensation.

4. The right of inheritance shall be guaranteed.

Article 36.

1. Citizens and their associations shall have the right to have land in private ownership.

2. The possession, use and management of land and other natural resources

shall be freely exercised by its owners, provided that this does not cause damage to the environment or infringe upon the rights and interests of other persons.

3. The terms and procedures for the use of land shall be determined on the basis of federal laws.

Article 37.

1. Labor shall be free. Everyone shall have the right to make free use of his or her abilities to work and to choose a type of activity and occupation.

2. Forced labor shall be prohibited.

3. Everyone shall have the right to work under conditions meeting the requirements of safety and hygiene, to remuneration for work without any discrimination whatsoever, at a rate of payment not below the statutory minimum, and also the right to security against unemployment.

4. The right to have individual and collective labor disputes resolved by means established by federal law, including the right to strike, shall be recognized.

5. Everyone shall have the right to rest and leisure. A person having a work contract shall be guaranteed the statutory duration of the work time, days off and holidays, and paid annual vacation.

Article 38.

1. Motherhood and childhood, and the family shall be under state protection.

2. Care for children and their upbringing shall be both the right and duty of parents.

3. Employable children who have reached 18 years old shall care for their non-employable parents.

Article 39.

1. Everyone shall be guaranteed social security in old age, in case of illness, invalidism, the loss of a breadwinner, for bringing up children, and in other cases established by law.

2. State pensions and social benefits shall be established by law.

3. Voluntary social insurance and the development of additional forms of social security and charity shall be encouraged.

Article 40.
1. Everyone shall have the right to a home. No one may be arbitrarily deprived of a home.
2. State bodies and organs of local self-government shall encourage home construction and create conditions for the realization of the right to a home.
3. The needy and other citizens designated by law who are in need of housing shall be provided housing free of charge or at reasonable rates from state, municipal and other housing funds in conformity with norms established by law.

Article 41.
1. Everyone shall have the right to health care and medical assistance. Medical assistance shall be made available free of charge in state and municipal health care institutions to citizens, the cost to be covered by funds from the relevant budget, insurance payments, and other revenues.
2. The Russian Federation shall finance federal health care and health-building programs, take measures to develop state, municipal and private health care systems, encourage activities contributing to the strengthening of a person's health, to the development of physical culture and sport, and to ecological, sanitary and epidemiologic welfare.
3. Concealment by officials of facts and circumstances posing hazards to human life and health shall involve liability in conformity with federal law.

Article 42.
Everyone shall have the right to a favorable environment, reliable information about its condition and to compensation for damage caused to his or her health or property by ecological violations.

Article 43.
1. Everyone shall have the right to education.
2. Openly accessible preschool, general secondary and vocational secondary education in public and municipal educational institutions and enterprises shall be guaranteed free of charge.
3. Everyone shall have the right to receive, free of charge and on a competitive basis, higher education in a state or municipal educational institution or enterprise.

4. Basic general education shall be mandatory. Parents or persons substituting for them shall make provision for their children to receive basic general education.

5. The Russian Federation shall institute federal state educational standards and support various forms of education and self-education.

Article 44.
1. Everyone shall be guaranteed freedom of literary, artistic, scientific, intellectual and other types of creative activity and instruction. Intellectual property shall be protected by law.
2. Everyone shall have the right to participate in cultural life, to use the institutions of culture, and to have access to cultural values.
3. Everyone shall care for the preservation of the historic and cultural heritage and safeguard landmarks of history and culture.

Article 45.
1. State protection for human rights and freedoms in the Russian Federation shall be guaranteed.
2. Everyone shall have the right to defend his or her rights and freedoms by any means not prohibited by law.

Article 46.
1. Everyone shall be guaranteed protection of his or her rights and freedoms in a court.
2. The decisions and actions (or inaction) of state organs, organs of local self-government, public associations and officials may be appealed in a court.
3. In conformity with the international treaties of the Russian Federation, everyone shall have the right to turn to interstate organs concerned with the protection of human rights and freedoms when all means of legal protection available within the state have been exhausted.

Article 47.
1. No one may be denied the right to have his or her case heard by the court and the judge under whose jurisdiction the case is placed by law.
2. Anyone charged with a crime has the right to have his or her case reviewed by a court, with the participation of jurors in cases stipulated by federal law.

Article 48.
1. Everyone shall be guaranteed the right to qualified legal counsel. Legal counsel shall be provided free of charge in cases provided by law.
2. Every person who has been detained, taken into custody, or charged with a crime shall have the right to legal counsel (a defense attorney) from the moment of being detained, taken into custody, or charged.

Article 49.
1. Any person accused of committing a crime shall be considered innocent until his or her guilt has been proven in conformity with the procedures stipulated by federal law and established by the sentence of a court that has entered into legal force.
2. The defendant shall not be obliged to prove his or her innocence.
3. The benefit of doubt shall be interpreted in favor of the defendant.

Article 50.
1. No one may be convicted twice for the same offense.
2. In the administration of justice no evidence obtained in violation of the federal law shall be permitted.
3. Everyone sentenced for a crime shall have the right to have the sentence reviewed by a higher court according to the procedure instituted by federal law, and also the right to plead for clemency or mitigation of punishment.

Article 51.
1. No one shall be obliged to give evidence against oneself, or against one's spouse or one's close relatives (the definition of which to be established by federal law).
2. The federal law may stipulate other exemptions from the obligation to give evidence.

Article 52.
The rights of victims of crimes and abuses of power shall be protected by the law. The state shall guarantee the victims access to justice and compensation for damage sustained.

Article 53.
Everyone shall have the right to compensation by the state for damage

caused by the unlawful actions (or inaction) of state organs or their officials.

Article 54.
1. A law that introduces or increases liability shall have no retroactive force.
2. No one may be held liable for an action which was not regarded as an offense when it was committed. If, after the offense has been committed, the extent of liability is lifted or mitigated, the new law shall apply.

Article 55.
1. The enumeration of basic rights and freedoms in the Constitution of the Russian Federation shall not be interpreted as denial or diminution of the other universally recognized rights and freedoms of the person and citizen.
2. No laws that abolish or diminish the rights and freedoms of the person and citizen may be adopted in the Russian Federation.
3. The rights and freedoms of the person and citizen may be limited by federal law only to the extent required for the protection of the fundamentals of the constitutional system, morality, health, rights and lawful interests of other persons, and for ensuring the defense of the country and the security of the state.

Article 56.
1. Under conditions of a state of emergency, in order to ensure the safety of citizens and the protection of the constitutional order, and in accordance with federal constitutional law, certain restrictions may be imposed on rights and freedoms, along with an indication of the limits and period of operation during which the restrictions are to operate.
2. A state of emergency throughout the territory of the Russian Federation and in individual areas thereof may be introduced in the circumstances and in conformity with the procedures defined by federal constitutional law.
3. The rights and freedoms stipulated by Articles 20, 21, 23 (part 1), 24, 28, 34 (part 1), 40 (part 1), 46–54 of the Constitution of the Russian Federation shall not be subject to restriction.

Article 57.
Everyone shall pay lawful taxes and fees. Laws introducing new taxes or worsening the situation of taxpayers shall not have retroactive force.

Article 58.
Everyone shall be obliged to preserve nature and the environment, and to treat natural resources with care.

Article 59.
1. Defense of the homeland shall be a duty and obligation of the citizen of the Russian Federation.
2. The citizen of the Russian Federation shall do military service in conformity with federal law.
3. The citizen of the Russian Federation whose convictions and faith are at odds with military service, and also in other cases stipulated by federal law, shall have the right to replace it with alternative civilian service.

Article 60.
A citizen of the Russian Federation may fully exercise all of his or her legal rights and duties upon reaching the age of 18.

Article 61.
1. A citizen of the Russian Federation may not be deported from Russia or extradited to another state.
2. The Russian Federation shall guarantee its citizens defense and protection beyond its borders.

Article 62.
1. The citizen of the Russian Federation may have citizenship of a foreign state (dual citizenship) in conformity with federal law or an international treaty of the Russian Federation.
2. Possession of the citizenship of a foreign state by the citizen of the Russian Federation shall not diminish his or her rights and freedoms or exempt him or her from the duties stemming from Russian citizenship, unless otherwise stipulated by federal law or an international treaty of the Russian Federation.
3. Foreign citizens and stateless persons in the Russian Federation shall enjoy the rights and bear the obligations of its citizens, except in those cases provided for by federal law or an international treaty of the Russian Federation.

Article 63.
1. The Russian Federation shall grant political asylum to foreign citizens and stateless citizens in conformity with the universally recognized norms of the international law.
2. The extradition to other states of persons persecuted for their political views or any actions (or inaction) which are not qualified as criminal by the law of the Russian Federation shall not be allowed in the Russian Federation. The extradition of persons charged with crimes and also the surrender of convicts to serve sentences in other countries shall be effected on the basis of federal law or an international treaty of the Russian Federation.

Article 64.
The provisions of these articles form the basis of personal rights in the Russian Federation and may not be changed other than by the means set forth in this Constitution.

Chapter 3. The Russian Federation

Article 65.
1. The Russian Federation shall consist of the subjects of the Federation: Republic of Adygeya (Adygeya), Republic of Altai, Republic of Bashkortostan, Republic of Buryatia, Republic of Dagestan, Ingush Republic, Kabardin-Balkar Republic, Republic of Kalmykia–Khalmg Tangch, Karachayevo-Cherkess Republic, Republic of Karelia, Republic of Komi, Republic of Mari El, Republic of Mordovia, Republic of Sakha (Yakutia), Republic of North Ossetia, Republic of Tatarstan (Tatarstan), Republic of Tuva, Udmurt Republic, Republic of Khakasia, Chechen Republic, Chuvash Republic–Chavash Republics;

Altai Territory, Krasnodar Territory, Krasnoyarsk Territory, Maritime Territory, Stavropol Territory, Khabarovsk Territory;

Amur Region, Arkhangelsk Region, Astrakhan Region, Belgorod Region, Bryansk Region, Vladimir Region, Volgograd Region, Vologda Region, Voronezh Region, Ivanovo Region, Irkutsk Region, Kaliningrad Region, Kaluga Region, Kamchatka Region, Kemerovo Region, Kirov Region, Kostroma Region, Kurgan Region, Kursk Region, Leningrad Region, Lipetsk Region, Magadan Region, Moscow Region, Murmansk Region,

Nizhny Novgorod Region, Novgorod Region, Novosibirsk Region, Omsk Region, Orenburg Region, Oryol Region, Penza Region, Perm Region, Pskov Region, Rostov Region, Ryazan Region, Samara Region, Saratov Region, Sakhalin Region, Sverdlovsk Region, Smolensk Region, Tambov Region, Tver Region, Tomsk Region, Tula Region, Tyumen Region, Ulyanovsk Region, Chelyabinsk Region, Chita Region, Yaroslavl Region;

Moscow, St. Petersburg—federal cities;

Jewish Autonomous Region;

Aginsky Buryat Autonomous Area, Komi-Permyak Autonomous Area, Koryak Autonomous Area, Nenets Autonomous Area, Taimyr (Dolgan-Nenets) Autonomous Area, Ust-Ordynsky Buryat Autonomous Area, Khanty-Mansi Autonomous Area, Chukchi Autonomous Area, Evenk Autonomous Area, Yamal-Nenets Autonomous Area.

2. Admission to the Russian Federation and the formation of a new subject of the Russian Federation shall be carried out according to the procedure established by federal constitutional law.

Article 66.
1. The status of a republic shall be defined by the Constitution of the Russian Federation and the constitution of the republic in question.
2. The status of a territory, region, federal city, autonomous region and autonomous area shall be determined by the Constitution of the Russian Federation and the Charter of the territory, region, city of federal importance, autonomous region, or autonomous area, adopted by the legislative (representative) body of the relevant subject of the Russian Federation.
3. A federal law on an autonomous region or autonomous area may be adopted upon a petition from the legislative and executive bodies of an autonomous region or autonomous area.
4. Relations between autonomous areas within a territory or region may be regulated by federal law and an agreement between bodies of state power of the autonomous and, correspondingly, bodies of state power of the territory or the region.
5. The status of a subject of the Russian Federation may be changed only with the mutual consent of the Russian Federation and the subject of the

Russian Federation in accordance with federal constitutional law.

Article 67.
1. The territory of the Russian Federation shall incorporate the territories of its subjects, the internal and territorial seas and the air space over them.
2. The Russian Federation shall have sovereign rights and exercise jurisdiction on the continental shelf and in the exclusive economic zone of the Russian Federation under the procedure stipulated by federal law and the norms of international law.
3. The boundaries between the subjects of the Russian Federation may be changed by their mutual agreement.

Article 68.
1. The state language of the Russian Federation throughout its territory shall be the Russian language.
2. The republics shall have the right to institute their own state languages. They shall be used alongside the state language of the Russian Federation in bodies of state power, bodies of local self-government and state institutions of the republics.
3. The Russian Federation shall guarantee all its peoples the right to preserve their native language and to create the conditions for its study and development.

Article 69.
The Russian Federation guarantees the rights of small indigenous peoples in accordance with the generally accepted principles and standards of international law and international treaties of the Russian Federation.

Article 70.
1. The state flag, state emblem, and the national anthem, their description and the procedure for their official use shall be established by federal constitutional law.
2. The capital of the Russian Federation is the city of Moscow. The status of the capital shall be established by the federal law.

Article 71.
The jurisdiction of the Russian Federation shall include:

a) the adoption and amendment of the Constitution of the Russian Federation and federal laws and supervision over compliance with them;
b) the federal structure and territory of the Russian Federation;
c) regulation and protection of the rights and freedoms of the person and citizen; citizenship of the Russian Federation; regulation and protection of the rights of national minorities;
d) establishment of the system of federal bodies of legislative, executive and judicial power, procedure for the organization and activities thereof; formation of federal bodies of state power;
e) federal and state property and management thereof;
f) determining the basic principles of federal policy and federal programs in the field of state structure, the economy, the environment, and the social, cultural and national development of the Russian Federation;
g) establishment of the legal framework for a single market; financial, monetary, credit and customs regulation, emission of money and guidelines for price policy; federal economic services, including federal banks;
h) the federal budget; federal taxes and levies; federal funds of regional development;
i) federal power grids, nuclear energy, fissionable materials; federal transport, railways, information and communications; space activities;
j) foreign policy and international relations of the Russian Federation, international treaties of the Russian Federation; questions of war and peace;
k) foreign trade relations of the Russian Federation;
l) defense and security; defense production; determining procedures for the sale and purchase of arms, ammunition, military hardware and other equipment; production of fissionable materials, toxic substances, narcotics and procedure for the use thereof;
m) defining the status and protection of the state border, territorial waters, air space, the exclusive economic zone and the continental shelf of the Russian Federation;
n) court structure; the procuracy; criminal, criminal-procedural and criminal-executive legislation; amnesty and pardon; civil, civil-procedural and arbitration-procedural legislation; legal regulation of intellectual property;
o) federal conflict of laws;

p) meteorological service; standards, models, the metric system and time measurement; geodesy and cartography; names of geographical objects; official statistics and accounting;

q) state decorations and honorary titles of the Russian Federation;

r) federal state service.

Article 72.

1. The joint jurisdiction of the Russian Federation and the subjects of the Russian Federation shall include:

a) ensuring compliance of the constitutions and laws of the republics, charters, laws, and other regulatory legal acts of the territories, regions, federal cities, the autonomous region and autonomous areas with the Constitution of the Russian Federation and the federal laws;

b) protection of the rights and freedoms of the person and citizen, protection of the rights of ethnic minorities; ensuring legality, law and order, and public safety; border zone regime;

c) issues of the possession, use and management of the land, mineral resources, water and other natural resources;

d) delimitation of state property;

e) management of natural resources, protection of the environment and ecological safety; specially protected nature preserves; protection of historical and cultural monuments;

f) general questions of upbringing, education, science, culture, physical culture and sports;

g) coordination of health issues, protection of family, motherhood, fatherhood and childhood; social protection including social security;

h) implementing measures to combat catastrophes, natural disasters, epidemics and eliminating the consequences thereof;

i) establishing general guidelines for taxation and levies in the Russian Federation;

j) administrative, administrative-procedural, labor, family, housing, land, water and forestry legislation; legislation on the subsurface and environmental protection;

k) cadres of judicial and law-enforcement agencies; the bar, the notary system;

l) protection of the original environment and traditional way of life of small ethnic communities;

m) establishment of general principles of the organization of the system of bodies of state power and local self-government;

n) coordination of the international and external economic relations of the subjects of the Russian Federation, and compliance with the international treaties of the Russian Federation.

2. The provisions of this Article shall apply equally to the republics, territories, regions, federal cities, the autonomous region and autonomous areas.

Article 73.

Outside the limits of authority of the Russian Federation and the powers of the Russian Federation on issues within the joint jurisdiction of the Russian Federation and the subjects of the Russian Federation, the subjects of the Russian Federation shall exercise full state power.

Article 74.

1. No customs frontiers, duties, levies, or any other barriers to the free movement of goods, services, or financial means may be established on the territory of the Russian Federation.

2. Restrictions on the movement of goods and services may be established under federal law, if this is necessary for the protection of the people's safety, their lives and health, or the protection of the environment and cultural values.

Article 75.

1. The monetary unit of the Russian Federation shall be the ruble. Monetary emissions shall be the exclusive responsibility of the Central Bank of the Russian Federation. No other currencies may be issued in the Russian Federation.

2. The protection and stability of the ruble is the main function of the Central Bank of the Russian Federation, which it shall exercise independently from other bodies of state power.

3. The system of taxes levied to the federal budget and the general principles of taxation and levies in the Russian Federation shall be established by federal law.

4. State loans shall be issued in accordance with the procedure established by federal law and distributed on a voluntary basis.

Article 76.
1. On issues within the jurisdiction of the Russian Federation, federal constitutional laws and federal laws shall be adopted that have direct effect throughout the territory of the Russian Federation.
2. On matters within the joint jurisdiction of the Russian Federation and the subjects of the Russian Federation, federal laws shall be issued and in accordance with them laws and other regulatory legal acts of the subjects of the Russian Federation shall be adopted.
3. Federal laws may not contravene federal constitutional laws.
4. Outside the limits of authority of the Russian Federation and the joint jurisdiction of the Russian Federation and the subjects of the Russian Federation, republics, territories, regions, federal cities, autonomous regions and autonomous areas shall effect their own legal regulation, including the adoption of laws and other regulatory legal acts. Laws and other regulatory legal acts of the subjects of the Russian Federation may not contravene federal laws adopted in accordance with parts 1 and 2 of this Article. In the event of a contradiction between a federal law and any other act issued in the Russian Federation, the federal law shall apply.
5. In the event of a contradiction between the federal law and a regulatory legal act of a subject of the Russian Federation issued in accordance with part 4 of this Article, the regulatory legal act of the subject of the Russian Federation shall apply.

Article 77.
1. The system of state power bodies of the republics, territories, regions, federal cities, the autonomous region, and autonomous areas shall be established by the subjects of the Russian Federation independently in accordance with the basic principles of the constitutional system of the Russian Federation and general principles of the organization of legislative and executive bodies of power as envisaged by federal law.
2. Within the jurisdiction of the Russian Federation and the powers of the Russian Federation on issues within the joint jurisdiction of the Russian Federation and the subjects of the Russian Federation, the federal bodies

of executive power and bodies of executive power of the subjects of the Russian Federation shall form a single system of executive power in the Russian Federation.

Article 78.
1. To exercise their powers, the federal bodies of executive power may set up their own territorial structures and appoint officials to them.
2. Federal organs of executive power, by agreement with organs of executive power of the subjects of the Russian Federation, may delegate some of their powers to the latter, provided that this does not conflict with the Constitution of the Russian Federation or federal laws.
3. Organs of executive power of the subjects of the Russian federation, by agreement with the federal organs of executive power, may delegate part of their powers to the latter.
4. The President of the Russian Federation and the Government of the Russian Federation shall, in accordance with the Constitution of the Russian Federation, provide for the implementation of federal state power throughout the territory of the Russian Federation.

Article 79.
The Russian Federation may participate in interstate associations and delegate some of its powers to them in accordance with international agreements, if this does not restrict rights and freedoms of the person and citizen or contravene the fundamentals of the constitutional system of the Russian Federation.

Chapter 4. President of the Russian Federation

Article 80.
1. The President of the Russian Federation shall be the head of state.
2. The President shall be the guarantor of the Constitution of the Russian Federation, and of human and civil rights and freedoms. In accordance with the procedure established by the Constitution of the Russian Federation, he shall take measures to protect the sovereignty of the Russian Federation, its independence and state integrity, and to ensure the concerted functioning

and interaction of all bodies of state power.

3. The President of the Russian Federation shall define the basic domestic and foreign policy guidelines of the state in accordance with the Constitution of the Russian Federation and federal laws.

4. The President of the Russian Federation as head of state shall represent the Russian Federation inside the country and in international relations.

Article 81.

1. The President of the Russian Federation shall be elected for a term of four years by the citizens of the Russian Federation on the basis of general, equal and direct vote by secret ballot.

2. A citizen of the Russian Federation not younger than 35, who has resided in the Russian Federation for not less than 10 years, may be elected President of the Russian Federation.

3. One and the same person may not hold the office of President of the Russian Federation for more than two consecutive terms.

4. The procedure for electing the President of the Russian Federation shall be determined by federal law.

Article 82.

1. At his inauguration the President of the Russian Federation shall take the following oath to the people: "I vow, in the performance of my powers as the President of the Russian Federation, to respect and protect the rights and freedoms of the person and citizen, to observe and protect the Constitution of the Russian Federation, to protect the sovereignty and independence, security and integrity of the state, and to serve the people faithfully."

2. The oath shall be taken in a solemn atmosphere in the presence of members of the Council of the Federation, deputies of the State Duma and judges of the Constitutional Court of the Russian Federation.

Article 83.

The President of the Russian Federation shall:

a) appoint the Chairman of the Government of the Russian Federation, subject to the consent of the State Duma;

b) have the right to preside over meetings of the Government of the Russian Federation;

c) decide on the resignation of the Government of the Russian Federation;

d) present to the State Duma a candidate for appointment to the office of Chairman of the Central Bank of the Russian Federation; submit to the State Duma a proposal on relieving the Chairman of the Central Bank of the Russian Federation of his duties;

e) appoint and dismiss deputy chairmen of the Government of the Russian Federation and federal ministers, as proposed by the Chairman of the Government of the Russian Federation;

f) submit to the Federation Council candidates for appointment to the office of judge of the Constitutional Court of the Russian Federation, the Supreme Court of the Russian Federation and the Supreme Arbitration Court of the Russian Federation as well as the candidate for Prosecutor-General of the Russian Federation; submit to the Federation Council a proposal on relieving the Prosecutor-General of the Russian Federation of his duties; appoint the judges of other federal courts;

g) form and head the Security Council of the Russian Federation, the status of which is determined by federal law;

h) endorse the military doctrine of the Russian Federation;

i) form the staff of the President of the Russian Federation;

j) appoint and dismiss plenipotentiary representatives of the President of the Russian Federation;

k) appoint and dismiss the Supreme Command of the Armed Forces of the Russian Federation;

l) appoint and recall, after consultation with the respective committees or commissions of the Federal Assembly, diplomatic representatives of the Russian Federation to foreign states and international organizations.

Article 84.

The President of the Russian Federation shall:

a) call elections to the State Duma in accordance with the Constitution of the Russian Federation and federal law;

b) dissolve the State Duma in cases and under procedures envisaged by the Constitution of the Russian Federation;

c) call referendums according to the procedure established by federal constitutional law;
d) submit draft laws to the State Duma;
e) sign and promulgate federal laws;
f) present an annual message to the Federal Assembly on the situation in the country and on basic directions of the domestic and foreign policies of the state.

Article 85.

1. The President of the Russian Federation may use dispute-settlement procedures to settle differences between organs of state power of the Russian Federation and organs of state power of the subjects of the Russian Federation, and also between organs of state power of the subjects of the Russian Federation. If no decision is agreed upon, he shall have the right to refer the dispute to the appropriate court.
2. The President of the Russian Federation shall have the right to suspend acts by organs of executive power of the subjects of the Russian Federation if such acts contravene the Constitution of the Russian Federation and federal laws, or with the international obligations of the Russian Federation, or violate the rights and freedoms of the person and citizen, pending the resolution of the issue in appropriate court.

Article 86.

The President of the Russian Federation shall:
a) supervise the conduct of the foreign policy of the Russian Federation;
b) conduct negotiations and sign international treaties of the Russian Federation;
c) sign instruments of ratification;
d) accept credentials and instruments of recall of diplomatic representatives accredited to his office.

Article 87.

1. The President of the Russian Federation shall be the Supreme Commander-in-Chief of the Armed Forces of the Russian Federation.
2. In the event of aggression against the Russian Federation or an immediate threat thereof, the President of the Russian Federation shall introduce

martial law on the territory of the Russian Federation or in areas thereof and shall immediately inform the Federation Council and the State Duma.
3. The regime of martial law shall be defined by federal constitutional law.

Article 88.
Under the circumstances and according to the procedure established by federal constitutional law, the President of the Russian Federation shall impose a state of emergency on the territory of the Russian Federation or in areas thereof and immediately inform the Federation Council and the State Duma.

Article 89.
The President of the Russian Federation shall:
a) resolve issues of citizenship of the Russian Federation and of granting political asylum;
b) award state decorations of the Russian Federation, confer honorary titles of the Russian Federation and supreme military and special titles;
c) grant pardon.

Article 90.
1. The President of the Russian Federation shall issue decrees and orders.
2. The decrees and orders of the President of the Russian Federation shall be binding throughout the territory of the Russian Federation.
3. The decrees and orders of the President of the Russian Federation may not contravene the Constitution of the Russian Federation or federal laws.

Article 91.
The President of the Russian Federation shall possess immunity.

Article 92.
1. The President of the Russian Federation shall assume his powers from the time he is sworn in and terminate his exercise of such powers with the expiry of his tenure of office and after a newly-elected President of the Russian Federation is sworn in.
2. The powers of the President of the Russian Federation shall be terminated in the event of his resignation or sustained inability due to health to discharge his powers or in the event of removal from office. In such cases

new elections of the President of the Russian Federation shall be held no later than three months from the time of the early termination of the President's powers.

3. In all cases when the President of the Russian Federation is unable to perform his duties, such duties shall be temporarily performed by the chairman of the Government of the Russian Federation. The acting president of the Russian Federation shall have no right to dissolve the State Duma, call a referendum, or make proposals on amending or revising the provisions of the Constitution of the Russian Federation.

Article 93.

1. The President of the Russian Federation may be removed from office by the Federation Council only on the basis of charges of high treason or some other grave crime, made against him by the State Duma, confirmed by a ruling of the Supreme Court of the Russian Federation on the presence of the indicia of crime in the President's actions, and by a ruling of the Constitutional Court of the Russian Federation confirming that the procedure for bringing charges was observed.

2. The decision of the State Duma on bringing charges and the decision of the Federation Council on removing the President must be adopted by the votes of two-thirds of the total number in each of the chambers at the initiative of at least one-third of the deputies of the State Duma and on the basis of a resolution of a special commission formed by the State Duma.

3. The decision of the Federation Council on removing the President of the Russian Federation must be adopted within three months of the time charges are brought against the President by the State Duma. If a decision of the Federation Council is not adopted within this time, the charges against the President shall be considered rejected.

Chapter 5. The Federal Assembly

Article 94.

The Federal Assembly—Parliament of the Russian Federation—shall be the supreme representative and legislative body of the Russian Federation.

Article 95.

1. The Federal Assembly shall consist of two chambers—the Federation

Council and the State Duma.

2. Two deputies from each subject of the Russian Federation shall be members of Federation Council: one from the representative and one from the executive bodies of state authority.

3. The State Duma shall consist of 450 deputies.

Article 96.

1. The State Duma shall be elected for a term of four years.

2. The procedure for forming the Federation Council and the procedure for electing deputies to the State Duma shall be established by federal law.

Article 97.

1. Any citizen of the Russian Federation aged 21or older who has the right to take part in elections may be elected deputy to the State Duma.

2. One and the same person may not concurrently be a member of the Federation Council and a deputy of the State Duma. A deputy of the State Duma may not be a deputy of other representative bodies of state power or bodies of local self-government.

3. The deputies of the State Duma shall work on a full-time professional basis. Deputies of the State Duma may not be employed in the civil service or engage in any activities for remuneration other than teaching, research or other creative activities.

Article 98.

1. Members of the Federation Council and deputies of the State Duma shall possess immunity during their terms in office. They may not be detained, arrested or searched, except when detained at the scene of a crime, and may not be subjected to personal search, except when such search is authorized by federal law to ensure the safety of other people.

2. The question of removing immunity shall be decided by the appropriate chamber of the Federal Assembly, on the recommendation of the Prosecutor-General of the Russian Federation.

Article 99.

1. The Federal Assembly shall be a permanently operating body.

2. The State Duma shall hold its first session on the 30th day after its election. The President of the Russian Federation may convene a session

of the State Duma before this term.

3. The first session of the State Duma shall be opened by its oldest deputy.

4. From the time that the new State Duma begins its work, the powers of the previous State Duma shall expire.

Article 100.

1. The Federation Council and the State Duma shall hold separate sessions.

2. The sessions of the Federation Council and the State Duma shall be open. In cases provided for by the procedural rules of a chamber, each chamber shall have the right to hold closed sessions.

3. The chambers may have joint sessions to hear the addresses of the President of the Russian Federation, addresses of the Constitutional Court of the Russian Federation, and speeches by leaders of foreign states.

Article 101.

1. The Federation Council shall elect from among its members the Chairman of the Federation Council and his deputies. The State Duma shall elect from among its members the Chairman of the State Duma and his deputies.

2. The Chairman of the Federation Council and his deputies, and the Chairman of the State Duma and his deputies shall preside over sessions and supervise the internal rules of the chamber.

3. The Federation Council and the State Duma shall form committees and commissions, exercise parliamentary supervision over issues within their jurisdiction, and hold parliamentary hearings.

4. Each chamber shall adopt its own rules and solve questions of internal organization and work.

5. In order to exercise control over the federal budget, the Federation Council and the State Duma shall form an Accounting Chamber, whose membership and rules of order shall be determined by federal law.

Article 102.

1. The jurisdiction of the Federation Council shall include:

a) approving changes of borders between the subjects of the Russian Federation;

b) approving a decree of the President of the Russian Federation on the introduction of martial law;

c) approving a decree of the President of the Russian Federation on the introduction of a state of emergency;

d) deciding on the possibility of the use of the Armed Forces of the Russian Federation outside the territory of the Russian Federation;

e) calling of elections of the President of the Russian Federation;

f) removing the President of the Russian Federation;

g) appointing judges of the Constitutional Court of the Russian Federation, the Supreme Court of the Russian Federation, and the Supreme Court of Arbitration of the Russian Federation;

h) appointing to office and removing from office the Prosecutor-General of the Russian Federation;

i) appointing to office and removing from office the deputy Chairman of the Accounting Chamber and half of its staff of auditors.

2. The Federation Council shall pass resolutions on the issues within its jurisdiction under the Constitution of the Russian Federation.

3. The decrees of the Federation Council shall be adopted by a majority of all deputies to the Federation Council unless otherwise provided for by the Constitution of the Russian Federation.

Article 103.

1. The jurisdiction of the State Duma shall include:

a) consenting to the nomination of the Chairman of the Government of the Russian Federation by the President of the Russian Federation;

b) deciding the issue of confidence in the Government of the Russian Federation;

c) appointing and dismissing the Chairman of the Central Bank of the Russian Federation;

d) appointing and dismissing the Chairman of the Accounting Chamber and half of its staff of auditors;

e) appointing and dismissing the Commissioner for Human Rights, who shall act in accordance with federal constitutional law;

f) granting amnesty;

g) bringing charges against the President of the Russian Federation for his removal from office.

2. The State Duma shall adopt resolutions on issues within its jurisdiction provided for by the Constitution of the Russian Federation.

3. The resolutions of the State Duma shall be adopted by a majority of

votes of all deputies of the State Duma unless otherwise provided for by the Constitution of the Russian Federation.

Article 104.
1. The President of the Russian Federation, the Federation Council, the members to the Federation Council, the deputies to the State Duma, the Government of the Russian Federation, and the legislative (representative) bodies of the subjects of the Russian Federation shall have the right of legislative initiative. The Constitutional Court of the Russian Federation, the Supreme Court of the Russian Federation and the Supreme Court of Arbitration of the Russian Federation shall also have the right of legislative initiative on issues within their competence.
2. Draft laws shall be introduced in the State Duma.
3. The draft laws on the introduction or abolishing of taxes, exemptions from the payment thereof, on the issue of state loans, on changes in the financial obligations of the state and other draft laws providing for expenditures covered from the federal budget may be introduced to the State Duma only with a corresponding resolution by the Government of the Russian Federation.

Article 105.
1. Federal laws shall be adopted by the State Duma.
2. Federal laws shall be adopted by a majority of votes of all deputies of the State Duma unless otherwise provided for by the Constitution of the Russian Federation.
3. Federal laws adopted by the State Duma shall be submitted to the Federation Council for consideration within five days.
4. A federal law shall be considered approved by the Federation Council if more than half of its deputies vote for it or, if within fourteen days, it has not been considered by the Federation Council. In the event that the Federation Council rejects a federal law, the chambers may set up a conciliation commission to settle the differences, after which the federal law shall be considered again by the State Duma.
5. In the event that the State Duma disagrees with the decision of the Federation Council, the federal law shall be considered adopted if, in the second vote, at least two-thirds of the total number of deputies to the State

Duma vote for it.

Article 106.
Federal laws adopted by the State Duma on the following issues must be examined by the Federation Council:

a) the federal budget;
b) federal taxes and levies;
c) financial, monetary, credit and customs regulations and money emission;
d) ratification and denunciation of international treaties of the Russian Federation;
e) the status and protection of the state border of the Russian Federation;
f) war and peace.

Article 107.
1. An adopted federal law shall be sent to the President of the Russian Federation for signing and promulgation within five days.
2. The President of the Russian Federation shall, within fourteen days, sign a federal law and promulgate it.
3. If the President rejects a federal law within fourteen days after the time it was sent to him, the State Duma and the Federation Council shall again consider the law in accordance with the procedure established by the Constitution of the Russian Federation. If, upon reconsideration, the federal law is approved in the previously adopted wording by majorities of not less than two thirds of the total number of members of the Federation Council and deputies of the State Duma, it must be signed by the President of the Russian Federation within seven days and promulgated.

Article 108.
1. Federal constitutional laws shall be adopted on issues provided for in the Constitution of the Russian Federation.
2. A federal constitutional law shall be considered adopted if it has been approved by a majority of at least three quarters of the total number of members of the Federation Council and at least two thirds of the total number of deputies of the State Duma. The adopted federal constitutional law shall be signed and promulgated by the President of the Russian Federation within fourteen days.

Article 109.

1. The State Duma may be dissolved by the President of the Russian Federation in cases envisaged by Articles 111 and 117 of the Constitution of the Russian Federation.

2. In the event that the State Duma is dissolved, the President of the Russian Federation shall announce the date of elections so that the newly elected State Duma may be convened no later than four months from the time of dissolution.

3. The State Duma may not be dissolved on grounds provided for by Article 117 of the Constitution of the Russian Federation within one year after its election.

4. The State Duma may not be dissolved from the time it brings charges against the President of the Russian Federation until the Federation Council adopts a decision on the issue.

5. The State Duma may not be dissolved during the period of a state of emergency or martial law throughout the territory of the Russian Federation, as well as during the last six months of the term of office of the President of the Russian Federation.

Chapter 6. The Government of the Russian Federation

Article 110.

1. Executive power in the Russian Federation shall be exercised by the Government of the Russian Federation.

2. The Government of the Russian Federation shall consist of the Chairman of the Government of the Russian Federation, Deputy Chairmen of the Government, and federal ministers.

Article 111.

1. The Chairman of the Government of the Russian Federation shall be appointed by the President of the Russian Federation with consent of the State Duma.

2. The proposal on the candidacy of the Chairman of the Government of the Russian Federation shall be made no later than two weeks after the inauguration of the newly elected President of the Russian Federation or

after the resignation of the Government of the Russian Federation or within one week after the rejection of a candidate by the State Duma. The State Duma shall consider the candidacy of the Chairman of the Government of the Russian Federation submitted by the President of the Russian Federation within one week after the nomination.

3. After the State Duma rejects candidates for Chairman of the Government of the Russian Federation nominated by the President of the Russian Federation three times, the President of the Russian Federation shall appoint a Chairman of the Government of the Russian Federation, dissolve the State Duma, and call a new election.

Article 112.
1. The Chairman of the Government of the Russian Federation shall, not later than one week after appointment, submit to the President of the Russian Federation proposals on the structures of the federal bodies of executive power.
2. The Chairman of the Government of the Russian Federation shall propose to the President of the Russian Federation candidates for the office of Deputy Chairmen of the Government of the Russian Federation and federal ministers.

Article 113.
The Chairman of the Government of the Russian Federation, in accordance with the Constitution of the Russian Federation, federal laws and decrees of the President of the Russian Federation, shall determine the guidelines of the work of the Government of the Russian Federation and shall organize its work.

Article 114.
1. The Government of the Russian Federation shall:
a) develop and submit the federal budget to the State Duma and ensure compliance therewith; submit a report on the execution of the federal budget to the State Duma;
b) ensure the implementation in the Russian Federation of a uniform financial, credit and monetary policy;
c) ensure the implementation in the Russian Federation of a uniform state

policy in the field of culture, science, education, health, social security and ecology;

d) manage federal property;

e) implement measures to ensure the country's defense, state security, and the implementation of the foreign policy of the Russian Federation;

f) implement measures to ensure legality, the rights and freedoms of citizens, the protection of property and public order, and the fight against crime;

g) exercise any other powers vested in it by the Constitution of the Russian Federation, federal laws and the decrees of the President of the Russian Federation.

2. The work of the Government of the Russian Federation shall be regulated by federal constitutional law.

Article 115.

1. On the basis of and pursuant to the Constitution of the Russian Federation, federal laws and normative decrees of the President of the Russian Federation, the Government of the Russian Federation shall issue decrees and orders and ensure their implementation.

2. The decrees and orders of the Government of the Russian Federation shall be binding throughout the Russian Federation.

3. The decrees and orders of the Government of the Russian Federation may be repealed by the President of the Russian Federation if they contravene the Constitution of the Russian Federation, federal laws, or decrees of the President of the Russian Federation.

Article 116.

The Government of the Russian Federation shall relinquish its powers before the newly elected President of the Russian Federation.

Article 117.

1. The Government of the Russian Federation may hand in its resignation, which may be accepted or rejected by the President of the Russian Federation.

2. The President of the Russian Federation may adopt a decision about the resignation of the Government of the Russian Federation.

3. The State Duma may express no-confidence in the Government of the Russian Federation. The no-confidence resolution shall be approved by a simple majority of deputies in the State Duma. In the event the State Duma shall again expresses no-confidence in the Government of the Russian Federation within three months, the President of the Russian Federation shall announce the resignation of the Government or dissolve the State Duma.

4. The Chairman of the Government of the Russian Federation may put the question of confidence in the Government of the Russian Federation before the State Duma. If the State Duma returns a vote of no-confidence, the President shall within seven days make a decision on the resignation of the Government of the Russian Federation or on the dissolution of the State Duma and the announcement of new elections.

5. In the event of the resignation or relinquishment of the powers of the Government of the Russian Federation, it shall continue to work, on the instructions by the President of the Russian Federation, until a new government of the Russian Federation is formed.

Chapter 7. Judicial Authority

Article 118.

1. Justice in the Russian Federation shall be administered only by courts.
2. Judicial power shall be exercised through constitutional, civil, administrative and criminal proceedings.
3. The judicial system of the Russian Federation shall be established by the Constitution of the Russian Federation and federal constitutional law. The creation of extraordinary courts shall not be permitted.

Article 119.

Citizens of the Russian Federation aged 25 and older, holding a law degree and having worked in the legal profession for at least five years may become judges. Federal law may establish additional requirements for judges in the courts of the Russian Federation.

Article 120.

1. Judges shall be independent and subordinate only to the Constitution of the Russian Federation and to federal law.

2. A court, having established in reviewing a case that an act of a state body or other organ was contrary to the law, shall adopt a decision in accordance with law.

Article 121.
1. Judges shall be unremovable.
2. A judge may not have his powers terminated or suspended except under procedures and on grounds established by federal law.

Article 122.
1. Judges shall possess immunity.
2. Criminal proceedings may not be brought against a judge except as provided for by federal law.

Article 123.
1. All trials in all courts shall be open. Cases may be heard in closed session in cases provided by federal law.
2. In absentia proceedings in criminal cases shall not be allowed except the cases provided for by federal law.
3. Judicial proceedings shall be conducted on the basis of adversarial principles and the equality of the parties.
4. In cases provided for by federal law, judicial proceedings shall be conducted with the participation of a jury.

Article 124.
Courts shall be financed only from the federal budget, and financing shall ensure full and independent administration of justice in accordance with federal law.

Article 125.
1. The Constitutional Court of the Russian Federation consists of 19 judges.
2. The Constitutional Court of the Russian Federation, on request by the President of the Russian Federation, the State Duma, one-fifth of the members of the Federation Council or deputies of the State Duma, the Government of the Russian Federation, the Supreme Court of the Russian Federation, the Supreme Arbitration Court of the Russian Federation, or bodies of legislative and executive power of subjects of the Russian

Federation shall resolve cases about the compliance with the Constitution of the Russian Federation of:

a) federal laws, normative acts of the President of the Russian Federation, the Federation Council, the State Duma, and the Government of the Russian Federation;

b) republican constitutions, the charters, as well as laws and other normative acts of subjects of the Russian Federation on issues pertaining to the jurisdiction of bodies of state power of the Russian Federation and joint jurisdiction of bodies of state power of the Russian Federation as well as bodies of state power of subjects of the Russian Federation;

c) agreements between bodies of state power of the Russian Federation and bodies of state power of subjects of the Russian Federation, agreements between bodies of state power of subjects of the Russian Federation;

d) international agreements of the Russian Federation that have not entered into force.

3. The Constitutional Court of the Russian Federation shall resolve disputes over jurisdiction:

a) between federal state bodies;

b) between state bodies of the Russian Federation and state bodies of the subjects of the Russian Federation;

c) between supreme state bodies of subjects of the Russian Federation.

4. The Constitutional Court of the Russian Federation, proceeding on the basis of complaints about the violation of constitutional rights and freedoms of citizens and on the basis of requests from courts shall review the constitutionality of the law applied or due to be applied in a specific case in accordance with procedures established by federal law.

5. The Constitutional Court of the Russian Federation on the basis of requests by the President of the Russian Federation, the Federation Council, the State Duma, the Government of the Russian Federation, and legislative bodies of subjects of the Russian Federation shall interpret the Constitution of the Russian Federation.

6. Acts or individual provisions thereof that are deemed unconstitutional shall lose force; international agreements of the Russian Federation may not be enforced and applied if they violate the Constitution of the Russian Federation.

7. The Constitutional Court of the Russian Federation, on the basis of a request by the Federation Council, shall render a conclusion regarding the observance of proscribed procedure in connection with a charge of state treason or the commission of another grave crime by the President of the Russian Federation.

Article 126.
The Supreme Court of the Russian Federation shall be the highest judicial body for resolving civil, criminal, administrative and other matters triable by general jurisdiction courts, and shall carry out judicial supervision over their activity in line with procedural forms provided by federal law, and shall offer explanations on questions of judicial practice.

Article 127.
The Supreme Arbitration Court of the Russian Federation shall be the highest judicial body for resolving economic disputes and other cases considered by arbitration courts, and shall carry out judicial supervision over their activity in line with legal procedures provided by federal law, and shall offer explanations on questions of judicial practice.

Article 128.
1. Judges of the Constitutional Court of the Russian Federation, the Supreme Court of the Russian Federation, and the Supreme Arbitration Court of the Russian Federation shall be appointed by the Federation Council following nomination by the President of the Russian Federation.
2. Judges of other federal courts shall be appointed by the President of the Russian Federation in accordance with procedures established by federal law.
3. The powers and procedure for the formation and activities of the Constitutional Court of the Russian Federation, the Supreme Court of the Russian Federation, and the Supreme Arbitration Court of the Russian Federation and other federal courts shall be established by federal constitutional law.

Article 129.
1. The Prosecutor's Office of the Russian Federation is a single centralized system in which lower prosecutors are subordinated to higher prosecutors

and to the Prosecutor-General of the Russian Federation.
2. The Prosecutor-General of the Russian Federation shall be appointed to his post and dismissed from it by the Federation Council, on the proposal of the President of the Russian Federation.
3. Prosecutors of subjects of the Russian Federation shall be appointed by the Prosecutor-General of the Russian Federation upon agreement with the subjects.
4. Other prosecutors shall be appointed by the Prosecutor-General of the Russian Federation.
5. The powers, organization and working procedure for the Prosecutor's Office of the Russian Federation shall be determined by federal law.

Chapter 8. Local Self-Government

Article 130.
1. Local self-government in the Russian Federation shall ensure independent decision by the population on local issues, as well as the ownership, use and disposal of municipal property.
2. Local self-government shall be exercised by citizens through referendums, elections and other forms of expression of their will, as well as through elected and other bodies of local self-government.

Article 131.
1. Local self-government shall be exercised in the cities, rural areas and other localities, taking into account historical and other local traditions. The structure of bodies of local self-government shall be determined by the population independently.
2. Changing the borders of territorial entities under local self- government shall be done only with the consent of the population of a given territory.

Article 132.
1. The bodies of local self-government shall independently manage municipal property, create, approve and execute the local budget, establish local taxes and levies, ensure law and order, and solve any other local issues.
2. The bodies of local self-government may be invested under law with certain state powers, with the transfer of material and financial resources required to exercise such powers. The exercise of the powers transferred

shall be supervised by the state.

Article 133.
Local self-government in the Russian Federation shall be guaranteed by the right to judicial protection and compensation for any additional expenses arising from the decisions adopted by the bodies of state power, and a ban on the restrictions of the rights of local self-government established by the Constitution of the Russian Federation and federal laws.

Chapter 9. Constitutional Amendments and Revisions

Article 134.
Proposals on amendments and revision of constitutional provisions may be made by the President of the Russian Federation, the Federation Council, the State Duma, the Government of the Russian Federation, and legislative (representative) bodies of the subjects of the Russian Federation, as well as groups of deputies numbering not less than one-fifth of the total number of deputies of the Federation Council or the State Duma.

Article 135.
1. The provisions of Chapters 1, 2 and 9 of the Constitution of the Russian Federation may not be revised by the Federal Assembly.
2. In the event that a proposal to revise any provisions in Chapters 1, 2 and 9 of the Constitution of the Russian Federation shall be supported by three-fifths of the total number of deputies of the Federation Council and the State Duma, a Constitutional Assembly shall be convened in accordance with federal constitutional law.
3. The Constitutional Assembly may either confirm the inviolability of the Constitution of the Russian Federation or develop a new draft of the Constitution of the Russian Federation, which shall be adopted by two-thirds of the total number of deputies to the Constitutional Assembly or submitted to a popular vote. The Constitution of the Russian Federation shall be considered adopted if, in the popular vote, more than half of those who participated voted for it, provided more than half of the electorate took part in the poll.

Article 136.
Amendments to Chapters 3–8 of the Constitution of the Russian Federation shall be adopted in accordance with the procedure established for the adoption of a federal constitutional law and shall come into force following the approval thereof by no less than two-thirds of the subjects of the Russian Federation.

Article 137.
1. Changes to Article 65 of the Constitution of the Russian Federation, which determines the composition of the Russian Federation, shall be made on the basis of a federal constitutional law on admission to the Russian Federation and the formation within the Russian Federation of a new subject and on a change of the constitutional-legal status of a subject of the Russian Federation.
2. In the event of a change in the name of a republic, territory, region, city of federal significance, autonomous region or autonomous area, the new name of the subject of the Russian Federation shall be included in Article 65 of the Constitution of the Russian Federation.

SECTION TWO

Concluding and Transitional Provisions

1. The Constitution of the Russian Federation shall take effect on the day of its official publication on the basis of the results of the national referendum. The day of the national referendum, December 12, 1993, is considered the day of adoption of the Constitution of the Russian Federation. Simultaneously, the Constitution (Fundamental Law) of the Russian Federation–Russia, adopted 12 April, 1978, with the changes and amendments that followed, loses effect. In the event of a situation of nonconformity between the Constitution of the Russian Federation and the Federal Treaty— the Treaty on the division of subjects of jurisdiction and powers between the federal bodies of State Power of the Russian Federation and the bodies of State power of the sovereign republics making up the Russian Federation, the Treaty on the division of subjects of jurisdiction and powers between the federal bodies of State power of the Russian Federation and

bodies of State power of the territories, regions, the cities of Moscow and St. Petersburg of the Russian Federation, the Treaty on the division of subjects of jurisdiction and powers between the federal bodies of State power of the Russian Federation and bodies of State power of the autonomous region, autonomous areas making up the Russian Federation, and similarly other treaties between the federal bodies of State power of the Russian Federation and bodies of State power of the subjects of the Russian Federation, and treaties between bodies of State power of the subjects of the Russian Federation—the provisions of the Constitution of the Russian Federation shall apply.

2. Laws and other legal acts in effect on the territory of the Russian Federation until the enactment of this Constitution are enforced insofar as they do not contravene the Constitution of the Russian Federation.

3. The President of the Russian Federation, elected in accordance with the Constitution (Fundamental Law) of the Russian Federation–Russia, from the day this Constitution takes effect exercises the powers set down in the Constitution until the end of his term for which he was elected.

4. The Council of Ministers—the Government of the Russian Federation—from the day this Constitution takes effect assumes the rights, duties and responsibilities of the Government of the Russian Federation set down in the Constitution of the Russian Federation and in future shall be designated as the Government of the Russian Federation.

5. Courts in the Russian Federation exercise the right to administer justice in accordance with their powers as set down in this Constitution. After the Constitution takes effect the judges of all courts of the Russian Federation preserve their powers until the end of the terms for which they were elected. Vacancies shall be filled in accordance with the procedures set down in this Constitution.

6. Until the adoption of a federal law setting forth the procedures for trial by jury, the prior procedure for conducting trials shall be retained. Until the criminal-procedural legislation of the Russian Federation has been brought into line with the provisions of this Constitution, the previous procedures

for the arrest, detention and custody of persons suspected of committing crimes shall apply.

7. The Federation Council and the State Duma of the first convocation shall be elected for a two-year term.

8. The Federation Council shall hold its first session on the 30th day after election. The first session of the Federation Council shall be opened by the President of the Russian Federation.

9. A deputy of the State Duma of the first convocation may simultaneously be a member of the Government of the Russian Federation. Deputies of the State Duma who are members of the Government of the Russian Federation are not covered by the provisions of this Constitution concerning deputies' immunity from responsibility for their activities (or their lack of activity) connected with the execution of their official duties. Deputies of the Federation Council of the first convocation shall exercise their powers on a temporary basis.

Appendix B
Chronology, 1985–2000

1985

March	Mikhail Gorbachev named general secretary of the Communist Party of the Soviet Union.
July	Eduard Shevardnadze named full member of Politburo and foreign minister.
	Boris Yeltsin named party central committee secretary.
December	Yeltsin named first secretary of Moscow party organization.

1986

February	Yeltsin named candidate Politburo member.
April	Chernobyl accident occurs. Vague and misleading statements about its seriousness are a blow to emerging glasnost policy.
November	The Law on Individual Labor Activity, an early reform measure, adopted.
December	Kazakhstan party chief, a Kazakh, is replaced by a Russian, prompting riots in the republic's capital.
	Gorbachev allows dissident physicist Andrei Sakharov to return to Moscow from exile in the city of Gorky.

1987

January	Gorbachev introduces first major ideas for political reform.
	Alexander Yakovlev named candidate Politburo member.
February	Yuri Churbanov, Leonid Brezhnev's son-in-law, is arrested for corruption.
May	Matthias Rust, a German teenager, lands a small plane in Moscow's Red Square. The political fallout includes the dismissal of the Soviet defense minister.
October	At a party Central Committee meeting, Yeltsin criticizes

Gorbachev and other party officials, as well as the pace of perestroika. He later loses both his Politburo post and his position as Moscow party chief.

1988

February	Bukharin and Rykov, high-ranking party leaders who were executed in the 1930s purges, are rehabilitated.
March	Ethnic violence connected with Nagorno-Karabakh, a largely Armenian enclave in Azerbaijan, bursts into the open.
April	Agreements on settling the war in Afghanistan are signed.
May	The Law on Cooperatives, another Gorbachev economic reform, is adopted.
June	The 19th Party Conference, which ushers in important reform, opens.
December	Gorbachev gives address at the United Nations in New York. Announces troop cuts, removal of some military forces in East Europe, and renunciation of the use of force. His Western Hemisphere visit is cut short by a major earthquake in Armenia.

1989

March	Nationwide elections for the new USSR Congress of People's Deputies take place. A number of party officials are defeated in the vote. Boris Yeltsin's political comeback commences with an easy win against a party-picked opponent.
May	New Soviet parliament opens. Gorbachev is chosen to the top post. Hungary creates an open border to the West, the first East European country to do so.
November	Berlin Wall is opened.
December	Andrei Sakharov dies.

1990

March	Soviet parliament creates USSR presidency and modifies article 6 of the Constitution, ending communist party's monopoly on political power. Gorbachev becomes first president of the Soviet Union. Elections for the new parliaments at the republic level take place.
May	Yeltsin named to the top post of the Russian parliament, Chairman of the Supreme Soviet.
June	Russian parliament declares primacy of its laws over those of the USSR, initiating so-called war of laws.
July	The 28th Congress of the Communist Party of the Soviet Union opens. Gorbachev retains post as general secretary. Yeltsin resigns from party. The "500 Days" economic reform plan is announced. Sponsored by the Russian republic, Gorbachev at first embraces the program but later abandons it.
October	East and West Germany reunited. Gorbachev receives the Nobel Peace Prize.
December	Foreign minister Shevardnadze resigns, warning of an "impending dictatorship."

1991

January	Soviet troops seize key buildings in Vilnius, Lithuania and Riga, Latvia, killing citizens in both countries. Gorbachev claims he knew nothing of the attack in Vilnius.
March	Referendum on Gorbachev's vague proposal for a renewed federal union takes place in nine republics. Over 75 percent support it. At the same time, voters in Russia also support a proposal to create a presidency in the republic.
June	Yeltsin wins election as Russia's first president.
August	A putsch aimed at removing Gorbachev and preventing the promulgation of a new union treaty fails. Yeltsin leads

	anti-coup forces, and emerges with heightened prestige. The coup plotters are arrested. Gorbachev resigns as party general secretary.
September	The Soviet government recognizes independence of Latvia, Lithuania and Estonia.
December	Leaders of Russia, Ukraine and Belarus sign agreement creating a Commonwealth of Independent States to replace the USSR. Eight other Soviet republics join in the agreement shortly thereafter. On December 25 Gorbachev resigns as USSR president. The Soviet Union ceases to exist.

1992

January	Price liberalization begins radical economic reform in Russia.
March	Yelstin names Yegor Gaidar first deputy prime minister, charges him with administering economic reform.
June	Gaidar named acting prime minister.
October	Voucher privatization begins.
December	Yeltsin nominates Gaidar for prime minister. When parliament refuses to approve him, Yeltsin nominates Viktor Chernomyrdin, who is approved.

1993

March	Parliament fails in vote to impeach Yeltsin.
April	In referendum, voters support Yeltsin's performance as president and his economic and social policies. They also vote in favor of early parliamentary elections, which parliament considers non-binding.
June-July	Constitutional conference convened by backers of the president. Conference supports Yeltsin's draft constitution.

September–October	Yeltsin issues decree dissolving parliament and ordering elections for December. The parliamentary leadership barricades itself in the White House (parliament building). Violent actions by hard-line supporters of parliament lead to the shelling of the White House by military units. The resistance is crushed and its leaders are arrested.
December	The new constitution is approved by referendum and a new parliament is elected.

1994

January	The new Russian parliament, the State Duma and the Federation Council, begin work.
February	The Duma adopts an amnesty freeing the 1991 coup plotters and those arrested in the October 1993 events.
October	"Black Tuesday," the value of the ruble plummets 25 percent against the dollar.
December	Russian troops enter Chechnya, initiating the 1994–1996 war.

1995

February	The Constitutional Court resumes activity, meeting for the first time in over a year, after its suspension by Yeltsin in connection with the September–October 1993 events.
June	The Duma votes no confidence in the government (a second no-confidence motion fails on July 1).
July	Yeltsin hospitalized with heart problems.
October	Yeltsin hospitalized after a heart attack.
December	Duma elections. Communists win largest representation, with 22.3 percent of proportional representation vote.

1996

February	Yeltsin announces that he will run for reelection as president.
May	A cease-fire in the Chechen war is announced, with broad autonomy to be granted to Chechnya. But the halt in fighting doesn't last.
June	Yeltsin leads in first round of presidential election, with 35 percent; Zyuganov, the communist, gets 32 percent, Lebed 14.5 percent. Yeltsin appoints Lebed national security advisor and secretary of the Security Council.
July	Yeltsin wins second term as president, with second-round vote of 53.8 percent, to 40.3 percent for Zyuganov.
August–September	A military disengagement in the Chechen war, largely engineered by Lebed, is achieved.
October	Yeltsin dismisses Lebed as national security advisor, citing insubordinate behavior.
November	Yeltsin undergoes quintuple bypass surgery.

1997

January	Aslan Maskhadov elected president of Chechnya.
February	Yeltsin delivers state-of-the-nation address, after months away from public activity in connection with illness.
May	Russian-Belarusian treaty of union signed.
	Yeltsin and Chechen president Maskhadov sign peace treaty.
	Yeltsin signs Founding Act on relations between Russia and NATO.
November	In a major government reshuffle, Yeltsin dismisses a number of ministers and aides.
December	Yeltsin falls ill, spends two weeks in hospital, then takes a two week vacation.

1998

March	Illness strikes Yeltsin. He spends a week away from the Kremlin.
	Yeltsin dismisses prime minister Chernomyrdin and most of the cabinet, nominates Sergei Kirienko to be prime minister.
April	After rejecting Kirienko twice, Duma confirms him. Yeltsin visits Japan in the midst of the confirmation process.
August	Kirienko dismissed as prime minister during financial crisis lasting much of the summer. Yeltsin nominates Chernomyrdin to return as prime minister. Duma rejects Chernomyrdin's nomination.
September	After the Duma's second rejection of Chernomyrdin, Yeltsin nominates foreign minister Yevgeny Primakov, who is quickly confirmed by the Duma.

1999

January	Yeltsin hospitalized with bleeding ulcer and other problems. Advised by doctors to refrain from flying for several months, but three weeks later flies to Jordan for King Hussein's funeral.
February	Yeltsin attempts to fire prosecutor general Skuratov, but Federation Council refuses to agree. Federation Council only assents to Skuratov's dismissal in April 2000, after Yeltsin has left the presidency.
March	Yeltsin returns to hospital, complaining of stomach pains.
April	Yeltsin publicly criticizes prime minister Primakov, who defends his record in a national television address.
May	Primakov dismissed as prime minister. Sergei Stepashin nominated in his place. Quickly confirmed by the Duma. Duma impeachment efforts against Yeltsin fall short.
August	Yeltsin dismisses prime minister Stepashin after only three

	months. Vladimir Putin named to replace him, and called his successor by Yeltsin. Putin is easily confirmed by Duma.

Incursions by Chechen rebels into the neighboring region of Daghestan repulsed by Russian military, which launches bombing raids on Chechen border towns.

Powerful explosion in underground shopping mall in Moscow causes considerable injury and property damage. The bombing is attributed in some quarters to Chechen terrorists. |
| September | Military action against Chechen militants in Daghestan continues, as do Russian bombing raids into Chechnya.

Further explosions in Moscow, elsewhere in Russia, heighten tensions. Chechen terrorists widely but not unanimously blamed. |
| December | In the Duma elections, the Communist Party of the Russian Federation retains first place, winning 24.3 percent of the proportional representation voting. Unity, the new party created in support of Putin, takes second, with 23.6 percent.

Boris Yeltsin resigns as Russian president, making prime minister Putin acting president. |

2000

January	Sergei Babitsky, a journalist for RFE/RL, disappears in Chechnya. He is returned to Moscow the next month, threatened with trial for violating Russian law. His case becomes a focal point of the regime's alleged harassment of the media.
March	Acting president Putin wins presidential election by collecting nearly 53 percent of the vote, thus avoiding the need for a runoff. Communist Zyuganov, the closest of ten other candidates, receives 29 percent.
May	Putin inaugurated as president of Russia.

June	For prime minister he nominates Mikhail Kasyanov, who wins speedy Duma approval. Putin moves quickly to strengthen the central government and rein in the regions. Media oligarch Vladimir Gusinskii is briefly thrown in prison. When released, he leaves Russia. Russian authorities later seek to have him extradited from Spain to face fraud charges.
July	Legislation adopted for reforming upper house of legislature, other Putin reforms.
August	The "Kursk" nuclear submarine sinks in the Barents Sea. Putin is criticized for remaining on vacation in the days immediately following the disaster.
September	Putin issues a decree creating a new State Council to advise him. The new body is made up of regional executive branch heads.
December	Putin announces that he will ask the Duma to readopt the national anthem of the Soviet period (but with different words) and other old national symbols.
	U.S. businessman Edmund Pope is found guilty of spying by the Moscow City Court and sentenced to 20 years in prison. Putin pardons Pope, who returns to the United States.

Index

('t' indicates a table)

A

Academy of Science (USSR), 26, 36
Afghanistan war, 39, 62, 234
Agrarian Party
  emergence of, 108, 109–110
  1993 election, 115t
Agro-Industrial Complex (*Gosagroprom*), 15, 30
Ahdieh, Robert, 83–84
Alcoholism
  campaign against, 15, 30
  public health problem, 156
amnesty, 145–146, 237
Andropov, Yuri Vladimirovich, 1, 2t, 5, 6, 7, 13
Anti-Semitism, in Russia, 37
Armenia
  and CIS, 54
  ethnic strife, 34
  Union treaty, 46
Article 6 (USSR), 41–42, 105, 235
Autonomous Soviet Socialist Republics (ASSRs), 73
"Autumn putsch," 55
Azerbaijan, 34, 54

B

Babitsky, Sergei, 240
Bakatin, Vadim, 44
ballots, marking of, 27
Beetham, David, 171
Belarus
  and CIS, 49, 51, 54
  nuclear policy, 56
  relations with Russia, 58–59, 238
Berlin Wall, 234
Bill of Rights, United States, 84
Black Sea Fleet, dispute over, 55, 56–57
Bolshevik Revolution, 1, 3, 8
Bolsheviks, 3, 7
Bonner, Elena, 182

Brezhnev Constitution, in RSFSR, 65–66
Brezhnev Doctrine, 39
  repudiation of, 39–40
Brezhnev, Leonid Ilich, 2t, 5–6, 7, 13
Brown, Archie, 16, 32, 49
Bukharin, Nikolai, 234

C

Cedar political party, 114, 115t
Central Asian Economic Community, 59
Central Committee (CPSU)
  and Article 6, 41
  Gorbachev's membership, 12, 13, 14, 16
  under Gorbachev, 17–18, 20–21
  1989 elections, 26
  role of, 8
Central Election Commission, 111, 113
"Chechen Case," 150
Chechen Republic, 74–75, 95, 96, 238
Chechen wars, 62, 87, 141–142, 182, 237, 238, 240
Chechen-Ingush Republic, 73, 74–75, 95
Chernenko, Konstantin Ustinovich, 1, 2t, 6–7
Chernobyl, 20, 233
Chernomyrdin, Victor, 109, 137–138, 139, 236, 239
Chubais, Anatoly, 138–139
Churbanov, Yuri, 233
"Cigarette riots," 40
"CIS sceptics," 54, 59
citizenship, Baltic states, 60
civil society, 174
"civilized divorce," 53
cohabitation, 92, 128
Committee for State Security, 135. *See also* KGB
Commonwealth of Independent States (CIS)
  corruption in, 161

creation of, 49, 51, 236
founding document, 51–52
military of, 55–56
nuclear policy, 54, 56
organs of, 52–53
Communist Party of the Russian Federation (CPRF)
emergence of, 107–108
1993 election, 115t
1995 election, 117, 118t, 119
1999 election, 120–121, 120t–121t, 240
Communist Party of the Soviet Union (CPSU)
absence of Russian, 36
and Article 6, 41–42, 105
coup participation, 48
under Gorbachev, 16, 20, 104
under Khrushchev, 5
limitations on, 47, 48
Nineteenth All-Union Party Conference, 21–22, 25
1989 election, 26, 27–28, 105
political power of, 1, 3, 7–11, 41, 66
in Russia, 43, 68, 69–70, 70, 72, 105
under Stalin, 4
Twentieth Party Congress, 4, 12
Twenty-Eighth Party Congress, 43, 68, 235
Comparative Constitutional Engineering, 85
Congress of People's Deputies (RSFSR)
1990 election, 43, 67–68, 105
role of, 70, 71, 72
Congress of People's Deputies (USSR)
creation of, 22, 25
demise of, 49
meetings of, 28–30, 35–36, 45
1989 election, 26–28, 35, 105, 234
role of, 67
Connor, Walter, 104
Constitutional Court
Constitution of 1993, 87, 90, 93, 224–226
and CPSU, 70
creation of, 71
membership of, 72
operation of, 149–150
role of, 65, 66, 71–72, 77, 84

"controlled democracy," 169
"convenience parties," 143–144
corruption
CIS countries, 161
in Russia, 144, 160–161
"corruption perceptions index," 160
Council of the Heads of State, CIS, 52
"creeping openness," 1
Crimea, dispute over, 56–58
Criminal justice system (RSFSR), 83, 149
Cuban Missile Crisis, 4–5
Czechoslovakia, 39

D

Dallin, Alexander, 183
Daniloff, Nicholas, 20
democracy
concepts of, 169–171
in Russia, 169, 182–183
Russian view of, 172–175
Democratic Russia alliance, 68
"dictatorship of law," 161
Duma
constitution of 1993, 214–216, 217–219, 220
corruption of, 144
elections to, 113, 116–119, 121, 146
functions of, 88, 89, 90, 91, 145–146, 151
inception of, 237
organization of, 89, 143–144
Duma Council, 143

E

election fraud, 2000 election, 126
elections
1989 USSR, 26–28, 35, 105
1990 RSFSR, 43, 47, 68–69, 105
1993 parliamentary, 112–116, 115t
1995 parliamentary, 112, 116–119, 118t, 237–238
1996 presidential, 112, 122–124, 238
1999 parliamentary, 112, 119–122, 121t–122t, 240
2000 presidential, 112, 125–126
and Russian democracy, 175–176
electoral law, features of, 27, 111–112

Index

"enlightened patriotism," 171
Estonia
    citizenship requirements, 60
    incorporation of, 35, 59
    independence of, 48, 60, 236
    1989 election, 35
    relations with Russia, 60–61
    Union treaty, 46
"Eurocentrism," 173
executive branch
    Putin era, 142, 151–152
    RSFSR, 91–92, 133–136
    under Yeltsin, 136–142

F

Fatherland-All Russia Movement
    emergence of, 108, 109–110
    1999 election, 120t
Federal Assembly
    1993 election, 113
    RSFSR, 77–78, 85, 89–90
Federal Security Service (FSB), 135
Federation Council
    constitution of 1993, 214–215, 216–217, 218, 219
    functions of, 86, 89–90, 147, 151
    inception of, 237
    membership of, 97, 143, 152
    1993 election, 78, 113, 116
    1995 election, 119
    operation of, 87, 89
Federation Treaty, 74–75, 95
Feshbach, Murray, 165
500 Days program, 32, 40, 235
"floating party system," 143–144
Foreign Intelligence Service (SRV), 135
Former Soviet Union (FSU), 51
France
    cohabitation, 92, 128
    organic law, 86–87
    political parties, 103, 128
Fund for Soviet Culture, 37

G

Gaidar, Yegor, 108, 137, 138, 169, 236
Georgia
    and CIS, 51, 54
    ethnic strife, 34
    Union treaty, 46
Germany, electoral system, 106, 114
glasnost (openness), 13, 16, 20, 21
    and economic sector, 31
    and ethnic grievances, 33–35
    and media freedom, 176–177
    and Russian nationalism, 36
Gorbachev, Mikhail Sergeevich,
    background of, 11–12
    Congress of People's Deputies, 28–30
    coup attempt, 47–48, 60, 69, 235
    criticism of, 42–43, 44–45
    democratization process, 20–22
    early career, 12–13
    early reforms, 13–16, 233
    economic reforms, 31–33
    electoral reform, 25–28
    foreign policy, 38–40
    nationality problems, 33–35
    1996 election, 123
    Nobel Peace Prize, 40, 235
    personnel policies, 16–19, 44
    radical reform, 19–22
    resignation of, 49, 54, 236
    and Russian nationalism, 36–37
    Soviet leader, 2t, 7, 233
    "turn to the right," 44–45, 59–60
    Union treaty, 45–47, 48–49
    United Nations speech, 39, 234
    USSR Presidency, 42, 43, 69
Gosagroprom, 15, 30
Grishin, Victor, 18
Gromyko, Andrei, 17–18, 37–38
Gusinskii, Vladimir, 177–178, 241
GUUAM (Georgia, Ukraine, Uzbekistan, Azerbaijan and Moldova), 59

H

human rights
    current policy, 178
    under Brezhnev, 5–6, 19
    under Gorbachev, 19–20
Hungary, 234
Huntington, Samuel P., 170
Huskey, Eugene, 134, 136

I

"incomplete democracy," 169
infant mortality, in Russia, 165, 166
"informals (*neformaly*)," 104–105
Ingushetia Republic, 74–75, 95
Inter-Regional Group, 30
"interlocking directorate," 9
Interparliamentary Assembly, CIS, 52–53
Interregional Movement Unity. *See* Unity

J

judiciary
    forms of, 85, 87, 147
    reform of, 149
    Russian view of, 147–148
jury systems, 148–149
Juviler, Peter, 1

K

Kaiser, Robert, 17
Kaliningrad, territorial dispute, 60
Kara-Murza, Alexy, 172–173
Karelia, 96
Kasyanov, Mikhail, 142, 241
Kazakhstan
    and Central Asian Economic
        Community, 59
    and CIS, 49, 54
    ethnic grievances, 33–34
    nuclear policy, 56
    Union treaty, 47, 48–49
KGB
    criticism of, 29
    Daniloff arrest, 20
    dissident campaign, 5
    economic crimes, 44
    reform of, 135
Khasbulatov, Ruslan
    amnesty for, 146
    coup attempt, 77
    Supreme Soviet, 68–69
    Yeltsin adversary, 75, 76, 137
Khrushchev, Nikita Sergeevich, 2t, 4–5, 6, 7, 30
Kirienko, Sergei, 108, 139, 239
komsomol, 12, 18
Kryuchkov, Vladimir, 44–45

Kursk accident, 241
Kyrgyzstan
    and Central Asian Economic
        Community, 59
    and CIS, 54

L

Language, in USSR, 36–37
Latvia
    citizenship requirements, 60
    incorporation of, 35, 59
    independence of, 48, 60, 236
    1989 election, 28, 35
    relations with Russia, 60
    Union treaty, 46
    USSR attack on, 45, 60, 235
Law on Cooperatives, 31–32, 234
Law on Individual Labor Activity, 31, 233
Law on the State Enterprise, 31
Lebed, Alexander, 123, 238
Lenin, Vladimir Ilich, 2t, 3, 7
Liberal Democratic Party of Russia (LDPR)
    emergence of, 110–111
    1993 election, 78, 114, 115t
    1995 election, 117, 118t, 119
Life expectancy, in Russia, 165, 166
Ligachev, Yegor, 17, 18, 19, 21, 43
Likhachev, Dmitri, 37
Lithuania
    incorporation of, 35, 59
    independence, 36, 40, 43, 48, 59–60, 236
    1989 election, 28, 35
    Union treaty, 46
    USSR attack on, 45, 60, 235
Lukin, Alexander, 173–174
Lukyanov, Anatoly, 47–48
Luzhkov, Yurii, 109–110

M

majority requirement, elections, 27
Malia, Martin, 183
"managed democracy," 169
Maskhadov, Aslan, 238
McFaul, Michael, 124

Index

media
  glasnost period, 177–178
  1989 elections, 27
Menon, Rajan, 62
military
  attack on Latvia/Lithuania, 45, 235
  of CIS, 55–56
  expanded role of, 44
  Soviet expenditures, 38
  USSR superpower status, 62
Moldavia, 34
Moldova
  and CIS, 54
  ethnic strife, 34–35
  Union treaty, 46

N

Nabokov, Vladimir, 20
Nagorno-Karabakh, ethnic grievances, 34, 54, 234
National Salvation Front (FNS), 76
Nationality movements, 1989 elections, 27
Nationality policy
  prior to Gorbachev, 72–73
  under Gorbachev, 33–37
  RSFSR, 94–97
NATO, 60, 238
Nazi-Soviet Pact, anniversary of, 35
Near Abroad, ethnic Russians, 51, 72
Nemtsov, Boris, 108
new thinking (*novoe myshlenie*), 38
New Economic Policy (NEP), 3, 4
Newly Independent States (NIS), 51
Nineteenth All-Union Party Conference, 21–22, 25, 234
  call for, 20–21
Nomenklatura, economic position of, 162
"*Nomenklatura* privatization," 160
Nomenklatura system, 10, 134

O

Our Home is Russia, 109, 117, 118t

P

Pamyat (Memory) society, 37
Party Congress (CPSU), 7–8, 20–21
Pasternak, Boris, 20

Pavlov, Valentin, 44, 47
perestroika (restructuring), 13, 14, 18, 19, 21
Perestroika: New Thinking for Our Country and the World, 14–15
Petro, Nicolai, 171
Podberiozkin, Aleksei, 172
Politburo (CPSU)
  criticism of, 29
  Gorbachev's membership, 12–13, 16
  under Gorbachev, 17–18
  role of, 8–9
political parties (RSFSR)
  characteristics of, 127–128, 143–144
  current Russian, 107–111
  development of, 105–107, 111–112, 128–129
  instability of, 103–104
  and Russian democracy, 176
Political Culture of the Russian "Democrats," The, 173
Pope, Edmund, 241
"power vertical," 153
"Prague Spring," suppression of, 6
presidency (RSFSR)
  Constitution of 1993, 85
  dual executive, 91–92, 133–136
  operation of, 144–147
  political power, 46, 65, 66, 69–71, 147
presidency (USSR), 42, 43, 69
Presidential Council, 44
Presidium of the Supreme Soviet, 38
"price liberalization," 75, 236
Primakov, Yevgenii, 110, 139–140, 239
primary party organization (PPO), CPSU, 7–8
privatization, economic reform, 138–139, 158, 160, 236
Procurator General, (RSFSR), Constitution of 1993, 94, 226–227
proportional representation (PR)
  electoral system, 113, 117
  1993 election, 113, 115–116
  1995 election, 116–117, 119
public health, decline in, 164–166
Pugo, Boris, 44
Putin, Vladimir
  and bureaucracy, 134, 135

and centralized power, 97, 151–153
and democracy, 179, 180–182
and Federation Council, 119
and legislature, 146
and media freedom, 177–178
and political parties, 129, 176
role of state, 174
selection of, 141–142, 240
"state of nation" address, 161, 166
support for, 108, 109, 120, 142
2000 election, 125–126, 142, 240
Yeltsin retirement, 124–125, 240

R

"red-brown" coalition, 76
referendum of 1993, 76–77
Remington, Thomas, 145, 146
"revolution from above," 4
Rose, Richard, 143–144
Russia (Russian Soviet Federated Socialist Republic [RSFSR])
    and CIS, 49, 51, 53–54, 55
    dual executive, 91–92, 133–136, 146
    economic inequality, 162–163
    electoral system, 106–107
    federal system, 65, 94–97, 151–152
    legal culture, 84
    nuclear policy, 56
    post-USSR, 61–62
    presidency, 46, 65, 66, 69–71, 135–136, 147. *See also* dual executive
    public health crisis, 164–166
    relations with Baltic states, 60–61
    relations with Belarus, 58–59, 238
    relations with Ukraine, 56–58
    Union treaty, 46–47
    unresolved constitutional issues, 66–67
    USSR successor state, 56
Russia, 66. *See also* Russia (RSFSR), Russian Federation
Russia Federation, 66, 87, 91. *See also* Russia, Russia (RSFSR)
Russia's Choice party, 108, 114, 115t
Russian "mafia," 159
Russian constitution (1978), 65–66, 75, 81
Russian constitution (1993)

adoption of, 77–78, 81
amendment process, 97–99, 151, 228–229
Federal Assembly, 85, 89–90, 214–220
federal system, 94–95, 96–97, 202–209
format of, 85
fundamental system, 187–191
government of, 85, 91–92, 220–223
judiciary, 85, 87, 92–94, 148, 223–227
local government, 227–228
obligations, 85, 196, 198, 200, 201
presidency, 85–88, 91–92, 209–214
rights/freedoms, 82, 83, 191–202
text of, 187–231
transitional provisions, 229–231
Russian legislature
    Constitution of 1993, 85, 88, 89–90, 144
    elections to, 77–78, 112–122, 115t, 119t, 121t–122t
    evolution of, 65, 66, 67–69,
    operation of, 144–147
    organization of, 142–144
Russian nationalism, growth of, 36–37
Russian Social Democratic Labor Party, 3
Russians, in FSU/NIS, 51
Rust, Matthias, 233
Rutland, Peter, 180, 183
Rutskoi, Alexander
    amnesty for, 146
    coup attempt, 77
    1991 election, 69
    Yeltsin adversary, 75–76, 137
Rykov, Nikolai, 234
Ryzhkov, Nikolai, 17, 44

S

Sajudis party, Lithuania, 35, 36, 40
Sakha Republic, 96. *See also* Yakutia Republic
Sakharov, Andrei
    and Article 6, 41
    human rights advocate, 19, 233, 234
    1989 elections, 26
Sakwa, Richard, 177

Index

Sartori, Giovanni, 85
secret protocols, Baltic states, 35
Secretariat (CPSU), 8, 9–10, 17
Shaposhnikov, Yevgeny, 55–56
Shatalin, Stanislav, 500 Days program, 32
Shevardnadze, Eduard
    foreign minister, 17–18, 37–38, 39
    and Gorbachev, 17, 233
    speech of, 45, 235
Shevtsova, Lilia, 138
Shoigu, Sergei, 109
single-member district plurality (SDP), 113, 116–117
Skuratov, Yuri, 125, 145, 239
Sobchak, Anatoly, 141, 181
"social democracy," 173
Solovyov, Yuri, 28
Soviet Constitution
    amendments to, 25
    Article 6, 41–42
    presidency, 42
    in RSFSR, 65–66
Stalin, Joseph Vissarionovich
    Brezhnev rehabilitation of, 5
    deportation of Tatars, 57
    Khrushchev attack on, 4
    Soviet leader, 2t, 3–4, 7
"State Committee for the State of Emergency," 47–48
State Council, 152–153, 241
State Duma. *See* Duma
Stepashin, Sergei, 140–141, 239–240
Strayer, Robert, 37
"superpresidential" system, 146
Supreme Arbitration Court (RSFSR)
    Constitution of 1993, 87, 94, 226
    membership, 147
Supreme Court (RSFSR)
    Constitution of 1993, 87, 90, 93–94, 226
    and Constitutional Court, 150
    membership, 147
    PR representation, 117
Supreme Soviet (RSFSR)
    1990 election, 43, 47, 68–69
    role of, 70, 74
Supreme Soviet (USSR)
    constitutional amendments, 25
    post-1989 operation, 29–30
    presidency, 42
    role of, 67

T

"tactical voting," 122
Tajikistan, 54, 59
Tatarstan Republic, 73, 74, 96
thaw, 4, 12
totalitarianism, in USSR, 4
Transdniestr Republic, 34–35
Transparency International, corruption index, 160
Tuleev, Aman, 125
Turkmenistan, 54
"turn to the right," 44–45, 59–60
Twentieth Party Congress
    attack on Stalin, 4
    children of, 12
Twenty-Eighth Party Congress, 43, 235

U

Ukazy (presidential decrees), 70–71, 87
Ukraine
    and CIS, 49, 51, 54
    military policy, 55
    nuclear policy, 56
    relations with RSFSR, 56–58, 59
    Union treaty, 46–47
Union of Right Forces party, 108, 120t
"Union of Sovereign States," 45–47, 48–49
Union of Soviet Socialist Republics (USSR)
    collapse of, 1, 49, 60
    coup attempt, 45, 47–48, 69–70, 235–236
    dissolution of, 40–41
    economic reforms, 157–158
    economic sector, 30, 40, 42, 237
    inequality in, 161–162
    leaders of, 1, 2t, 3–7
    legislature of, 67
    public health system, 164
Union treaty, 45–47, 48–49
United Nations, Gorbachev speech, 39, 234
Unity, parliamentary group, 44
Unity party
    emergence of, 109

1999 elections, 120–121, 120t–121t
Uskorenie (acceleration), 15, 31
Uzbekistan
    and Central Asian Economic
        Community, 59
    and CIS, 54
    Union treaty, 47

W

"war of laws," 41, 43, 235
Warsaw Pact, Czechoslovakian invasion, 39
West, Russian view of, 171–172
White, Stephen, 127
Women of Russia, 109, 115t

Y

Yabloko party
    emergence of, 108
    1993 election, 115t
    1995 election, 117, 118t
    1999 election, 120t, 121
Yakovlev, Alexander, 17, 38
Yakutia Republic, ASSR, 73, 74, 96
Yanaev, Grennady, 44
Yavlinsky, Grigory, 32, 108, 123, 200
Yeltsin, Boris
    Baltic independence, 60
    CIS, 49, 55
    constitutional crisis, 75–78, 237
    coup resistance, 48, 70, 235–236
    and democracy, 179–180
    early career, 18–19, 233–234
    500 Days program, 32
    and judiciary, 150
    limitations on CPSU, 47, 48
    media support, 177
    ministerial relations, 88, 92, 120, 136–142, 238–239
    "national idea," 171
    nationalities policy, 73–75, 95
    Nineteenth All-Union Party
        Conference, 21
    1989 elections, 28, 234
    1991 election, 28, 122, 136, 235
    1996 election, 122–124, 238
    presidency of, 69–71, 136, 146
    resignation of, 124, 142, 240
    RSFSR jurisdiction, 54–55
    Russian nationalism, 37
    and Supreme Soviet (USSR), 29, 20, 68, 235
    Twenty-Eighth Party Congress, 43, 68

Z

Zhirinovsky Bloc
    emergence of, 111
    1999 election, 120t, 121–122
Zhirinovsky, Vladimir
    and LDPR, 78, 110, 114, 119
    1991 election, 47, 78, 122
    1993 election, 114
    1995 election, 119
    1996 election, 122, 123
    2000 election, 125
Zorkin, Valery, 72, 150
Zyuganov, Gennadii, 107, 123, 125, 238, 240